"I love food that brings people together, and this book does exactly that. Erin's recipes are full of heart—comforting, fun, and the kind you'll want to make again and again. Reading this book feels like being invited to her family table, and I'm glad I came hungry."

—PHIL ROSENTHAL
***New York Times* bestselling author**
and host of *Somebody Feed Phil*

"*Dig In!* is packed with the kind of recipes you'll actually want to cook—comforting, classic, and ridiculously delicious. And as if the recipes weren't enough, there's a carefully and expertly selected wine pairing for each one! Erin keeps it simple and approachable, with recipes that have been loved in her family for generations (and will quickly become your family's greatest hits, too). These are the dishes you'll cook for friends, pass down to family, and never get tired of eating."

—CARISSA STANTON
***New York Times* bestselling author**
of *Seriously, So Good*

"Every recipe in *Dig In!* is vibrant, fresh, and full of flavor. What I love most is Erin's approach: it's warm and inviting, and makes cooking feel exciting rather than intimidating. This is the kind of cookbook that will live on your counter, not your bookshelf—because once you start, you will not want to stop digging in."

—KYLIE SAKAIDA
***New York Times* bestselling author**
of *So Easy So Good*

"Erin's first cookbook is absolutely stunning. Every page is filled with beauty, inspiration, and the kind of recipes that make you want to linger in the kitchen. I couldn't be more excited for her!"

—GABY DALKIN
***New York Times* bestselling author**
and founder of What's Gaby Cooking

DIG IN!

DIG IN!

OVER 100 EASY, DELICIOUS, AND STRESS-FREE RECIPES TO MAKE ON REPEAT

ERIN O'BRIEN

Photography by
MATT ARMENDARIZ

SIMON ELEMENT
NEW YORK AMSTERDAM/ANTWERP LONDON TORONTO SYDNEY/MELBOURNE NEW DELHI

For you.
Thank you for inviting me into
your kitchens, your homes, and your hearts.
Food is always better when shared,
and I'm so grateful to be part of your table.
And, of course, to my incredible family—
my first and forever inspiration.

CONTENTS

INTRODUCTION

HOW IT ALL STARTED

Dig In! is all about connection—the kind that happens over a sizzling pan, a well-worn cutting board, or a group chat that suddenly turns into a full-blown dinner party. It starts with the women who raised me, running restaurants and home kitchens with equal parts skill and heart. It stretches through childhood, where I cooked alongside them, soaking up their wisdom (and sneaking bites like a kitchen thief along the way). And it stretches across travels with my husband, Andrew, as we ate our way through the country and beyond, collecting flavors and kitchen secrets like souvenirs.

And then there was my kitchen during the Covid-19 pandemic, where cooking (and, let's be honest, drinking) videos turned into a whole online dinner party—one that never really ended. We swapped recipes, shared tips, hacked our way through limited pantry staples, and somehow, in the middle of it all, went viral. When the world cracked back open, I found myself stepping into a new kind of life—one even more centered around food, friendship, and the magic that happens when you share both.

Nana with Mom on her lap and Mom's siblings in their immigration photo.

Somewhere along the way, I realized how much I love to dig in—to figure out that one thing, that secret ingredient, technique, or little tweak that makes a dish sing. Why is this sauce so velvety? What makes this pasta taste unforgettable? How is this simple salad so darn good? That curiosity has led me to grill waiters and chefs, mid-meal; spend fifteen hours tweaking a single cookie recipe; and deep-dive into cookbooks, articles, and chats with my online food community. That's how I've learned—by asking, testing, tasting, and obsessing until I get it just right. And now, with this book, I can finally share it with YOU!

Because, sure, we all love to eat—but it's the passing of plates, the "wait, you have to try this" moments, the desperate late-night texts to Mom about the best way to crisp chicken skin, whether in person or through a screen, that make food mean something. That's what this book is: an invitation to dig in—together.

But first, let me back up a little. I'm a Mexican American Southern California girl who inherited my obsession with food from the best chefs (and strongest women) I know: my mom, grandmother, and great-grandmother. They didn't just cook—they built lives, businesses, and communities around food. In our family, feeding people wasn't just an act of love; it was survival, celebration, and sometimes, reinvention. So it's no surprise that food became my ultimate love language.

It all started in Mexico, with my great-grandmother, Jesús de Romero, or Guela, who was as fearless as they come. She once rode horseback from Tepic, Nayarit, Mexico, into Santiago Ixcuintla just to give birth to my nana—a journey that takes an hour by car, for context. She sold home-cooked meals from her doorstep to help support her family, but in 1959, she made an even bigger leap, moving to San Diego with my great-grandfather and their kids to start fresh. There, she opened Lupita's Café, a tiny lunch counter serving comforting, home-style Mexican dishes. She was the first in our family to prove that food could change lives—and she wouldn't be the last.

Nana is on the right.

Her daughter, my nana, Manuela, carried that same unstoppable spirit. After raising three kids on her own in Tijuana, she fought for a fresh start, securing a divorce (which was almost unheard of for a Mexican woman in the '60s) and moving to San Diego. There, she opened her own restaurant, Lupita's La Jolla, a small but mighty spot that became known for her carnitas, Signature Green Enchiladas (page 123), and was even a favorite spot of Mother Teresa's when she was in town! Nana had a way of making simple ingredients taste unforgettable—she challenged herself to create dishes that became

instant favorites, like her Iconic Crunchy Lemon Parm Salad (page 59) and Cure-All Fideo (Mexican Noodle Soup) (page 191). She inspired me to do the same, blending tradition with my own creations. It brings her so much joy seeing how our dishes have become just as beloved—if not viral—all over again.

My mom, Guadalupe, grew up in that restaurant, learning from Nana and carrying on the family magic in the kitchen. By the time I came along, she had mastered the art of making something incredible out of whatever was in the fridge. It looked effortless, whether it was her neighborhood-famous Secret Salsa (page 31), Classic Chilaquiles Verdes (page 95), or Loaded Twice-Baked Broccoli Cheddar Potatoes (page 143). And she didn't stop there—after years in the medical field, she became a nanny, which pretty much evolved into a role as a private chef, turning everyday groceries into restaurant-quality meals for the wonderful family she cooked for. I wish she had filmed those recipes!

But back at home, our kitchen was always the heart of everything. Whether it was family, friends, or the student-athletes my dad coached—including Andrew—there was always a seat at the table and something delicious and comforting on the stove. In fact, my parents introduced Andrew and me over my mom's Family Favorite Pot Roast (page 136), proving once again that food has a way of bringing people together in ways you never expect. And now, through this book, I get to do the same, with recipes like the community fave Red Wine–Braised Short Ribs (page 90) and One-Pan Sicilian Baked Cod with Roasted Tomatoes & Olives (page 140), while also sharing many new dishes like The Only Roast Chicken You'll Need (page 113) and Easy Burrata Lasagna (page 172).

I grew up surrounded by all this—women who cooked with intuition, never measured a thing, and ran their kitchens with the kind of confidence I

could only hope to have. But I didn't realize how much I had absorbed from them until much later.

In my early twenties, while working in real estate and figuring out my next move, Andrew and I stretched every dollar to travel whenever we could—even when it meant sacrificing in other places. From Mexico to France, Italy to Greece, we ate our way through cities, falling hard for new flavors and dishes that excited me in a way I hadn't felt before. I wanted to bring those tastes home, so I did what I'd always done when I got curious—I asked a lot of questions. I quizzed chefs and waiters mid-meal, scribbling on napkins as I tried to decode what made each dish special. They also told me something my nana had shared with me years ago: The best dishes aren't about fancy ingredients. They're about knowing how to use what you have and understanding that sometimes the simplest dishes are the most delicious.

That stuck with me. I started cooking more at home, pulling from my family's recipes and my travels, and obsessing over the small details that could take a dish from good to great. A tiny tweak in technique, a new shortcut, or a smarter way to layer flavors—it all mattered. Even the simplest dishes had a secret.

Of course, learning from my mom and nana came with one small challenge: They never measured anything. My mom always says, "I measure with my heart, my hands, and my head," which is poetic . . . but not exactly helpful when you're trying to write down a recipe. Still, I was determined. I spent hours testing, adjusting, and figuring out how to translate those instinctive recipes into something everyone could follow. And in the end, I guess I'm actually thankful they never measured . . . words I never thought I would say!

Sharing the finished dish with friends and family was deeply fulfilling, and I became obsessed with the creative, intuitive spark I felt doing it all. I wanted others like me—who might not feel confident enough to have fun in the kitchen—to feel empowered to learn. If I could do it, I was certain anyone could.

In 2019, I started posting my recipes online—not just to share what I was cooking, but to spill the little secrets tucked inside every great dish. Years later, what started as a leap of faith and an all-consuming after-hours hobby had grown into something much bigger—an incredible community of people just like me, hungry for easy, delicious, stress-free recipes to make on repeat and share with loved ones. That community helped shape every single aspect of this book.

Sharing my family's time-tested recipes alongside new favorites is my way of doing what Nana and my mom always did—bringing people together through food. Whether it's a dish straight from my childhood family kitchen, a flavor-packed weeknight win, or something inspired by my travels, I hope these recipes help you cook with confidence, creativity, and ease.

And now, you're officially part of the family—the kind that always has room for one more at the table.

So, grab a plate—let's Dig In!

Glam at age four!

Nana and her cousin, Javier.

Nana and me.

Mom, Nana, Dad, and me!

Always ready to blend.

Mom and me.

Diamond Crystal
KOSHER SALT
Barilla
GIADZY
Maldon
Barilla

LITTLE THINGS THAT MAKE A BIG DIFFERENCE

Great cooking isn't about flashy tricks—it's about knowing a few secrets and making smart choices. The right ingredients and tools do the heavy lifting, turning simple dishes into something special with minimal effort. You'll find plenty of easy techniques and clever tips woven into the recipes, but before we get there, I want to set you up with my go-to essentials—the game-changers that will make your everyday cooking faster, tastier, and just plain better. This includes ingredients, tools, and tips and even the garnishes that take a recipe from good to great.

One quick HOT TIP before we dive in (there are many of them throughout the book): **Always read the recipe start to finish.** It's the simplest way to cook with confidence and avoid last-minute surprises. It's the map for success—don't skip this step!

Now, let's talk about the kitchen staples that pull the most weight and will make the biggest impact in your kitchen.

INGREDIENTS

Stocking the right ingredients—and knowing how to put them to work—is the secret to making food so good and so effortless that you actually look forward to making dinner. These are the key ingredients you'll need for the recipes.

Bouillon Powder: A flavor booster commonly used in Mexican cuisine, bouillon powder quickly adds complex flavor to a dish. It's a pantry powerhouse for soups, stews, salsas, sauces, and grains. Can't find it? Swap in the same amount of bouillon paste.

Butter: Melted into pasta sauce, browned and whipped into frosting, or basted over steak, butter makes everything better! Use unsalted butter for depth of flavor, richness of texture, and full salt control. Only have salted butter? Slightly reduce the amount of salt called for in the recipe.

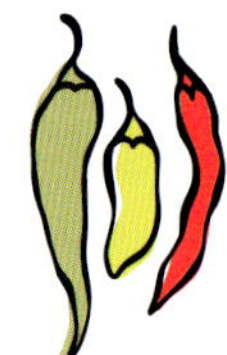

Chile Peppers (Dried): Dried chiles—like de árbol, guajillo, and ancho—add depth to sauces and stews with rich, smoky notes. De árbol is the spiciest, while guajillo and ancho are milder, with fruitier undertones ranging from plums to raisins.

Chile Peppers (Fresh): Jalapeño, serrano, poblano, Anaheim (or California), güero (yellow, or Sante Fe Grande), and Fresno peppers—each fresh chile brings its own balance of heat and flavor but isn't always easy to find. If your local grocer doesn't come through, try Mexican, Italian, or Asian markets—or online outlets. HOT TIPS: Spicier fresh peppers often have red or orange markings, or dry white lines on their exterior. Also, use disposable nitrile gloves to handle peppers to avoid spreading the heat.

Extra-Virgin Olive Oil: Extra-virgin olive oil is my go-to for dressings, finishing dishes, and pretty much all my cooking. Look for single-origin, cold-pressed oil, and you can't go wrong keeping a couple varieties on hand: one for cooking (mild and buttery) and the other peppier and bright for drizzling.

Garlic: I believe garlic is at the root of most great recipes, and always have some nearby. It adds a punch of flavor in so many forms—raw, cooked, lightly fried, roasted, and any other way you can think of. The more garlic, the better!

Parmigiano-Reggiano: People ask what brand of Parmesan cheese I use. The answer? None! If it doesn't say Parmigiano-Reggiano, it's not the real deal. Authentic Parmigiano-Reggiano is DOP-certified (short for *Denominazione d'Origine Protetta*, which guarantees the origin and quality), aged twelve to thirty-six months, and stamped on the rind. The flavor? Sharper, nuttier, and leagues beyond standard Parmesan. Cheese labeled parmesan (often US-made) doesn't compare in flavor, texture, or its ability to meld into sauces and dressings. Also, make sure you avoid pre-grated Parm (see below).

Grate Your Cheese, please! Though the convenience of pre-grated cheese is tempting, that convenience comes with a cost: Those anti-clumping preservatives and starches stop it from melting properly. When it comes to grating Parm, size matters. If you want ooey gooey melted cheese, pick up a block and grate it by hand—or use a food processor. For recipes that call for a light, feathery texture, reach for a Microplane zester or the finest side of a box grater—finely grated cheese melts more seamlessly and coats more evenly. This is one of those "more work but worth it" moments, I promise!

Pasta: For the full noodle know-how, twirl your way over to Pasta 101 (page 150)—your crash course in all things saucy, starchy, and perfectly al dente.

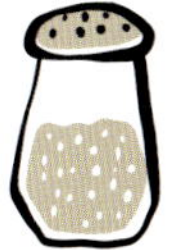

Salt: Salt unlocks flavor—savory, sweet, and everything in between. Season as you cook to build depth and always taste as you go. If you wonder whether a dish needs more salt, it probably does. I reach for Diamond Crystal kosher salt for everyday cooking and flaky sea salt for finishing. (If you use Morton kosher salt, halve the amount, as it is saltier.) I never use fine table salt.

Vinegar: Acid is as important as salt when it comes to balance and enhancing flavor, so good vinegar is crucial. My core lineup: balsamic vinegar, balsamic glaze, white balsamic vinegar, champagne vinegar, red wine vinegar, and rice wine vinegar. Each one brings a different lift to your recipes—experiment to find your favorites.

Wine: Cooking with wine adds layers of complexity to sauces, braises, and more. Feel free to use up anything lurking in your fridge, or select varietals that are medium-bodied and dry (nothing too tannic that might make the dish bitter, or too sweet). My go-tos: Red: Cabernet Sauvignon, Merlot, Chianti. White: Sauvignon Blanc, Pinot Grigio.

FLAVOR BOMBS

What do capers, kalamata olives, pepperoncini, roasted red peppers, crushed Calabrian peppers, freshly squeezed citrus, and anchovies have in common? They're the easiest way to pump up flavor in simple recipes. A splash, spoonful, or sprinkle of these adds instant dimension.

GARNISH YOUR HEART OUT

For me, most dishes aren't complete without an extra touch. Just like any good outfit, they need to be accessorized with all the right toppings.

- Acid (citrus, salsa, vinegar)
- Crunch (cabbage, breadcrumbs, pepitas [pumpkin seeds], peanuts)
- Dairy (sour cream, queso fresco, feta, burrata)
- Fresh herbs (basil, cilantro, chives, dill, flat-leaf parsley)
- Parmigiano-Reggiano (freshly grated, of course)

SOURCING INGREDIENTS

A little exploring can open up a whole new world of flavors—don't be shy about asking for help. If you can't find an ingredient at the grocery store, stop by your favorite restaurant that offers that cuisine to see if they have tips, visit a specialty market, or look online. Specialty Mexican, Italian, and international markets often offer the freshest produce, herbs, spices, chiles, cheeses, and unique pasta shapes—sometimes at better prices, too.

TOOLS—THE REAL KITCHEN MVPS

These kitchen basics make cooking a breeze and will last decades, improve your mood and experience in the kitchen, and make your food taste better. They're worth the investment!

Blenders: Investing in a good high-speed blender and an immersion blender makes soups, sauces, salsas, hummus, frozen cocktails, and more a joy to whip up. I prefer the high-speed for the airiest hummus and dips, but a standard blender is a solid choice.

Colander, Fine Mesh Strainer & Spider Strainer: Strain, scoop, fry, blanch, or transfer—each tool has its job. This book leans on the colander for pasta, but use what works for you. Just make sure to save that pasta water.

Food Processor: If you've got the space and budget, a food processor is a prep time hero. It slices, dices, purees, makes doughs and dips in no time, and my favorite—finely grates cheese in bulk.

Knives: A sharp 7- to 8-inch chef's knife and a smaller paring knife can take on nearly all your slicing and dicing—no need for an arsenal of blades! Add a serrated knife for crusty bread and delicate tomatoes, and you've got a rock-solid kitchen lineup. Sharpen them every few months, either at home or professionally—check for a stall at the farmers' market or try the mail-in sharpening services.

Mandoline: For uniform, paper-thin veggie slices in seconds, an inexpensive mandoline is a game-changer. Just do yourself a favor—buy a cut-proof glove and save your fingertips!

Meat Thermometer: Guesswork? Gone. A meat thermometer ensures perfect doneness, every time. Check your recipes for target temps and bookmark this temp chart for precision cooking.

Microplane Zester: Tiny tool, big impact. Essential for zesting citrus and grating garlic so it's more pungent and melts completely into dishes, or tackling my fave—finely grating Parmigiano-Reggiano—to make the best sauces.

Parchment Paper: My go-to over aluminum foil, for lining cake pans, roasting vegetables, baking meatballs for even cooking, minimal sticking, perfect caramelization, and making cleanup a breeze.

Skillets, Pots & Pans: These recipes are built to work with what you have, but a few go-to pieces make all the difference. Stainless steel, cast-iron skillets, and ceramic-coated Dutch ovens handle high heat and sear like a dream. Properly preheated, stainless steel and cast-iron can mimic nonstick: Just heat over medium-high and flick a few drops of water onto the surface—if they dance instead of evaporating, you're good to go.

Wire Rack: A kitchen lifesaver: cools cakes, cookies, and all your baked goods, and doubles as an oven rack for roasting extra-crispy veggies, bacon, or prosciutto.

INTERNAL MEAT TEMP CHEAT SHEET

Steak & Red Meat	
Rare	120° to 125°F
Medium Rare	125° to 130°F
Medium	140° to 145°F
Medium Well	150° to 155°F
Well Done	160°F
Chicken & Poultry	
165°F (or 160°F plus 10 minutes resting in the oven or pan, heat off, to reach 165°F)	
Fish & Seafood	
White Fish	145°F
Salmon	125° to 145°F depending on desired doneness
Shrimp	Cook just until they lose transparency, begin to turn pink, and form a C-shape rather than an O-shape, which signals they're overcooked
Scallops	Cook until opaque inside and firm to the touch; 120°F for seared scallops (plus 2 to 3 minutes resting out of the skillet to reach 125°F)
Pork	
Chops & Roasts	145° to 160°F

CHEERS! IT'S WINE TIME

A good meal begins long before the first bite—it begins in the kitchen, often with the satisfying pop of a cork. Whether you're cooking with friends, catching up over App-y Hour (page 29), or simply unwinding, wine doesn't just enhance food—it elevates the entire experience. It creates moments of connection, something I realized during the Covid-19 pandemic when I started popping bottles in my videos. What began as a way for me to learn and share quickly became a way to create community.

One of the most memorable moments? Discovering a hidden gem like Kings of Prohibition, the $8.99 Australian Cabernet Shiraz rec of mine from Trader Joe's that flew off the shelves after I shared it. The winery was so thrilled that they sent us 150 bottles. In that same spirit, we paid it forward, gifting them to our best friends for their wedding. That single bottle connected so many people, both online and in person!

It's important to understand that I'm no sommelier—just a wine lover who knows how confusing the world of wine can be, especially when you're trying to find a great bottle that won't break the bank. That's why I teamed up with Helen Johannesen, the coolest sommelier I know, of Helen's Wines in Los Angeles to make wine feel much less intimidating and more fun. We've put together an approachable guide to wine, along with expertly paired wine (and cocktail!) recs for almost every recipe in the book. They take the guesswork out of finding wine for any dish and can make every meal way more delicious. I've got you covered; just look for the PERFECT PAIRING at the bottom of each recipe and start popping!

ERIN'S HOT TIPS BEFORE YOU SIP

1. There are no rules! You don't need an expensive bottle or an impressive label—if you like how it tastes, you're doing it right. Surprise yourself: Try a natural wine (see Pét Nats, page 26), a local bottle, or explore the globe.

2. Trust your taste buds. You learn by tasting. Pay attention to what you like and don't overthink it. It's not that serious!

3. It's a balancing act. Wine pairing is about balancing intensity, acidity (including tannins, compounds that give you that bitter, dry sensation like over-steeped tea), and sweetness. Think about the dish—is it rich, fresh, tangy, or bold? Match or counterbalance with your wine choice. (See the Perfect Pairings cheat sheet on page 27!)

4. What grows together goes together. When in doubt, match the wine's origin to its cuisine. Wine's flavor is influenced by terroir: the way the soil, elements, and climate of a place affect the grape's growth and the wine's fermentation and create the perfect match. Serving One-Pan Sicilian Baked Cod (page 140)? Try an Etna Bianco. What to pour with Famous Brown Butter Lemon Chicken (page 101)? Reach for a Chianti Classico or Rosso di Montalcino from Tuscany.

5. Pop the bottle now! Waiting for the "perfect" moment? Don't. I once saved a fancy French bottle for years only to find it had gone bad. Carpe diem, and open that bottle. The occasion is now.

WINE 101: THE BASICS

What is wine, anyway? At its core, wine is fermented grape juice. Good wine begins with gorgeous grapes, which are grown, harvested, sorted, crushed, and left to ferment as yeast transforms the sugary sweet juice into alcohol. The process can take nuance, skill, technique, and aging to produce an amazing wine.

There are six main types of wine: red, rosé, white, orange, sparkling, and dessert.

RED

Made by crushing or pressing grapes, their skins and seeds (and sometimes even their stems) macerate (soften in a soaking liquid), which gives the wine its color, flavor, and tannins. Fermentation lasts from ten to sixty days, the fruit matter is removed, and the wine is aged from a few months to many years.

Light Red: Delicate, bright, mineral driven, less tannins, lower alcohol content, lighter color, juicy, soft, fresh, elegant, pretty, transparent, and typically has notes of fresh red fruits and berries. (Grape examples: Frappato, Gamay, Pinot Noir)

Medium Red: Moderate level of tannins and alcohol content, can feel lighter or heavier depending on varietal and how it's made, medium acidity, textured, and typically has notes of dark red and blue fruit, and a bit more spice. (Grape examples: Grenache, Sangiovese, Barbera, Merlot)

Bold Red: Rich, velvety, lush, full, higher alcohol content, more tannins, darker color, heavier feel, jammy, and typically has notes of black fruits and berries, oak, and spice. (Grape examples: Nebbiolo, Malbec, Cabernet Sauvignon, Syrah)

Ideal serving temp: 15 minutes in a standard fridge or 60° to 65°F in a wine fridge.

ROSÉ

Made just like red wine but with less skin contact—the grapes macerate for just a few hours, or none at all, rather than days or weeks. Rosé can be either light, soft, and creamy; acidic, lively, and fresh; or robust and full of texture and tannins.

Light Rosé: Fresh, crisp, refreshing, bright, more delicate, higher acidity, and typically has notes of citrus, floral, red fruit, and melon. (Grape examples: Pinot Noir, Grenache, Cinsault)

Full Rosé: Fresh, light, rich, more intense, longer finish, higher alcohol content, more tannins, and typically has notes of citrus, floral, red fruit, berries, melon, and spices. (Grape examples: Zinfandel, Syrah, Nebbiolo, Mourvèdre)

Ideal serving temp: Fridge cold or 50°F in wine fridge.

WHITE

Made by separating the grape juice from the skins either immediately or within hours after pressing, adding texture and body. After the juice is finished fermenting, it's aged in tanks or barrels before bottling. Lower in tannins and can be fresh, bright, and citrus-zested, soft and stone-fruit juicy, or balanced, round, and light as air.

Light White: Crisp, citrusy, zesty, mineral driven, fresh, bright, more acidic, lighter in color. (Grape examples: Albariño, Riesling, Pinot Grigio, Chenin Blanc, Sauvignon Blanc, Vermentino)

Full White: Creamy, rich, luscious, buttery, full-bodied, deeper in color, and typically has notes of vanilla and oak. (Grape examples: Gewürztraminer, Viognier, Chardonnay)

Ideal serving temp: Fridge cold or 45° to 55°F in a wine fridge.

ORANGE

Spoiler: Orange wine isn't made from oranges! Its color and flavor come from processing white wine grapes like a red wine, leaving the skins in extended contact with the juice during maceration. Fun fact: Orange wine is thought to be the very first wine made on earth.

Orange wines have good acidity, range from light- to full-bodied, have a unique texture with small or big tannins, and boast citrus, tropical, or stone fruit notes.

Characteristics: Higher tannins, fuller bodied, bold, dry, and typically has notes of citrus, fruits, honey, nuts, herbs, minerality, and a bit of sourness and can be a bit "funky." (Grape examples: Chardonnay, Sauvignon Blanc, Pinot Grigio, Muscat, Riesling)

Ideal serving temp: Fridge cold or 50° to 60°F in a wine fridge.

SPARKLING

There are bubbly variations of white, rosé, orange, and red wine from all over the world. They pair with almost anything and instantly make any meal feel like a celebration. A variety of methods are used in their production, but every technique features a second round of fermentation to add complexity and fizz. Sparkling wines play with the balance of acidity and creaminess, can be bone-dry or sweet, fruity or tannic, and may be mineral-driven or fruit-forward. Only sparkling wine produced in France's Champagne region can legally be called Champagne. Within Champagne (and many other sparkling wines), sweetness levels vary.

If you've spotted terms like Extra Brut, Brut, or Demi-Sec on your bottle, they indicate the amount of sugar that remains after fermentation, offering you a guide to the wine's dryness or sweetness.

Extra Brut: The driest.

Brut: Still dry, but slightly less so.

Demi-Sec: Sweeter, often enjoyed with desserts.

Characteristics: Dry, zesty, zippy, light, and typically has floral, citrusy, fruity, nutty, and toasty notes. (Grape examples: Chardonnay, Pinot Noir, and Pinot Meunier [Champagne], Glera [Prosecco], Xarel-lo [Cava])

What about those Pét Nats that are all the rage now? Pétillant naturels are lightly sparkling wines that can be white, orange, rosé, or even red, like some Lambruscos. Unlike the traditional method, which involves two distinct fermentations, Pét Nats follows the ancestral method—bottled before the first fermentation is complete, trapping natural bubbles. This process is less refined, often yielding cloudy, unfiltered wines with a wild, casual character.

Ideal serving temp: Fridge cold or 40°F in a wine fridge.

DESSERT

Dessert wine is a broad category of sweet wines typically served with or after dessert. These wines have higher residual sugar, making them richer, more intense, and often syrupy in texture. They can be sparkling or still, light or rich, red or white, and are typically sweet, often with nutty, honeyed, or dried-fruit flavored notes.

Late-Harvest Wines: Grapes are left on the vine longer, allowing them to develop more sugar. (Grape examples: Sauternes, Riesling, Chenin Blanc)

Fortified Wines: Brandy or spirits are added to stop fermentation, preserving natural sweetness and boosting alcohol content. (Grape examples: Port, Madeira, Sherry, Vin Santo)

Ice Wine (Eiswein): Made from grapes that naturally freeze on the vine, concentrating their sugars. (Grape examples: Canadian Ice Wine, German Eiswein)

Sparkling Dessert Wines: Light, fizzy, and sweet, these are perfect for a celebratory toast. (Grape examples: Moscato d'Asti, Brachetto d'Acqui)

Ideal serving temp: Varies from 40° to 65°F depending on the style of dessert wine.

WHERE TO FIND GREAT WINE

Wine adventures start anywhere—from that cute new wine shop in town, to Costco or Trader Joe's, or a winery (online or in person) and virtual retailers. Shopping locally? Ask questions! Many shops and wine bars offer tastings and flights to help you explore new styles.

A properly paired wine balances acidity, tannins, and richness so neither the food nor the wine overwhelms the other. With my Perfect Pairings at the bottom of most recipes, you can't go wrong. They were specially curated so that you can just chill!

As Helen says: Relax and have fun! Food and wine pairings are meant to be an adventure—step out of your comfort zone and most importantly, enjoy the moment with people you love.

Happy sipping!

PERFECT PAIRINGS:

CHEAT SHEET

Greens/Salads

Dry white (Sauvignon Blanc) or sparkling (Prosecco or Cava)

Pasta & Other Carbs

Mineral white (Pinot Grigio) or light red (Gamay)

Fish

Dry white (Chenin Blanc or Albariño) or sparkling (Champagne)

Shellfish & Seafood

Rich white (Viognier or Chardonnay) or rosé (especially one from Provence)

Beef & Pork

Medium-bold red (Sangiovese or Cabernet Sauvignon)

Veggies

Dry white (Vermentino) or orange wine (especially one from France)

Dessert

Sweet wine (Moscato d'Asti or Sauternes)

APP-Y HOUR

When I first started sharing recipes online, I broke the ice the same way I do at any gathering—with a good appetizer. Just like a clever conversation starter, the right app sets the tone, sparks curiosity, and gets people leaning in. It's the first spark before the meal, the opening move that says, this is going to be good. A well-chosen appetizer is more than just a bite—it's a glimpse into what's to come and a reflection of the cook behind it. Maybe it's a coveted family recipe (like my mom's never-before-shared Secret Salsa, page 31), a dish inspired by a recent adventure (hello, Faux-caccia, page 36), or the nonnegotiable favorite that friends and family expect to see on the table (can't beat Auntie Bug's Caramelized Almond & Orange Baked Brie, page 45). It's also an opportunity to try something new and see how it goes (like Green Goddess Hummus with Feta, page 50).

This chapter is packed with inventive yet simple recipes that can be prepared ahead and deliver huge flavor with minimal effort because hosting (or just making Tuesday night special) should be about connection, not kitchen stress. Whether you're setting the stage for a full feast or turning a lineup of hearty apps into a meal, there's something here to keep the conversation flowing, like the Mini Pineapple Teriyaki Meatballs (page 53), Chile Mango Halibut Ceviche (page 49), Saucy Chicken (or tofu) Lettuce Cups (page 40), or my favorite Cheesy Baked White Bean & Artichoke Dip (page 39). Ready, set, app!

The Holy Trinity Mom's Secret Salsa

SERVES 8 TO 10 (MAKES 3 CUPS) • **TOTAL TIME** 10 MINUTES

- 2 fresh güero (yellow) chiles or fresh jalapeño peppers
- 1 fresh serrano pepper
- 1 (28-ounce) can fire-roasted diced tomatoes
- 1 large bunch fresh cilantro, with 1-inch tender stems
- 3 garlic cloves, coarsely chopped
- 1 dried chile de árbol, stemmed
- 1 tablespoon fresh lime juice (about ½ lime)
- ¾ teaspoon kosher salt
- ½ teaspoon chicken bouillon powder
- ½ teaspoon ground cumin
- ½ teaspoon dried oregano

PERFECT PAIRING (FOR THE TRINITY)

The Spicy Watermelon Pine-Aperol Margarita (page 284), a Frozen Coconut Mojito (page 295), or an ice-cold beer!

This is the kind of recipe that disappears as soon as it hits the table. It's smoky, spicy, and layered with deep, savory flavors that make it almost impossible to stop eating. Everyone who tries it immediately asks my mom to bottle it up and sell it. There are a few "secrets" here, kicking off with a trio of chiles—güero, de árbol, and serrano—each bringing their own distinct personality to the mix. The güero chiles add a mellow, slightly sweet heat, the de árbol delivers a sharp, fiery punch, and the serrano brings that fresh, grassy spice that lingers just enough. Plus, there's a surprising secret weapon—chicken bouillon. And speaking from experience, this Secret Salsa is far more effective than any Marry Me Chicken!

1. For a gas stove, use tongs to carefully roast the güero chiles and serrano pepper over an open flame, rotating them every 45 seconds to 1 minute to ensure all sides are mostly charred, about 5 minutes total. Or, preheat your broiler on high and move a rack to the upper third of the oven. Place the güero chiles and serrano pepper on a lined sheet pan, and broil, rotating every 3 to 4 minutes, until they are charred on both sides, 6 to 8 minutes.
2. Allow the chiles and pepper to cool, and remove the stems. For Mom's classic spicy salsa, leave the seeds and veins intact. For a mild or medium salsa, with a pair of gloves, remove the seeds by slicing the chile in half and scooping the seeds out with a small spoon.
3. In a blender or food processor, add the charred chiles and pepper, tomatoes, cilantro, garlic, chile de árbol, lime juice, salt, bouillon powder, cumin, and oregano. Blend or pulse until lightly chunky, 15 to 30 seconds.
4. Chill before serving. The salsa will keep for up to a week in the fridge when stored in an airtight container.

HOT TIP

Start with the minimum number of peppers recommended and adjust to your tolerance (see page 18 for more hot tips on handling chiles). If possible, make your salsa the night before so the flavors can develop.

Salsa Verde

SERVES 8 TO 10 (MAKES ABOUT 3 CUPS) • **TOTAL TIME** 20 MINUTES

- 10 tomatillos (about 1 pound), husked and rinsed
- ½ small white onion, peeled and halved
- 1 fresh serrano pepper, stemmed and halved lengthwise
- 1 fresh jalapeño pepper, stemmed and halved lengthwise
- 1 fresh poblano or Anaheim pepper stemmed, halved lengthwise, seeded, and deveined
- 2 tablespoons avocado or other neutral oil
- 1¼ teaspoons kosher salt
- 1 bunch fresh cilantro, with 1-inch tender stems
- 1 tablespoon fresh lime juice (about ½ lime)
- 2 garlic cloves, coarsely chopped
- 1¼ teaspoons chicken bouillon powder

This is another family classic—bright, smoky, and undeniably delicious. It starts with roasted tomatillos, their tartness mellowed by the char, blending seamlessly with a bold mix of serrano, jalapeño, and poblano peppers. The serrano brings a clean, sharp heat, the jalapeño adds a grassy warmth, and the poblano pepper introduces a deeper, almost earthy richness that rounds out the salsa beautifully. Just like Mom's Secret Salsa, this one has people asking to bottle it up. It's the kind of salsa that feels at home on everything—drizzled over tacos, spooned onto chilaquiles, or mixed into dishes that need a little extra kick.

---

1. Place an oven rack in the top third of the oven and preheat the broiler to high. Line a sheet pan with parchment paper.
2. Place the tomatillos, onion, and serrano, jalapeño, and poblano peppers on the lined sheet pan. Drizzle with the oil, sprinkle with the salt, and toss until thoroughly coated. Broil for 6 to 8 minutes per side, until the veggies are slightly charred.
3. Transfer the charred veggies (including the juices!) into a blender (with the steam vent in the top open) or food processor along with the cilantro, ½ cup water, lime juice, garlic, and bouillon powder. Blend or pulse until slightly chunky, 15 to 30 seconds.
4. Chill before serving. The salsa will keep for up to a week in the fridge when stored in an airtight container.

Go-To Guac

SERVES 4 TO 6 • **TOTAL TIME** 10 MINUTES

½ small red onion, finely diced

1 fresh serrano pepper, stemmed, seeded, and finely diced

2 tablespoons fresh lime juice (about 1 lime)

1½ teaspoons kosher salt

4 Hass avocados, halved (see Hot Tips)

½ cup chopped fresh cilantro, plus more for garnish

Salted roasted pepitas (pumpkin seeds), for garnish

This is more like a run-to guac, because it's a true original. It also has a little trick up its sleeve—a quick lime juice marinade that tames the bite of the serrano and onion, smoothly melding their flavors. Salty pepitas (pumpkin seeds) add a satisfying crunch, balancing out the creamy avocado and fresh cilantro for a guacamole that's anything but ordinary. Serve it up with your favorite tortilla chips, and use them on everything from eggs to migas, beans and rice, quesadillas, and more—it's one of those staples that instantly makes everything better.

1. In a medium bowl, add the onion, serrano pepper, lime juice, and salt. Stir to combine and let sit for at least 5 minutes and no longer than 10 minutes. Add the avocado and, using a fork, gently mash until mostly smooth with some chunks throughout to create texture. Gently fold in the cilantro.
2. Transfer to a serving bowl and top with the chopped cilantro and pepitas. Enjoy immediately.

HOT TIPS

For a safe and easy way to get the avocado pit out, cut the ripe avocado in half and use your thumbs to press down on the back side of the avocado, pushing the pit out.

If you have leftover guacamole, level out the top and squeeze lime juice over it to prevent oxidation, then cover with plastic wrap. This will change the flavor, so adjust salt levels before serving.

Sweet & Savory Balsamic Peach Bruschetta

SERVES 8 TO 10 • **TOTAL TIME** 30 MINUTES

- 2 medium yellow peaches, pitted and finely diced
- 1 cup cherry tomatoes (about 6 ounces), quartered
- 1 cup chopped fresh basil, plus more for garnish
- ½ small red onion, finely chopped (see Hot Tip)
- ¼ cup extra-virgin olive oil, divided
- 1 teaspoon kosher salt
- ½ teaspoon freshly ground black pepper, plus more for garnish
- 1 baguette, cut into about 24 (½-inch) slices
- 1 garlic clove, peeled and halved
- 1 (8-ounce) ball burrata cheese, at room temperature
- Balsamic glaze, for serving
- Flaky sea salt, for serving

When stone fruit and tomatoes peak, their juicy sweetness perfectly contrasts with the savory red onion, basil, the hint of garlic, and drizzle of balsamic. Piled on top of olive oil–toasted baguettes slathered with creamy burrata, it's the kind of bite that stops the conversation—sweet, salty, rich, and bright all at once. The peach-and-tomato mixture is so good you'll be tempted to eat it by the spoonful. No peaches? Swap in nectarines, plums, or cherries—or omit the stone fruit and go full savory with extra tomatoes. Easy to assemble and impossible to resist, these are made for entertaining—especially alongside a glass of wine or a cocktail (see the Perfect Pairing).

1. Preheat the oven to 400°F. Line a sheet pan with parchment paper.
2. In a large bowl, add the peaches, tomatoes, basil, red onion, 2 tablespoons of the oil, the salt, and the black pepper. Gently toss and marinate on the counter for at least 10 minutes.
3. Meanwhile, place the baguette slices onto the sheet pan and brush the tops with the remaining 2 tablespoons oil. Bake until golden brown and crispy, 10 to 12 minutes. Rub the garlic onto the top of each slice of toasted baguette.
4. **TO SERVE:** Place the toasts on a serving platter. Tear the burrata into about 2 teaspoon pieces and spread onto each toast. Top each with a heaping spoonful of the peach mixture. Garnish with basil, balsamic glaze, flaky salt, and a few twists of black pepper.

PERFECT PAIRING

A California or Washington State rosé made from Grenache or Syrah, or the Slice of Heaven Rossini (page 296).

HOT TIP

To mellow the pungency of raw onion, soak chopped onion in ice water for 10 minutes, drain, and pat dry.

Faux-caccia

SERVES 4 TO 6 • **TOTAL TIME** 40 MINUTES PLUS REST TIME

- 3 tablespoons extra-virgin olive oil, divided, plus more for serving
- 1 pound store-bought pizza dough
- ¾ cup cherry tomatoes, halved
- Leaves from 2 sprigs fresh rosemary
- 1 teaspoon flaky sea salt
- Balsamic vinegar, for serving

PERFECT PAIRING

A light and dry Italian red wine like a Nebbiolo or Rossese from Liguria, or a Cucumber Basil Martini (page 288).

Focaccia—golden, airy, and olive oil–drenched—is the kind of bread that lingers in your memory. I still think about the slices we devoured in Cinque Terre. But let's be real: Making it from scratch takes time and patience, and sometimes you want that pillowy, salty, crispy-edged bite without all the effort. Enter faux-caccia. One night I grabbed store-bought pizza dough for an impromptu dinner party. It was good, but I set out to perfect the method, adding plenty of olive oil, fresh rosemary, cherry tomatoes, and flaky salt. It's not focaccia, but it's pretty darn close. Serve with extra-virgin olive oil and balsamic for dipping, or alongside the Magic Meatballs & Marinara (page 96). Play with your fave toppings—Italian oregano and olives? Don't stop there!

1. Coat the bottom and sides of a 10- or 11-inch cast-iron skillet with 1 tablespoon of the olive oil. Place the pizza dough in the skillet and cover with a damp kitchen towel or plastic wrap in a warm spot and let the dough rest and rise until it looks soft and pillowy—a minimum of 1½ and up to 3 hours.
2. Preheat the oven to 425°F. Remove the towel or plastic wrap. Drizzle 1 tablespoon of the olive oil over the dough. Sprinkle the surface of the dough with a few flicks of water and use your hands to spread the dough to the edges of the skillet. Press your fingertips into the dough (but not all the way to the bottom), creating the signature focaccia dimples. They may bounce back, and that's ok. Drizzle the remaining 1 tablespoon of oil over the top and press the tomatoes, cut side up, evenly across the dough. Sprinkle with the rosemary leaves and flaky salt.
3. Bake for 28 to 30 minutes, until light golden brown. Using a spatula, lift the bread from the skillet and transfer to a wire rack to cool for 10 minutes.
4. **TO SERVE:** Slice the bread in half and cut crosswise into 2-inch-wide strips alongside your favorite extra-virgin olive oil and balsamic vinegar for dipping.

Cheesy Baked White Bean & Artichoke Dip

SERVES 8 TO 10 • **TOTAL TIME** 30 MINUTES

- 1 stick (8 tablespoons) unsalted butter
- ½ medium yellow onion, finely chopped
- 3 garlic cloves, finely chopped
- ¼ cup all-purpose flour
- 2 cups whole milk
- 1½ teaspoons garlic powder
- 1½ teaspoons onion powder
- 1 teaspoon kosher salt
- ½ teaspoon freshly ground black pepper
- ½ teaspoon cayenne pepper
- 1 cup freshly grated sharp white cheddar cheese, divided
- ¾ cup finely grated Parmigiano-Reggiano cheese, divided
- ¼ cup sour cream, at room temperature
- 1 (15-ounce) can cannellini beans, drained and rinsed
- 1 (14.5-ounce) jar marinated artichoke hearts, drained and coarsely chopped
- Chopped fresh flat-leaf parsley or fresh dill, for garnish
- Pita chips or tortilla chips, for serving

PERFECT PAIRING

A high-acid white wine like a Sauvignon Blanc, Txakolina, or an Albariño are all phenomenal counter-points to the tangy artichoke.

A hot bubbling dish of garlicky cheddar and Parm, tender cannellini beans, and briny artichoke? Heavenly! This decadent dip is always the first thing to go at a party. It's totally vegetarian, but thanks to the savory flavor mix, people swear there's bacon hiding in there! And bonus—it's packed with protein and fiber from the beans and can be prepped ahead. Serve it when dinner is on the lighter side, or when you need a snack that keeps a crowd happy and distracted while you cook! Best enjoyed with crunchy pita or tortilla chips for dipping.

1. Place one oven rack in the top third of the oven and one in the middle and preheat the oven to 375°F.
2. In a medium pot, melt the butter over medium-high heat. Add the onion and garlic and cook, stirring occasionally, until the onions are translucent and starting to brown, about 5 minutes. Add the flour and cook, whisking constantly, until the mixture is very light golden in color, 1 to 2 minutes.
3. Add the milk and cook, whisking constantly, until the sauce has thickened and is beginning to bubble rapidly around the edges of the pot, 1 to 2 minutes.
4. Off heat, stir in the garlic powder, onion powder, salt, black pepper, and cayenne pepper. Stir in ¾ cup of the cheddar and ½ cup of the Parmigiano-Reggiano until melted. Stir in the sour cream, beans, and artichoke hearts to thoroughly combine.
5. Transfer to a medium 8 x 8-inch baking dish and sprinkle the remaining ¼ cup of cheddar and ¼ cup of Parmigiano-Reggiano over the top.
6. Bake in the middle rack for 15 to 18 minutes, until bubbling. Carefully move the dish to the top rack, turn the broiler on high, and broil for 1 to 2 minutes, until golden brown spots appear.
7. Garnish with the parsley or dill. Serve hot with pita chips or tortilla chips.

Saucy Chicken Lettuce Cups
with Thai-Inspired Mango Salsa

SERVES 8 TO 10 AS AN APPETIZER, OR 4 TO 6 FOR DINNER • **TOTAL TIME** 50 MINUTES

FOR THE THAI-INSPIRED MANGO SALSA

1 large mango, diced

2 tablespoons chopped fresh cilantro

2 tablespoons chopped fresh mint

1 tablespoon chopped fresh basil

1 tablespoon fresh lime juice (about ½ lime)

1 small fresh red Thai chile or Fresno pepper, stemmed, seeded, deveined, and finely chopped (optional)

1 teaspoon granulated sugar

¼ teaspoon kosher salt

FOR THE CHICKEN LETTUCE CUPS

¼ cup fresh lime juice (about 2 limes)

¼ cup reduced-sodium soy sauce

2 tablespoons toasted sesame oil

4 garlic cloves, grated or finely chopped

4 green onions (white and green parts), chopped, plus more for garnish

1 tablespoon peeled and grated fresh ginger

1 teaspoon crushed red pepper

I love a lettuce cup: They remind me of going to P.F. Chang's as a kid, where I'd order their crunchy, savory classic chicken version. This Thai-inspired take is a weeknight favorite, packed with flavor and texture. Ground chicken (or tofu; see Variation) gets cooked with mushrooms, carrots, ginger, garlic, and sesame, then spooned into crisp lettuce leaves. The fresh mango salsa topping with mint, basil, and cilantro adds sweetness and zing. You can prep the filling and salsa ahead, then assemble in minutes for an easy meal or crowd-friendly appetizer.

1. **MAKE THE THAI-INSPIRED MANGO SALSA:** In a medium bowl, add the mango, cilantro, mint, basil, lime juice, red Thai chile (if using), sugar, and salt. Gently mix and let marinate on the counter while you make the lettuce cups.
2. **MAKE THE CHICKEN LETTUCE CUPS:** In a large measuring cup, whisk the lime juice, soy sauce, sesame oil, garlic, green onions, ginger, and crushed red pepper until combined and set aside.
3. Heat 5 tablespoons of the oil in a large skillet over high heat. Once shimmering, add the chicken and, using a wooden spoon, break up the larger pieces. Cook, stirring occasionally, until browned, 6 to 8 minutes. Push the chicken to one side of the skillet and add the remaining tablespoon of oil to the opposite side, along with the mushrooms and carrot. Cook, stirring the vegetables occasionally, until they soften and the mushrooms are slightly browned, 5 to 7 minutes.
4. Reduce the heat to medium, add the reserved sauce, and stir to combine. Cook, stirring occasionally, until the sauce is mostly absorbed, 3 to 4 minutes.
5. **TO SERVE:** Place 2 heaping tablespoons of the chicken mixture onto each of the lettuce leaves followed by a generous spoonful of the salsa and place on a platter or individual plates. Garnish with more green onions and the peanuts.

(recipe continues)

¼ cup plus 2 tablespoons avocado or other neutral oil, divided

1 pound ground chicken (or 1 [12-ounce] block of extra-firm tofu for variation)

8 ounces chopped baby bella or cremini mushrooms

1 large carrot, peeled and diced

20 medium Bibb lettuce leaves (from 2 medium heads Bibb lettuce; iceberg and romaine also work great), for serving

Coarsely chopped salted roasted peanuts, for serving

PERFECT PAIRING

An aromatic white wine with a little sweetness to play off the Thai influence, like a Riesling, off-dry Chenin Blanc, or Viognier.

Tofu Variation

1. Swap the chicken for a 12-ounce block of extra-firm tofu.
2. Press the tofu between double-lined paper towels to remove excess moisture and break up into small pieces.
3. Proceed with recipe using tofu instead of chicken.

Auntie Bug's Caramelized Almond & Orange Baked Brie

SERVES 6 TO 8 • **TOTAL TIME** 25 MINUTES

- 1 (10-ounce) wheel Brie cheese
- ½ cup sliced almonds
- ½ stick (4 tablespoons) unsalted butter, cold
- 2 tablespoons light brown sugar
- 1 tablespoon fresh orange juice
- ½ teaspoon kosher salt
- ½ teaspoon freshly ground black pepper
- 2 tablespoons honey
- 1 teaspoon grated orange zest, plus more for garnish
- Leaves from 2 sprigs fresh thyme
- Flaky sea salt, for garnish
- 1 baguette, cut into about 24 (½-inch) slices and toasted (see Hot Tip) or crackers, for serving

PERFECT PAIRING

Get the party started with a dry Champagne or sparkling wine, like a Crémant from France or Cava from Spain.

When I started sharing recipes online, my mom's best friend—Auntie Bug—became my unofficial recipe scout. She would send me hilarious home videos of dishes, including an outrageous baked Brie with just honey, almonds, and a healthy amount of butter. The only catch? Like my mom, Auntie Bug didn't believe in measuring. I finally landed on a version that was a gooey, caramelized dream. I shared it even without the measurements, and boom—it went viral! This (measured) version levels it up with brown sugar, fresh orange, and black pepper for a sweet-savory twist.

1. Preheat the oven to 350°F.
2. Place the Brie into a small, oven-safe baking dish and bake for 15 to 20 minutes, until the top is soft and squishy.
3. Meanwhile, heat a medium, dry skillet over medium heat. Add the almonds and toast, stirring constantly, until fragrant and light golden brown, 3 to 4 minutes. Add the butter and stir constantly until melted. Add the brown sugar, orange juice, salt, and black pepper and cook, stirring occasionally, until the mixture thickens and becomes deep golden brown, 4 to 5 minutes.
4. Reduce the heat to low, add the honey and orange zest, and stir until melted. Keep warm on low until the Brie is ready.
5. When the Brie is done, using a paring knife, remove the top rind by cutting around the edges (leaving an edge to keep the cheese from spilling out), then use tongs to discard. Pour the honey mixture directly over the exposed Brie.
6. Garnish with more orange zest, thyme leaves, flaky salt, and black pepper. Serve with the toasted baguette or crackers for dipping.

HOT TIP

If serving with baguette slices, you can toast them in the oven while the Brie is baking, on a sheet pan lined with parchment paper. Place the baguette slices on the sheet pan and brush the top of each slice with extra-virgin olive oil. Bake on a rack below the Brie for 10 to 15 minutes, until crispy and light golden brown, flipping the toasts midway.

Crispy Pecorino Zucchini Fries

SERVES 4 TO 6 • **TOTAL TIME** 40 MINUTES (PLUS 30 MINUTES OF ZUCCHINI REST TIME)

3 medium zucchini (about 1 pound), cut into 3 x ½-inch fries

2 ½ teaspoons kosher salt, divided

¾ cup tapioca flour (or cornstarch)

1 teaspoon garlic powder

½ teaspoon freshly ground black pepper

2 large eggs

2 teaspoons grated orange zest, plus more for garnish

1 ½ cups panko breadcrumbs

½ cup finely grated Pecorino Romano cheese, plus more for garnish

½ teaspoon paprika

Olive oil spray, as needed

Leaves from 2 sprigs fresh thyme, for garnish

Flaky sea salt, for garnish

Go-To Marinara (page 171) or Calabrian Chili Romesco (page 221) (optional), for serving

PERFECT PAIRING

A fresh orange wine with distinct tannins, or a light-bodied red like a Pinot Noir.

Orange zest and salty Pecorino Romano might not be an obvious match, but once you try them together, you'll wonder why you waited so long. Inspired by a version I had in Rome at Il Vero Alfredo, I took the flavors and ran with them, swapping the fryer for a crisp panko coating and a high-heat roast. The result? A crunchy golden exterior and a tender center without the hassle of frying. Even better with Go-To Marinara (page 171) or Calabrian Chili Romesco (page 221) for dipping.

---

1. Preheat the oven to 425°F.
2. Line a sheet pan with paper towels, arrange the zucchini skin side down, and season with 1 teaspoon of the salt. Cover with another layer of paper towels, pressing down lightly. Let the zucchini "sweat" at room temperature for 30 minutes, replacing the top layer of paper towels halfway through, pressing down firmly to release moisture. Press one final time before dredging. This is crucial for crispy fries!
3. Place an oven-safe wire rack on top of a sheet pan.
4. In a shallow bowl, whisk the tapioca flour, ½ teaspoon of the salt, the garlic powder, and black pepper. In a second bowl, whisk the eggs and orange zest. In a third bowl, mix the panko, Pecorino Romano, paprika, and the remaining 1 teaspoon salt.
5. Using your left (dry) hand, add a few zucchini fries to the tapioca mixture, turn to coat, then shake off any excess. With your right (wet) hand, dip the fries in the egg mixture and allow any excess to drip off, then add to the panko mixture and toss with the dry hand to ensure all sides are well coated. Place the fries in a single layer on the prepared wire rack, and repeat with the remaining fries. Spritz a thin coating of olive oil spray over the fries for extra crispiness.
6. Bake for 20 to 25 minutes, until golden brown and crispy, rotating the pan halfway through.
7. Transfer the fries to a serving platter and garnish with the Pecorino Romano, thyme leaves, flaky salt, and orange zest. Serve with sauce for dipping, if desired.

HOT TIP

To air fry, bake in batches at 400°F until golden and crispy, 10 minutes.

VINO BIANCO

Chile Mango Halibut Ceviche

SERVES 6 • **TOTAL TIME** 15 MINUTES (PLUS MARINATING TIME)

- ¾ cup fresh lime juice (about 6 limes)
- 2 tablespoons blanco tequila (I love LALO)
- 1 pound sashimi-grade halibut, cut into ½-inch cubes
- 2 medium Hass avocados, cut into ½-inch cubes
- 1 medium mango, cut into ½-inch cubes
- 3 medium fresh Fresno or jalapeño peppers, stemmed and seeded, 2 finely chopped and 1 thinly sliced, for garnish (see Hot Tips)
- 2 medium fresh güero (yellow) or jalapeño peppers, stemmed, seeded, and finely chopped (see Hot Tips)
- ½ small red onion, finely chopped
- ½ cup chopped fresh cilantro, for garnish
- 1 teaspoon kosher salt
- Lime wedges, for serving
- Tostadas or tortilla chips, for serving

PERFECT PAIRING

A Melon de Bourgogne like Muscadet, Sauvignon Blanc from Chile or New Zealand, or the Spicy Watermelon Pine-Aperol Margarita (page 284)!

Inspired by a ceviche in Punta Mita, Mexico, this dish brings just the right amount of heat, sweetness, and acidity. Sashimi-grade halibut meets mango, avocado, lime, red onion, Fresno and güero chiles, cilantro, and tequila (my secret ingredient!) for a bright, well-balanced bite. It's delicate, refreshing, and so simple to make. Though it's not cooked, you can control how much the fish cures by adjusting the marinating time (details in method and Hot Tips). Be sure to buy the freshest, sashimi-grade fish the day you plan to serve it. For a stylish presentation, serve in martini glasses or shallow bowls, paired with plenty of tostadas or tortilla chips!

1. In a large glass bowl, combine the lime juice and tequila. Submerge the halibut in the mixture, cover, and refrigerate until the fish becomes opaque and slightly firmer in texture, a minimum of 30 minutes for medium-rare or a maximum of 3 hours for well done, based on preference.
2. When ready to serve, remove the marinated halibut from the fridge and add the avocado, mango, chiles, red onion, cilantro, and salt. Using a spoon, gently mix until well combined. Divide the ceviche among six individual martini glasses or bowls or transfer to a serving platter. Garnish with the Fresno (or jalapeño) pepper slices and chopped cilantro. Serve with lime wedges and tostadas or tortilla chips.

HOT TIPS

Be sure not to exceed 3 hours of cure time for the ceviche or the fish will become tough.

If you prefer less heat, devein the chiles when you remove the seeds. If you prefer a spicier ceviche, you can add or substitute with fresh serrano peppers.

Green Goddess Hummus with Feta

SERVES 4 TO 6 • **TOTAL TIME** 15 MINUTES

- 1 (15-ounce) can chickpeas, drained and rinsed
- 1 cup fresh flat-leaf parsley
- ½ cup coarsely chopped fresh chives
- ¼ cup fresh mint
- ¼ cup extra-virgin olive oil, plus more for serving
- 1 medium fresh jalapeño pepper, stemmed, seeded, deveined, and coarsely chopped
- 2 garlic cloves, coarsely chopped
- 3 tablespoons fresh lemon juice (about 1½ lemons)
- 2 teaspoons grated lemon zest
- 3 tablespoons ice water, plus more as needed
- 1 tablespoon tahini
- 1¾ teaspoons kosher salt
- ¼ teaspoon freshly ground black pepper
- 4 medium ice cubes
- 2 tablespoons crumbled feta (from feta in brine), for garnish
- Ground sumac, for garnish (see Hot Tips)
- Pita chips, for serving
- Crudités, for serving

PERFECT PAIRING

A Sauvignon Blanc from the Central Coast of California to complete the green goddess vibe!

If hummus had a cooler older cousin, this would be it. Herb-packed, zippy, and just spicy enough, it blends parsley, chives, mint, and jalapeño into a smooth, flavor-loaded dip. A crumble of feta and a dusting of sumac take it up a notch. It's the kind of app that feels effortlessly impressive—far more than the reality that you just tossed together some ingredients. The ice and a high-speed blender give it that extra-fluffy texture, but a food processor works too. Serve with pita chips or crudité, and watch it disappear.

---

1. In a high-speed blender (or food processor), add the chickpeas, parsley, chives, mint, oil, jalapeño, garlic, lemon juice and zest, water (see Hot Tips), tahini, salt, and black pepper and blend on high for 30 seconds to 1 minute to break down the chickpeas. Add the ice cubes and blend until completely smooth and fluffy, scraping down the sides as needed, 1 to 2 minutes.
2. Transfer the hummus to a serving bowl. Top with the feta, sumac, and a drizzle of olive oil. Serve with the pita chips and crudités.

HOT TIPS

If you're finding the mixture too dry, add 1 tablespoon of ice water at a time to help it along.

This hummus is at its best after chilling for 30 minutes in the fridge.

Ground sumac is a tart and lemony spice from the Middle East. Garnish with more lemon zest and a pinch of cayenne if you can't find it.

ampelos

Mini Pineapple Teriyaki Meatballs

SERVES 10 AS AN APPETIZER, OR 4 TO 6 FOR DINNER • **TOTAL TIME** 45 MINUTES

FOR THE MEATBALLS

1 tablespoon avocado or other neutral oil, plus more for shaping

1 large egg plus 1 large egg yolk

4 green onions (white and green parts), thinly sliced, plus more for garnish

¾ cup panko breadcrumbs

3 garlic cloves, grated or finely chopped

3 tablespoons pineapple juice (from 6-ounce can, remainder used below)

1 tablespoon peeled and grated fresh ginger

1 teaspoon garlic powder

1 teaspoon kosher salt

½ teaspoon freshly ground black pepper

1½ pounds ground chicken (preferably dark meat)

Toasted sesame seeds, for garnish

There's something about mini meatballs that just hits different—they're bite-size, juicy, and perfect for snacking or piling onto a plate. These glazed teriyaki chicken meatballs bring layered flavor in every bite, thanks to pineapple juice, green onion, and plenty of ginger and garlic. The glaze? A quick blend of soy sauce, rice vinegar, pineapple juice, brown sugar, and a little cornstarch for that glossy, sticky finish. It all comes together in just 45 minutes—the glaze simmers while the meatballs bake, and the sheet pan method keeps cleanup a breeze. They're the perfect pregame to a meal or served as the main event over Steamed Rice (page 244) with extra glaze—an appetizer and weeknight favorite in one!

1. **MAKE THE MEATBALLS:** Place one oven rack in the top third of the oven and one in the middle and preheat the oven to 400°F. Line a large sheet pan with parchment paper, and coat the paper with 1 tablespoon of the oil.
2. In a large bowl, whisk the egg and egg yolk until combined. Add the green onions, panko, garlic, pineapple juice, fresh ginger, garlic powder, salt, and black pepper and stir to combine. Add the chicken and mix well.
3. Using a ½-ounce cookie scoop or 1 tablespoon measure, portion the mixture into about 45 heaping tablespoon-sized balls and place directly on the oiled parchment paper. Lightly oil your hands and roll the meatballs between your palms until they're smooth and return to the pan, spacing 1 inch apart.
4. Bake on the middle rack, using tongs to flip the meatballs over halfway through, about 24 minutes total, until the meatballs are light golden brown and cooked through. Turn the broiler on high and move the sheet pan to the upper oven rack. Broil for 3 to 4 minutes, just until the color deepens and the meatballs are slightly crisper.

(recipe continues)

FOR THE PINEAPPLE TERIYAKI GLAZE

Pineapple juice (remainder from 6-ounce can, used above)

½ cup reduced-sodium soy sauce

⅓ cup packed light brown sugar

3 tablespoons honey

2 tablespoons rice vinegar

2 tablespoons cornstarch

PERFECT PAIRING

A medium-bodied California or French rosé made from Pinot Noir grapes.

5. **MAKE THE PINEAPPLE TERIYAKI GLAZE:** Meanwhile, in a large skillet over medium-high heat, combine the pineapple juice, soy sauce, brown sugar, honey, and rice vinegar and bring to a rapid simmer.
6. In a small bowl, whisk ½ cup cold water and the cornstarch until no clumps remain to create a slurry. Once the glaze is simmering, slowly pour in the slurry until combined, whisking constantly. Cook, stirring occasionally, until the mixture thickens enough to coat the back of a spoon, about 2 minutes. Reduce the heat to low, add the meatballs and gently toss them with a spatula or spoon until evenly coated.
7. **TO SERVE:** Transfer the meatballs to a serving platter and garnish with the sesame seeds and green onions. Place cocktail picks in each meatball.

SALAD PARTY

I was that quirky kid who preferred salads to candy, so trust me when I say salads deserve the spotlight. With the right mix of ingredients and a knockout dressing, a salad can be vibrant, flavor-packed, nourishing, and downright celebratory. And like any great party, the key is balance—contrasting salty, sweet, and tangy flavors, mixing up textures, and (more often than not) inviting cheese to join the fun.

This lineup brings the crowd-pleasers: family favorites like Nana's Iconic Crunchy Lemon Parm Salad (page 59) and Sweet & Spicy Mexican Fruit Salad with Tajín Vinaigrette (page 67), globetrotting inspirations like Tuscan Zucchini & Arugula Salad with Parm Crisps (page 72), and full-on meal-worthy bowls like My Favorite Chinese Chicken Salad (page 63), My Big Fat Italian Chopped Salad (page 80), and Spiced Chicken & Black Bean Taco Salad (page 75).

The best part? Salads are a choose-your-own-adventure kind of dish—an open invitation to play with flavors, what's in season, and riff on what you crave. This chapter is a well-dressed party mix of crisp, refreshing, hearty, and bold recipes, proving that salads can be just as exciting as any main course. So let's mix it up and get this salad party started!

Nana's Iconic Crunchy Lemon Parm Salad

SERVES 4 TO 6 • **TOTAL TIME** 15 MINUTES (PLUS CHILL TIME)

5 medium romaine hearts, bottoms trimmed (see Hot Tips)

½ cup extra-virgin olive oil

2 cups fresh, finely grated Parmigiano-Reggiano cheese, plus more for garnish (see Hot Tips)

¼ cup plus 2 tablespoons fresh lemon juice (about 3 lemons)

Freshly ground black pepper

Flaky sea salt (optional)

PERFECT PAIRING

A bright and fresh white wine like Sauvignon Blanc, or an Aligoté from France.

This salad has always been the star of our family gatherings—and after sharing it with my online community, it was clear you all felt the same way. With over 70 million views, it practically broke the internet! Every day, I get messages and videos from people marveling at how a salad with so few ingredients can taste this incredible. We like to call it Nana's magic touch, but the real secret lies in top-quality ingredients and her tried-and-true technique. First, the romaine is washed and chilled for maximum crunch. Next, it's coated in extra-virgin olive oil, allowing freshly grated Parmigiano-Reggiano to cling to the leaves before a toss in lemon juice. Repeating this process layers flavor and creates the signature creamy dressing—no blender, no fuss, and now you have the magic touch, too. I love topping this with chicken or shrimp, but make it your own with whatever protein you're craving. It goes with too many dishes to list here!

1. Separate the romaine leaves, wash, shake off excess water, and tightly wrap them with a kitchen towel or paper towels. Place in the fridge for at least 20 minutes (and up to overnight) to crisp up, preferably in a crisper drawer. This step is critical!
2. Roughly chop the chilled romaine leaves (about 10 cups) and place in a large bowl. Drizzle with half of the oil and using your hands or tongs, toss until thoroughly coated. Add half of the Parmigiano-Reggiano and toss again. Add half of the lemon juice and toss again. Repeat this process with the remaining olive oil, Parmigiano-Reggiano, and lemon juice, evenly coating each leaf with every ingredient.
3. **TO SERVE:** Divide among serving bowls and garnish with more Parmigiano-Reggiano, a few twists of black pepper, and a tiny pinch of flaky salt, if desired.

HOT TIPS

Using whole romaine hearts is essential to this salad's magical crunch, but if you can't find them, pre-chopped romaine hearts will do—use 10 cups pre-chopped romaine hearts, from about 2 (10-ounce) bags.

This is a recipe where the extra effort for fresh, finely grated Parm really improves the dish.

Summer Stone Fruit Salad

with Basil Mint Vinaigrette

SERVES 4 • **TOTAL TIME** 20 MINUTES

FOR THE BASIL MINT VINAIGRETTE

- ¾ cup extra-virgin olive oil
- ¼ cup plus 1 tablespoon white balsamic vinegar
- 1 cup fresh basil
- ½ cup fresh mint
- 1 small shallot, quartered
- 2 tablespoons honey
- 1 teaspoon kosher salt
- ¾ teaspoon freshly ground black pepper

FOR THE SALAD

- 1 (5-ounce) container baby arugula (about 5 cups packed)
- 1 (4-ounce) ball burrata cheese, at room temperature
- 1 cup cherry tomatoes (about 6 ounces), halved
- 1 peach, pitted and sliced ¾-inch thick
- 1 nectarine, pitted and sliced ¾-inch thick
- 1 plum, pitted and sliced ¾-inch thick
- Chopped salted roasted pistachios, for garnish
- Flaky sea salt, for serving

PERFECT PAIRING

A Côtes de Provence rosé is perfect! Or try a rosé from Cassis or Bandol!

This vibrant salad is a love letter to summer—peak-season stone fruit, peppery baby arugula, and luscious burrata, all tied together with an herbaceous white balsamic vinaigrette so good, you'll want to drink it. Fresh basil, mint, and savory shallots balance the sweetness of cherry tomatoes and ripe stone fruit, while a scattering of salty, roasted pistachios add an irresistible crunch. Want to switch it up? Swap in whatever's in season or excites you—think berries, cherries, crisp apples, pears, or persimmons. No matter the variation, this salad is guaranteed to be chic, endlessly adaptable, and the kind of dish that demands a spot on your table (and maybe your Instagram feed).

1. **MAKE THE BASIL MINT VINAIGRETTE:** In a blender, add the olive oil, vinegar, basil, mint, shallot, honey, salt, and black pepper. Blend on high until smooth and uniform in color, 1 to 2 minutes. Set aside (see Hot Tip).
2. **MAKE THE SALAD:** Just before serving, in a large bowl, add the arugula and add half the basil mint vinaigrette. Using your hands or tongs, toss to combine.
3. **TO SERVE:** Transfer to a large serving dish. Tear the burrata over the salad and top with the tomatoes and stone fruit. Drizzle the remaining vinaigrette over the salad, to taste. Garnish with plenty of pistachios and flaky salt.

HOT TIP

This vinaigrette transforms roasted vegetables, steamed potatoes, or pan-roasted fish. Store it in an airtight container in the refrigerator for up to 4 days.

My Favorite Chinese Chicken Salad

SERVES 4 TO 6 • **TOTAL TIME** 45 MINUTES

FOR THE TOASTED SESAME DRESSING

- ¼ cup rice vinegar
- 1 tablespoon reduced-sodium soy sauce
- 2 tablespoons honey
- ¾ teaspoon kosher salt
- ½ teaspoon freshly ground black pepper
- ¼ cup plus 2 tablespoons extra-virgin olive oil
- 2 tablespoons toasted sesame oil

FOR THE CRISPY CHICKEN

- 6 (3-ounce) chicken breast tenderloins
- 2 teaspoons kosher salt, divided
- ½ teaspoon freshly ground black pepper
- ½ cup all-purpose flour
- 2 large eggs
- 1 cup panko breadcrumbs
- ¼ cup avocado or other neutral oil, plus more as needed
- 1 tablespoon toasted sesame oil

Los Angeles has been serving up versions of this classic since the 1950s! If you've ever craved that perfect mix of crisp greens, crunchy toppings, and a sweet-savory punch, this one's for you. Inspired by the iconic version at Joan's on Third in LA, my take delivers all the texture, flavor, and nostalgia—no trip to West Hollywood required. With this salad, more is more, and even the chicken tenders get a glow-up: panko-breaded and shallow-fried in toasted sesame oil. Prefer to skip the chicken? Try it with fried tofu or a jammy boiled egg. However you make it, this salad is a guaranteed favorite.

---

1. Preheat the oven to 350°F. Line a sheet pan with parchment paper and set an oven-safe wire rack over a second sheet pan.
2. **MAKE THE TOASTED SESAME DRESSING:** In a medium bowl, whisk the vinegar, soy sauce, honey, salt, and black pepper. Slowly stream in the olive oil and toasted sesame oil, whisking constantly to thoroughly combine, about 1 minute. Set aside.
3. **MAKE THE CRISPY CHICKEN:** Place the chicken tenderloins on a large plate and season both sides with 1 teaspoon of the salt and the black pepper.
4. Set up a dredging station using 3 shallow bowls. In the first bowl, whisk the flour and ½ teaspoon of the salt. In the second, whisk the eggs until well combined. In the third bowl, stir together the panko and the remaining ½ teaspoon of salt. Using your left (dry) hand, add a few chicken tenders at a time to the flour mixture, turn to coat, then shake off any excess. Using your right (wet) hand, dip the chicken into the egg mixture and allow any excess to drip off, and add to the panko mixture. Use the dry hand to thoroughly coat the chicken in the panko mixture. Transfer to the parchment-lined sheet pan. Repeat with the remaining tenders.
5. In a large skillet, heat the avocado and sesame oil over medium-high heat. Once shimmering, add as many tenders as will comfortably fit, working in batches as to not overcrowd the pan. Add more oil in between batches, if needed, so the bottom of the pan is fully coated. Cook until very crispy and deeply golden brown on both sides, about 2 minutes per side. They will finish cooking in the oven.

(recipe continues)

FOR THE SALAD

- 1 small head iceberg lettuce, finely chopped (about 5 cups)
- ½ medium head Napa cabbage, thinly sliced (about 5 cups)
- 1 cup thinly sliced snap peas
- 1 small bunch green onions (white and green parts), thinly sliced
- 1 cup crunchy wonton strips
- 2 small mandarin oranges, peeled, and cut into supremes (see Hot Tip) or 1 (11-ounce) can, drained (optional)
- ½ cup coarsely chopped fresh cilantro
- ½ cup toasted sliced almonds
- ¼ cup toasted sesame seeds

PERFECT PAIRING

A Riesling with apple-skin notes, the tiniest touch of sweetness, and lots of ripe fruit flavor.

6. Place the cooked tenders on the wire rack and transfer to the oven.
7. Bake for about 5 minutes, until firm when pressed and cooked through, reaching an internal temperature of 165°F. Remove and cool slightly on the wire rack.
8. **MAKE THE SALAD:** In a large bowl, combine the iceberg, cabbage, snap peas, green onions, wonton strips, mandarins (if using), cilantro, almonds, and sesame seeds.
9. Whisk the toasted sesame dressing, pour over the salad, and mix well. Chop the chicken into large, bite-size pieces.
10. **TO SERVE:** Evenly divide the salad among serving bowls and top with the chopped crispy chicken.

HOT TIP

Adding freshly peeled mandarin segments is definitely an extra step, but it's one that delivers. To get those gorgeous sections without the pith, you'll need to supreme the mandarin. A sharp knife is key. Start by slicing off the top and bottom to create flat edges. Stand the fruit upright and use a sharp knife to cut away the peel and pith, following the fruit's curve. Then, hold the peeled mandarin over a bowl and carefully slice between the membranes to release the clean, juicy segments.

Sweet & Spicy Mexican Fruit Salad

with Tajín Vinaigrette

SERVES 6 TO 8 • **TOTAL TIME** 25 MINUTES

In Mexico or Southern California, few things hit the spot like a roadside fruit stand—bright, juicy slices piled high and finished with a squeeze of lime and a generous shake of Tajín, the zesty chile-lime seasoning that adds a tangy, spicy kick to every bite. This version takes it a step further with a Tajín vinaigrette, fresh jalapeño (for medium heat) or serrano (for a real kick), mild queso fresco or salty cotija, crunchy pepitas, and fresh mint over a vibrant mix of not just fruit but also veggies. Just be sure to toss with the dressing right before serving to keep the fruit crisp.

FOR THE TAJÍN VINAIGRETTE

- ½ cup fresh lime juice (about 5 to 6 limes)
- 2 tablespoons agave nectar or honey
- 2 teaspoons grated lime zest
- 2 teaspoons Tajín seasoning, plus more for garnish
- 1 teaspoon kosher salt
- ¼ cup mild extra-virgin olive oil

FOR THE FRUIT SALAD

- 3 cups (1½-inch cubed) watermelon
- 1½ cups (1½-inch cubed) cantaloupe
- 1½ cups (peeled and 1-inch cubed) jicama
- 1½ cups (1½-inch cubed) pineapple
- 1¼ cups (halved and 1-inch cubed) unpeeled Persian (mini) cucumbers
- 1 small fresh serrano or jalapeño pepper, stemmed, seeded, and very thinly sliced
- ½ cup crumbled queso fresco or cotija cheese
- Salted roasted pepitas (pumpkin seeds), for garnish
- Fresh torn mint, for garnish

1. **MAKE THE TAJÍN VINAIGRETTE:** In a large bowl, whisk the lime juice, agave, lime zest, Tajín, and salt. Slowly drizzle in the oil, whisking constantly until thoroughly combined. Set aside.
2. **MAKE THE FRUIT SALAD:** Into the bowl with the dressing, add the watermelon, cantaloupe, jicama, pineapple, cucumbers, and serrano or jalapeño pepper and gently toss to combine.
3. **TO SERVE:** Transfer the salad to a serving dish and top with the queso fresco or cotija. Garnish with the pepitas, Tajín, and torn mint.

HOT TIPS

If you're making the salad ahead of time, mix the Tajín Vinaigrette in a sealable jar and dress the salad just before you serve.

PERFECT PAIRING

A sparkling wine, like Cava, or a Prosecco!

Zesty Fattoush Salad

with Lemony Feta Vinaigrette

SERVES 6 TO 8 • **TOTAL TIME** 30 MINUTES

FOR THE LEMONY FETA VINAIGRETTE

- 1½ cups crumbled feta
- ½ cup extra-virgin olive oil
- ¼ cup fresh lemon juice (about 2 lemons)
- 2 garlic cloves, grated or finely chopped
- 2 teaspoons pomegranate molasses
- 2 teaspoons ground sumac
- ½ teaspoon dried mint
- ½ teaspoon dried oregano
- ½ teaspoon kosher salt
- ½ teaspoon freshly ground black pepper

FOR THE PITA CHIPS

- ¼ cup extra-virgin olive oil
- 3 (6- to 8-inch) rounds pita bread, torn into bite-size pieces
- 1 teaspoon kosher salt

FOR THE SALAD

- 6 cups chopped romaine (from 2 to 3 medium romaine hearts)
- 4 Persian cucumbers, unpeeled and diced
- 3 large tomatoes, diced
- ½ large red onion, thinly sliced
- ½ cup chopped fresh mint, plus more for garnish
- 4 small radishes, tops trimmed and thinly sliced
- ¾ cup crumbled feta

I became obsessed with fattoush—the Levantine chopped salad of crisp lettuce, cucumbers, tomatoes, onions, fresh herbs, and fried pita—while working my first job at a Mediterranean restaurant as a teenager. Though feta isn't traditional, its creamy saltiness works beautifully here. Tangy pomegranate molasses and citrusy sumac add depth and brightness. You can find both in the specialty grocery section, a Middle Eastern market, or online. No luck? If you can't find the pomegranate, swap in balsamic glaze and replace the sumac with an extra squeeze of lemon and a pinch of cayenne. Homemade pita chips are always a win, but if you're short on time and want to grab a bag at the store—no judgment!

1. Preheat the oven to 425°F. Line a sheet pan with parchment paper.
2. **MAKE THE LEMONY FETA VINAIGRETTE:** In a large bowl, whisk the feta, oil, lemon juice, garlic, pomegranate molasses, sumac, mint, oregano, salt, and black pepper until thickened with small bits of feta, 1 to 2 minutes.
3. **MAKE THE PITA CHIPS:** Place the pita pieces in a single layer on the prepared sheet pan. Drizzle with the oil and sprinkle with the salt. Using your hands or tongs, toss until thoroughly coated. Bake for 8 to 12 minutes, until golden brown and crispy, depending on chip size.
4. **ASSEMBLE THE SALAD:** To the large bowl with the lemony feta vinaigrette, add the romaine, cucumbers, tomatoes, red onion, mint, and pita chips. Toss until thoroughly coated, and transfer to a serving bowl or platter. Top with the radish and feta and sprinkle with chopped mint.

PERFECT PAIRING

A lemony, high-acid Assyrtiko (a white grape grown mostly in Greece) or a Sauvignon Blanc from France would be perfect!

HOT TIP

Of course you can buy pre-crumbled feta, but for this recipe, you'll want to use the creamiest cheese, which is feta in brine.

Best Ever Pasta Salad

SERVES 8 TO 10 • **TOTAL TIME** 35 MINUTES

FOR THE ZESTY RED WINE VINAIGRETTE

- 3/4 cup extra-virgin olive oil
- 1/4 cup plus 2 tablespoons red wine vinegar
- 1 garlic clove, grated
- 1 1/2 teaspoons kosher salt
- 1 teaspoon dried basil
- 1 teaspoon dried oregano
- 1/2 teaspoon crushed red pepper
- 1/2 teaspoon freshly ground black pepper
- 1/4 teaspoon sugar

FOR THE PASTA SALAD

- 2 tablespoons kosher salt
- 16 ounces dried fusilli
- 1 (15-ounce) can chickpeas, drained and rinsed
- 2 cups cherry tomatoes, halved
- 3 small Persian cucumbers, diced
- 2 celery stalks, diced
- 2 bell peppers, diced
- 1/2 red onion, diced
- 1/2 cup grated Asiago cheese
- 1/2 cup (1/2-inch cubed) Genoa salami
- 1/2 cup (1/2-inch cubed) Parmigiano-Reggiano
- 1/2 cup finely grated Parmigiano-Reggiano, plus more for garnish
- 1/2 cup chopped fresh cilantro, plus more for garnish

My mom's signature pasta salad holds a very special place in my heart—it was the first recipe I ever shared online, and to this day, it remains a community favorite. I love hearing how it's racked up potluck victories, thanks to a zesty red wine vinaigrette that ties everything together, coating crisp veggies, hearty chickpeas, savory salami, and cheese. Yes, there's a bit of prep here, so blast some music, grab a glass of vino, and get chopping—it's worth it! Bring this to your next barbecue or potluck and let me know if it wins any awards!

---

1. **MAKE THE ZESTY RED WINE VINAIGRETTE:** In a sealable pint-size jar or container, add the oil, vinegar, garlic, salt, basil, oregano, crushed red pepper, black pepper, and sugar. Close the lid and shake vigorously until thickened, about 1 minute.
2. **MAKE THE PASTA SALAD:** Bring a large pot of water with the salt to a boil. Add the fusilli and cook until al dente according to package directions. Using a colander, drain the pasta and immediately run under cold water until completely cool.
3. In a large bowl, add the pasta and a generous splash of the vinaigrette and toss. Add the chickpeas, tomatoes, cucumbers, celery, bell peppers, red onion, Asiago, salami, cubed and grated Parmigiano-Reggiano, and cilantro or parsley. Add the remaining vinaigrette and toss until all the ingredients are well distributed and thoroughly coated.
4. Serve immediately or chill in the fridge, covered, for a few hours or overnight before serving. Garnish with a generous shower of Parmigiano-Reggiano, cilantro, or parsley.

PERFECT PAIRING

A light and zesty Trebbiano, Pecorino, or Pinot Grigio with higher acidity and notes of citrus are the perfect sip for every flavor-packed bite.

Tuscan Zucchini & Arugula Salad

with Parm Crisps

SERVES 6 • **TOTAL TIME** 20 MINUTES

FOR THE PARM CRISPS

1½ cups fresh, finely grated Parmigiano-Reggiano cheese (see Hot Tips)

FOR THE ZUCCHINI AND ARUGULA SALAD

2 small zucchini, very thinly sliced into rounds (see Hot Tips)

2 yellow summer squash, very thinly sliced into rounds (see Hot Tips)

¼ cup plus 2 tablespoons extra-virgin olive oil, divided

2 tablespoons fresh lemon juice (about 1 lemon)

¾ teaspoon kosher salt, divided

½ teaspoon freshly ground black pepper, plus more for garnish

¾ cup fresh, finely grated Parmigiano-Reggiano cheese, divided (see Hot Tips)

1 (5-ounce) container baby arugula (about 5 cups packed)

Flaky sea salt, for garnish

PERFECT PAIRING

A cold, fizzy, dry Lambrusco from Emilia-Romagna is this salad's destiny!

This salad will completely change the way you think about raw zucchini—it's not just for crudité. With only a few high-quality ingredients and the right technique, this salad really shines. One very important note: If you skip the real-deal Parmigiano-Reggiano for the crisps, you risk ending up with a rubbery mess—trust me, it's worth getting the good stuff.

1. **MAKE THE PARM CRISPS:** Preheat the oven to 425°F. Line a sheet pan with parchment paper.
2. Spread the Parmigiano-Reggiano onto the parchment paper, creating an even square, about 10 x 10 inches and ⅛ inch in height. Bake for 7 to 8 minutes, until golden brown and crispy. Allow to cool completely on the sheet pan, then use your hands to break the crisp into imperfect 1-inch-sized pieces.
3. **MAKE THE ZUCCHINI AND ARUGULA SALAD:** In a medium bowl, add the zucchini and squash rounds, ¼ cup of the oil, lemon juice, ½ teaspoon of the salt, and the black pepper. Using your hands or tongs, gently toss until thoroughly coated. Add ½ cup of the Parmigiano-Reggiano and toss again until the cheese is clinging to every surface.
4. On a serving platter, lay out the arugula and toss with the remaining 2 tablespoons of oil and remaining ¼ teaspoon of salt. Top the arugula with the dressed zucchini and squash, leaving some of the arugula peeking out around the edges. Sprinkle the remaining ¼ cup of Parmigiano-Reggiano and the Parm crisps over the top. Garnish with a few twists of black pepper and a sprinkle of flaky salt.

HOT TIPS

If you don't have time to make the Parm crisps, use some crushed croutons instead.

Break out your mandoline to create perfectly even, super-thin slices of zucchini and squash. Don't forget to wear your cut-proof glove!

This is a recipe where real fresh, finely grated Parm is crucial for the texture.

Spiced Chicken & Black Bean Taco Salad
with Cilantro Lime Vinaigrette

SERVES 4 • **TOTAL TIME** 40 MINUTES

FOR THE CILANTRO LIME VINAIGRETTE

½ cup finely chopped fresh cilantro

⅓ cup fresh lime juice (about 3 to 4 limes)

2 garlic cloves, grated or finely chopped

2 teaspoons agave nectar or honey

2 teaspoons Tajín seasoning (see Hot Tip)

½ teaspoon kosher salt

½ teaspoon freshly ground black pepper

¾ cup extra-virgin olive oil

FOR THE SALAD

1 (15-ounce) can black beans, drained and rinsed

1 cup fresh corn kernels (from 1 cob), or frozen, thawed

1 bell pepper, seeded and diced

½ small red onion, thinly sliced

This taco salad brings a little extra play to the salad bowl—fresh, flavorful, and just the right amount of fun (hello, crushed tortilla chips!). A vibrant mix of black beans, fresh corn, peppers, avocado, cotija cheese, and pepitas gets tossed in a tangy cilantro vinaigrette, whisked directly in the bowl for minimal cleanup. Seared chicken thighs—coated in a subtly smoky herb seasoning—make it a satisfying meal. (Bonus: These thighs are just as good on any salad or grain bowl.) Short on time? Grab a rotisserie chicken and call it a day!

---

1. **MAKE THE CILANTRO LIME VINAIGRETTE:** In a large bowl, whisk the cilantro, lime juice, garlic, agave, Tajín, salt, and black pepper until well combined. Whisking constantly, slowly stream in the olive oil.
2. **MAKE THE SALAD:** To the vinaigrette, add the black beans, corn, bell pepper, and red onion and mix well. Set aside.

(recipe continues)

FOR THE SPICED CHICKEN

1½ teaspoons kosher salt

1 teaspoon garlic powder

1 teaspoon dried oregano

1 teaspoon smoked paprika

½ teaspoon freshly ground black pepper

½ teaspoon ground cumin

1½ pounds boneless, skinless chicken thighs

2 tablespoons avocado or other neutral oil

FOR ASSEMBLY

8 heaping cups chopped romaine lettuce (from about 2 medium heads)

1 cup crushed tortilla chips, plus more for garnish

½ cup crumbled cotija cheese, plus more for garnish

½ cup salted roasted pepitas (pumpkin seeds)

1 Hass avocado, diced

2 teaspoons Tajín seasoning, for garnish (see Hot Tip)

Lime wedges, for serving

PERFECT PAIRING

A chilled, lighter-bodied red wine like a Gamay, Pinot Noir, or Barbera—or the Summer Berry Sangria (page 287)!

3. **MAKE THE SPICED CHICKEN:** In a small bowl, mix the salt, garlic powder, oregano, smoked paprika, black pepper, and cumin. Pat the chicken thighs dry with a paper towel and place on a large plate. Press the spice mixture onto both sides.
4. Heat the oil in a large skillet over medium-high heat. Once shimmering, add the chicken, working in batches as to not overcrowd the pan, and cook, undisturbed, until golden brown and slightly crisp, 5 to 7 minutes. Flip and cook until the chicken reaches an internal temperature of 165°F, 6 to 8 minutes. Transfer the chicken to a plate and let it rest for at least 10 minutes. Cut the chicken into 1-inch cubes (reserve the juices!).
5. **TO ASSEMBLE:** In the bowl with the vinaigrette and vegetable mixture, add the romaine, tortilla chips, cotija, and pepitas. Gently toss to evenly coat. Divide among four bowls and top with the chicken and reserved juices and avocado. Garnish with more crushed tortilla chips, cotija, pepitas, and Tajín, and serve with lime wedges.

HOT TIP

No Tajín? Use a chile-lime seasoning (with salt) or make your own using 1 tablespoon fine chile flakes, ¾ teaspoon kosher salt, and 1 teaspoon grated lime zest.

Peach, Kale & Crunchy Quinoa Salad

with White Balsamic Vinaigrette

SERVES 4 TO 6 • **TOTAL TIME** 35 MINUTES

FOR THE WHITE BALSAMIC VINAIGRETTE

3 tablespoons white balsamic vinegar

2 tablespoons honey

1 tablespoon fresh lemon juice (about ½ lemon)

1 tablespoon whole grain mustard

1 teaspoon kosher salt

½ teaspoon freshly ground black pepper

½ cup extra-virgin olive oil

FOR THE SALAD

1 cup cooked and cooled quinoa (see Hot Tips)

2 large bunches lacinato kale, stems removed, leaves finely chopped

3 peaches, pitted and diced

2 Hass avocados, cubed

½ small red onion, thinly sliced

1 cup store-bought candied pecans, coarsely chopped

¾ cup crumbled goat cheese or feta, divided

Freshly ground black pepper

PERFECT PAIRING

A vibrant white wine from Portugal like Vinho Verde or the Blackberry Bourbon Smash (page 292)!

This is the kale salad to win over skeptics—tender kale tossed in a white balsamic vinaigrette (see Hot Tips), with juicy peaches, creamy goat cheese, avocado, sweet candied pecans, and crunchy oven-roasted quinoa. The vinaigrette balances kale's earthy bite, while ripe fruit (peaches, berries, or whatever's in season) adds a fresh, juicy contrast. And the crispy, nutty roasted quinoa? Absolutely worth turning on the oven. This salad is perfect as is, but if you're looking for something heartier, add chicken or steak.

---

1. **MAKE THE WHITE BALSAMIC VINAIGRETTE:** In a medium bowl or measuring cup, whisk the vinegar, honey, lemon juice, mustard, salt, and black pepper. Slowly drizzle in olive oil while whisking to thoroughly combine and set aside.
2. **MAKE THE SALAD:** Preheat the oven to 400°F. Line a sheet pan with parchment paper.
3. Spread the cooked quinoa in a thin layer across the prepared sheet pan. Bake, tossing halfway through, for about 20 minutes, until deep golden brown and crispy. If using an air fryer, bake at 375°F, tossing halfway through, for about 20 minutes total.
4. In a large bowl, add the kale and a quarter of the white balsamic vinaigrette. Using your hands, massage the kale until it starts to become tender, 1 to 2 minutes. Add the peaches, avocados, onion, candied pecans, toasted quinoa, and ½ cup of the cheese. Add the remaining vinaigrette and toss well.
5. **TO SERVE:** Transfer to a serving platter or bowl and top with the remaining ¼ cup cheese and a few twists of black pepper.

HOT TIPS

White balsamic vinegar is lighter and less sweet than traditional balsamic vinegar. If you can't find it, use white wine vinegar or champagne vinegar.

To cook quinoa: Bring 2 cups of water or chicken stock to a boil. Add 1 cup quinoa and stir to combine. Reduce the heat to medium-low and simmer, covered, until the quinoa is tender and the liquid has evaporated, about 20 minutes. Remove from the heat and fluff with a fork.

My Big Fat Italian Chopped Salad

SERVES 6 • **TOTAL TIME** 30 MINUTES

FOR THE ITALIAN VINAIGRETTE

- ⅓ cup red wine vinegar
- 2 tablespoons jarred pepperoncini brine
- 2 garlic cloves, grated
- 1½ teaspoons kosher salt
- 1 teaspoon Dijon mustard
- 1 teaspoon dried oregano
- ½ teaspoon freshly ground black pepper
- ½ teaspoon dried basil
- ½ teaspoon sugar
- ¼ teaspoon crushed red pepper
- ¾ cup extra-virgin olive oil

FOR THE SALAD

- 3 romaine hearts, chopped
- 1 small head of radicchio, chopped
- 2 cups cherry tomatoes, halved (about 12 ounces)
- 1 (15-ounce) can chickpeas, drained and rinsed
- 1 cup sliced Castelvetrano olives
- 1 cup sliced pepperoncini
- 2 celery stalks, diced
- 4 ounces Genoa salami, cut into ½-inch cubes (see Hot Tip)
- ½ medium red onion, thinly sliced
- 1 cup (½-inch cubes) Asiago cheese
- 1½ cups finely grated Parmigiano-Reggiano cheese

This fully loaded Italian chopped salad is my ode to the bold, briny, and craveable restaurant salads I grew up on. It all starts with a zesty homemade dressing—pepperoncini brine, herbs, mustard, garlic, and just a kiss of sugar. Radicchio and celery mix with romaine for layers of flavor and crunch, while cubed Asiago, grated Parm, and buttery Castelvetrano olives bring salty richness. Chickpeas and Genoa salami add heft and spice, making it a guaranteed crowd-pleaser. Go vegetarian with extra chickpeas or your favorite beans.

1. **MAKE THE ITALIAN VINAIGRETTE:** In a large bowl, whisk the vinegar, pepperoncini brine, garlic, salt, mustard, oregano, black pepper, basil, sugar, and crushed red pepper. Whisking constantly, slowly stream in the olive oil to combine, 1 to 2 minutes.
2. **MAKE THE SALAD:** In the same bowl, add the romaine, radicchio, tomatoes, chickpeas, olives, pepperoncini, celery, salami, red onion, Asiago, and Parmigiano-Reggiano. Toss to combine.
3. **TO SERVE:** Divide among six plates and top with additional Parmigiano-Reggiano to taste.

PERFECT PAIRING

An aromatic Ribolla Gialla from Friuli, or a Sauvignon Blanc or Pinot Blanc.

HOT TIP

If you can buy whole Genoa salami and cube it, great, but pre-sliced chopped salami will work just as well!

Easy Brussels Sprouts Salad

with Honey Shallot Vinaigrette

SERVES 6 TO 8 • **TOTAL TIME** 25 MINUTES

FOR THE HONEY SHALLOT VINAIGRETTE

- ½ cup extra-virgin olive oil
- 1 medium shallot, finely chopped
- 3 tablespoons white balsamic vinegar
- 2 tablespoons fresh lemon juice (about 1 lemon)
- 2 tablespoons honey
- 1 teaspoon kosher salt
- ½ teaspoon freshly ground black pepper

FOR THE BRUSSELS SPROUTS SALAD

- 10 cups thinly shaved brussels sprouts (about 1½ pounds whole or 24 ounces store-bought shredded)
- ⅓ cup pine nuts
- 1¼ cups finely grated Parmigiano-Reggiano cheese, plus more for garnish
- 1 large Honeycrisp or Fuji apple, cored and diced
- ½ cup sweetened dried cranberries
- ½ cup pomegranate seeds, plus more for garnish

This salad won over the brussels sprouts holdouts at our Thanksgiving table a few years ago, and it's been a staple ever since. The secret is in the method: First, the leaves get a good massage with a shallot and honey-infused vinaigrette (think: veg spa treatment), tenderizing them while packing in flavor. Pops of sweetness from apples, pomegranate seeds, and dried cranberries balance the salty bite of Parmigiano-Reggiano and the richness of toasted pine nuts. Incredibly versatile, this salad welcomes any mix of fresh or dried fruits and nuts—and bonus, it's a great make-ahead option. Who knew brussels could be this good!

1. **MAKE THE HONEY SHALLOT VINAIGRETTE:** In a sealable pint-size jar or container, combine the oil, shallot, vinegar, lemon juice, honey, salt, and black pepper. Close and shake vigorously until thickened, about 1 minute. Set aside.
2. **MAKE THE BRUSSELS SPROUTS SALAD:** In a large serving bowl, add the brussels sprouts and half of the honey shallot vinaigrette. Using your hands, gently massage just until they soften, 1 to 2 minutes. Set aside until ready to assemble.
3. Heat a small, dry skillet over medium heat. Add the pine nuts and toast, stirring frequently, until fragrant and golden brown, 2 to 3 minutes. Immediately transfer to a bowl and set aside to cool.
4. To the bowl with the brussels sprouts, add the Parmigiano-Reggiano, apple, cranberries, pomegranate seeds, and pine nuts and toss to combine.
5. **TO SERVE:** Pour the remaining vinaigrette over the prepared salad and toss well. Top with additional Parmigiano-Reggiano and pomegranate seeds.

PERFECT PAIRING

A lighter-bodied Gamay, Cinsault, or Pinot Noir.

Little Gem Caesar Wedge
with Lime-Zested Breadcrumbs

SERVES 4 • **TOTAL TIME** 25 MINUTES

FOR THE SALAD

4 heads little gem lettuce

3 tablespoons extra-virgin olive oil

2 heaping tablespoons drained capers

½ cup finely grated Parmigiano-Reggiano cheese, plus more for garnish

FOR THE LIME-ZESTED BREADCRUMBS

¾ cup panko breadcrumbs

½ teaspoon kosher salt

1 teaspoon grated lime zest

Legend has it that back in 1924 at Caesar's Restaurant in Tijuana, Italian chef Caesar Cardini ran out of ingredients for his house dressing and improvised a tableside salad for hungry customers. Using what he had on hand, he blended lime juice, egg yolk, Parmigiano-Reggiano, anchovies, Worcestershire sauce, mustard, and seasonings to create his now world-famous dressing. Caesar's ingenuity and commitment to making something amazing with what he had in the kitchen is how my mom (born in Tijuana, just like the salad) and Nana taught me to cook. This updated version features buttery little gem wedges showered with a healthy amount of Parm, zesty lime breadcrumbs for added texture, and crispy fried capers. A savory salad that's so good for parties and trust me, it tastes even better when you eat the wedges with your hands!

---

1. **MAKE THE SALAD:** Fill a large bowl with water and submerge each head of lettuce upside down, shaking and agitating the leaves to dislodge any dirt. Remove, shake off the excess water, and transfer to a cutting board. Slice the heads in half lengthwise and dry well. Pile the wedges on top of a kitchen towel or paper towels, roll up tightly, and place into the refrigerator until ready to serve.
2. Have a paper towel–lined plate near the stove. Heat the oil in a medium skillet over medium-high heat. Once shimmering, add the capers and fry, stirring occasionally, until crispy and golden, 3 to 4 minutes. Using a slotted spoon, transfer to the lined plate. Reserve the oil in the pan.
3. **MAKE THE LIME-ZESTED BREADCRUMBS:** Reduce the heat to medium. Once the oil is shimmering, add the panko and salt and cook, stirring occasionally, until deep golden brown, 2 to 3 minutes. Remove from heat, stir in the lime zest, and transfer the breadcrumbs to a plate.

(recipe continues)

FOR THE CAESAR DRESSING

3 tablespoons finely grated Parmigiano-Reggiano cheese

2 tablespoons fresh lime juice (about 1 lime)

3 anchovy fillets

1 large raw egg yolk (see Hot Tip for cooked yolk)

2 garlic cloves, grated or finely chopped

1 teaspoon honey

1 teaspoon Dijon or whole grain mustard

1 teaspoon Worcestershire sauce

¾ teaspoon freshly ground black pepper

¼ teaspoon kosher salt

¼ teaspoon crushed red pepper

½ cup extra-virgin olive oil

4. **MAKE THE CAESAR DRESSING:** In a blender or food processor, add the Parmigiano-Reggiano, lime juice, anchovies, egg yolk, garlic, honey, mustard, Worcestershire sauce, black pepper, salt, and crushed red pepper and blend on low just until broken down, 5 to 10 seconds. Continue to blend on low and slowly stream in the oil until a smooth and slightly thick dressing forms, about 30 seconds. Don't over-blend, as the dressing may break.
5. **TO SERVE:** Remove the little gem wedges from the fridge and dry again. Place 2 wedges on each of four plates. Sprinkle each wedge with 1 tablespoon of the Parmigiano-Reggiano and, using your fingers, push the cheese into the nooks and crannies of the lettuce. Drizzle with the Caesar dressing, top with the breadcrumbs, and garnish with more Parmigiano-Reggiano, black pepper, and the fried capers.

HOT TIP

If you prefer not to use a raw egg yolk, coddle your egg by cooking a whole egg in boiling water for 1 minute and submerging in an ice bath for 1 minute. Use only the yolk for the dressing.

PERFECT PAIRING

A citrusy and herbaceous white wine like Vermentino, Sauvignon Blanc, or Albariño.

WTF TO MAKE FOR DINNER

I'm here to help you answer the eternal question: WTF to make for dinner? Even better, I want to make dinnertime easy, fun, and delicious—the highlight of your day and never stressful. With the right recipes, joy in the kitchen is actually possible, I promise. I've collected twenty-two of my all-time favorite standout dishes to take the guesswork out of the dinner dilemma. Every recipe here is bold, achievable, and deeply satisfying, whether it's a 30-minute meal or a knockout dish for a dinner party. You'll find elevated comfort food classics—think Foolproof Date-Night Steak with Creamy Peppercorn Sauce (page 108) and One-Pan Chicken Marsala & Orzo (page 107)—alongside cherished recipes from my Mexican and Irish roots, like Nana's Signature Green Enchiladas (page 123), Guinness Irish Beef & Veggie Stew (page 147), and Mom's Classic Chilaquiles Verdes (page 95). There are also dishes inspired by my travels and go-to hometown spots—hello, Magic Meatballs & Marinara (page 96), One-Pan Sicilian Baked Cod with Roasted Tomatoes & Olives (page 140), and Yellow Chicken Curry & Coconut Rice (page 130), plus my forever favorite, Famous Brown Butter Lemon Chicken (page 101).

Every recipe is designed to be approachable, reliable, and flavor-packed. My hope is that these meals will also become your favorites that you can turn to again and again. And remember, they're flexible, so that, over time, you can riff off the OG and personalize them based on whatever you're in the mood for or have on hand. Not a fan of red onions on your Italian Smash Burger (page 120)? Caramelize them! Feeling chicken tacos instead of fish? That no-fuss recipe is your perfect jumping-off point. Looking for vegetarian options? I've got some great swaps for you. Bottom line: It's time to get these pages dirty and get cooking!

Red Wine–Braised Short Ribs

SERVES 4 TO 6 • **TOTAL TIME** 3 HOURS 45 MINUTES

- 5 pounds bone-in beef short ribs (about 3-inch pieces)
- 1 tablespoon kosher salt
- 1 tablespoon freshly ground black pepper
- ¼ cup avocado or other neutral oil
- 2 large carrots, peeled and diced
- 1 medium yellow onion, diced
- 3 tablespoons tomato paste
- 1 (750 ml) bottle dry red wine (Cabernet Sauvignon)
- 4 cups beef stock
- 1 head of garlic, top cut off and discarded
- 1 bunch fresh thyme, plus a few leaves for garnish
- 5 sprigs fresh oregano
- 3 sprigs fresh rosemary
- 2 tablespoons cornstarch
- 2 tablespoons unsalted butter, cold
- Chopped fresh flat-leaf parsley, for garnish
- Easy Creamy Parm Polenta (page 218)

PERFECT PAIRING

A blend of Syrah and Grenache, like a cozy Côtes du Rhône.

These short ribs are the definition of low effort, high reward. They're deep, complex perfection with minimal hands-on time—rich, fall-apart tender, and just as fitting for a cozy Sunday spread as for a special occasion celebration, delivering a restaurant-quality knockout. Braising the ribs in red wine with fresh herbs and a whole head of garlic yields deep, bold flavor. Even better, they only improve with time, making them ideal for prepping ahead. Serve with Easy Creamy Parm Polenta (page 218) and the Little Gem Caesar Wedge (page 84).

---

1. Preheat the oven to 350°F.
2. Using a paper towel, pat the short ribs dry and season all over with the salt and black pepper.
3. Heat the oil in a large Dutch oven or oven-safe lidded pot over medium-high heat. Once shimmering, add the short ribs. Cook all sides of the meat until golden brown, working in batches if needed, 1 to 2 minutes per side. Transfer to a plate.
4. Discard all but 2 tablespoons of the oil and add the carrots and onion and cook, stirring occasionally, until the onion is translucent and the carrots are slightly tender, 8 to 10 minutes. Add the tomato paste and cook, stirring constantly and scraping the bottom of the pot to prevent burning, until the mixture darkens and becomes fragrant, 3 to 5 minutes.
5. Add 1 cup of the red wine to the pot, scraping up any bits from the bottom. Allow the wine to almost fully reduce, stirring occasionally, until a thick paste remains, 2 to 3 minutes. Add another cup of wine and repeat the same process, about 5 minutes. Add the remainder of the bottle and reduce until half the liquid remains, 5 to 8 minutes.
6. Add the beef stock, raise the heat to high, and bring to a boil. Add the short ribs and their juices to the pot along with the head of garlic, thyme, oregano, and rosemary, and return to a boil. Cover and braise in the oven for 2½ to 3 hours, until the ribs are fork tender.

(recipe continues)

7. Transfer the ribs to a plate. Skim off any fat from the top layer of the pot and discard. Place a fine mesh strainer over a large bowl and strain, discarding the veggies, garlic, and herbs. Return the strained liquid to the pot and bring to a simmer over medium-high heat.
8. In a small bowl, whisk ¼ cup water and the cornstarch until smooth to create a slurry. Set aside.
9. Whisking constantly, add the butter until incorporated. Slowly pour in the cornstarch slurry and whisk until the mixture is thick enough to coat the back of a spoon, about 3 minutes.
10. Divide the polenta among four bowls, top with ribs, and spoon the sauce over the ribs. Garnish with chopped fresh parsley and thyme leaves.

Mom's Classic Chilaquiles Verdes

SERVES 4 • **TOTAL TIME** 30 MINUTES

FOR THE CHILAQUILES

¾ cup avocado or other neutral oil, for frying, plus more as needed

12 (6-inch) corn tortillas, cut into 8 triangles

Kosher salt

FOR THE FRIED EGGS

4 large eggs

Kosher salt

1½ cups Salsa Verde (page 32)

FOR SERVING

Crema or sour cream

Crumbled cotija cheese

Crumbled queso fresco

Finely chopped white onion

Chopped fresh cilantro

Thinly sliced radishes

PERFECT PAIRING

An orange wine from Alsace, a drier Riesling from Germany or New York, or the Spicy Watermelon Pine-Aperol Margarita (page 284).

Chilaquiles are one of my favorite breakfasts, but I'd happily eat my mom's version for dinner any night of the week. Lightly fried tortillas soak up our signature Salsa Verde (page 32), topped with crema, a combination of Mexican cheeses, cilantro, onion, radish, and of course, fried eggs. A few shortcuts make them even easier—use your favorite store-bought salsa and thick-cut tortilla chips if you're short on time. Serve alongside Brothy Frijoles de la Olla (page 241) and Mexican Rice (page 242).

---

1. **MAKE THE CHILAQUILES:** Line a sheet pan with paper towels.
2. Heat the oil in a large skillet over medium heat. Once shimmering, check for readiness by placing a wooden spoon or the tip of a tortilla triangle in the oil: It will bubble when ready! Fry the tortillas in batches as to not overcrowd the pan, using tongs to flip halfway through, until golden brown and crispy, 2 to 3 minutes per side. Using a slotted spoon or tongs, transfer the fried tortillas to the lined sheet pan. Immediately sprinkle the tortilla chips with salt. Repeat this process, spreading the finished chips in one layer to keep them crispy. Discard all but 2 tablespoons of the oil or add more if needed.
3. **MAKE THE FRIED EGGS:** Heat the oil in the same skillet over medium heat. Crack in the eggs and cook until the whites of the eggs are golden brown around the edges, and the yolks are cooked to your preference, 3 to 5 minutes. Transfer to a plate and season with salt.
4. Return the skillet to low heat and add more oil to equal two tablespoons. Return the tortilla chips to the skillet along with the salsa verde. Gently toss with a wooden spoon until the chips are coated. Remove from the heat, cover, and allow to soften slightly, 1 to 2 minutes.
5. **TO SERVE IN THE SKILLET:** Transfer the fried eggs directly on top of the chilaquiles, or divide the chilaquiles among four plates and top each with a fried egg. Drizzle with the crema or dollops of sour cream and garnish with the cotija, queso fresco, onion, chopped cilantro, and radishes.

Magic Meatballs & Marinara

SERVES 4 TO 6 (MAKES 18 TO 20 MEATBALLS) • **TOTAL TIME** 1 HOUR

- 4 slices white sandwich bread
- 1 pound 80% lean ground beef (remove from refrigerator 30 minutes before cooking)
- ¼ cup finely chopped fresh flat-leaf parsley
- 3 garlic cloves, grated or finely chopped
- 1½ teaspoons kosher salt
- 1 teaspoon freshly ground black pepper
- ½ teaspoon dried oregano
- ½ teaspoon crushed red pepper
- 1 large egg
- 1¼ cups finely grated Parmigiano-Reggiano cheese, plus more for serving
- 2 cups extra-virgin olive oil, plus more for shaping
- 4 cups Go-To Marinara (page 171) or store-bought sauce
- Fresh basil, for garnish
- Toasted baguette, for serving

PERFECT PAIRING

A rich red wine like Aglianico, Negroamaro, Nero d'Avola, or Sangiovese.

I always pick up a few tricks when traveling, and sometimes the simplest ones are the biggest game-changers. In Positano, I learned that swapping breadcrumbs for water-soaked bread (yes, water, not milk!), makes for impossibly light and pillowy meatballs. Frying, rather than baking, delivers that crisp exterior while keeping them tender inside. Let them soak in my favorite Go-To Marinara (page 171) and serve over spaghetti, and if you'd like, round it out with My Big Fat Italian Chopped Salad (page 80) or the Perfect Green Bean Salad (page 232).

---

1. Line a sheet pan with parchment paper. Line a second sheet pan with paper towels.
2. Fill a medium bowl with a few inches of cold water and soak 2 slices of the bread until completely tender, about 5 seconds. Squeeze out the liquid and place the soaked bread into a large bowl. Repeat with the remaining bread and discard any leftover water.
3. To the bowl with the soaked bread, add the ground beef, parsley, garlic, salt, black pepper, oregano, and crushed red pepper. Mix with your hands until evenly combined, without bread clumps.
4. Create a well in the center of the bowl and add the egg. Using your fingers (if you must, use a fork, but this is the authentic way!), stir the egg until smooth. Sprinkle the cheese over the entire bowl and using your hands, stir to incorporate the meat, egg, and cheese until a uniform paste forms, 1 to 2 minutes. This should be a bit of an arm workout!
5. Scoop about 2 heaping tablespoons and gently roll between lightly oiled palms into 18 to 20 golf ball–sized meatballs and transfer to the parchment-lined sheet pan. Set aside. Heat the oil in a large pot over medium-high heat. Once shimmering, check for readiness by placing a wooden spoon or small amount of the meatball mixture in the oil: It will bubble when ready!

(recipe continues)

HOT TIP

If you have an extra Parm rind, add it to the marinara sauce for extra flavor.

6. Using a large slotted spoon for the entire cooking process, add the meatballs to the hot oil, working in batches if needed as to not overcrowd the pan, and cook until the bottom of the meatballs are golden brown, 2 to 3 minutes. Gently flip the meatballs and cook until the entire surface area is golden brown, 2 to 3 minutes more. Transfer the meatballs to the paper towel–lined sheet pan. Repeat this process with the rest of the meatballs. Carefully transfer the oil into a small bowl, let cool and discard.
7. In the same pot over medium-low heat, add the marinara sauce and cook until gently simmering. Transfer the meatballs to the sauce, bring to a gentle simmer, and cook covered, stirring occasionally to prevent sticking, until the meatballs are cooked through but still tender with an internal temperature of 160°F, about 25 minutes.
8. **TO SERVE:** Transfer the meatballs and sauce to a serving dish and top with a generous amount of grated Parmigiano-Reggiano and basil. Serve with toasted baguette slices for dipping.

Famous Brown Butter Lemon Chicken

SERVES 2 • **TOTAL TIME** 40 MINUTES

- 2 (8-ounce) boneless, skinless chicken breasts
- 1½ teaspoons kosher salt, divided
- 1 teaspoon freshly ground black pepper, divided
- 1 large egg
- 1 tablespoon milk
- ⅓ cup all-purpose flour
- 1 tablespoon avocado or other neutral oil
- 1 stick (8 tablespoons) unsalted butter, cold
- 1 lemon, halved, seeds removed
- Lemon wedges, for serving
- Arugula and tomatoes, for serving (see Hot Tip)

PERFECT PAIRING

A rustic and earthy but elegant red wine from Sangiovese grapes: think Chianti Classico or Rosso di Montalcino.

HOT TIP

I love to serve this over a bed of arugula dressed with extra-virgin olive oil, lemon juice, and finely grated Parm, alongside cherry tomatoes, whole or sliced.

It took me nearly a year to get this right, and now it's yours for the making. I first had this chicken at Trattoria Sostanza, a Florentine gem dating back to 1869. It's no exaggeration to say that one bite changed my idea of chicken forever. Savory, nutty brown butter melds with zesty lemon, coating juicy, tender, perfectly salted chicken. After peppering our server with questions and countless rounds of testing, I'm sharing the magic with you, which is to brown the chicken before dredging. I promise it's worth it! Serve with Tuscan Zucchini & Arugula Salad (page 72) and Limoncello Tiramisu (page 268) for an Italian date night.

1. Preheat the oven to 350°F. Have a parchment-lined sheet pan near the stove.
2. Place the chicken breasts between two layers of plastic wrap or in a plastic bag and lightly pound with a meat mallet or rolling pin until each piece is evenly about ⅓-inch thick. Remove the chicken from the plastic, pat dry with a paper towel, and generously season both sides with 1 teaspoon of the salt and ½ teaspoon of the black pepper. Transfer to a plate and set aside.
3. In a shallow bowl, whisk the egg and milk until fully combined. In a second shallow bowl, add the flour and stir in the remaining ½ teaspoon salt and remaining ½ teaspoon black pepper.
4. Heat the oil in an ovenproof skillet over medium-high heat. Once shimmering, add the chicken and cook until golden brown and it easily releases from the pan, about 2 minutes per side. Transfer to one half of the lined sheet pan.
5. While the chicken is still warm, dip and coat it generously in the flour mixture, shake off excess flour, and dip in the egg mixture. Transfer to the other half of the lined sheet pan in a single layer.
6. In the same skillet over medium-high heat, add the butter and melt, stirring occasionally, until it begins to turn slightly golden brown and fragrant, about 2 minutes. Return the chicken breasts to the skillet and cook until deep golden brown, about 3 minutes per side.
7. Transfer the skillet to the oven and bake until the chicken is cooked through, firm yet tender, with an internal temperature of 165°F, 5 to 8 minutes.
8. Transfer the chicken to a serving platter. Pour the brown butter pan sauce over the chicken and finish by squeezing both halves of the lemon directly onto the chicken. Serve with lemon wedges.

Spice-Rubbed Fish Tacos
with Cilantro Cabbage Slaw

SERVES 4 TO 6 • **TOTAL TIME** 40 MINUTES

FOR THE FISH

- 1 teaspoon kosher salt
- 1 teaspoon chili powder
- ½ teaspoon ground cumin
- ½ teaspoon garlic powder
- ½ teaspoon smoked paprika
- ¼ teaspoon cayenne pepper (optional)
- 2 tablespoons unsalted butter
- 1 garlic clove, grated or finely chopped
- 4 (6-ounce) cod fillets, about 1 inch thick, skin and small bones removed

FOR THE CILANTRO CABBAGE SLAW

- 3 tablespoons fresh lime juice (about 1½ limes)
- 2 teaspoons agave nectar or honey
- ½ teaspoon kosher salt
- ¼ teaspoon freshly ground black pepper
- ½ small head red or green cabbage, thinly shredded (about 3 cups)
- 2 Roma (plum) tomatoes, seeded and diced
- 4 green onions (white and green parts), thinly sliced

There's no denying fish tacos taste better at the beach, but this version with a smoky spice blend will hold you over until those sunny days. I've ditched the stress and mess by baking instead of frying, keeping things crisp without the hassle. The herby, tangy cilantro slaw gets a quick cure from lime juice, agave, and salt, while avocado, crema, radish, and extra cilantro bring the crunch and creaminess. Use any white fish you like—just adjust the cook time based on thickness. Serve with Mexican Rice (page 242), No-Mayo Esquites (Mexican Street Corn Salad) (page 233), and the Holy Trinity (page 31) for taco bar heaven.

1. **MAKE THE FISH:** Preheat the oven to 425°F. Have a parchment-lined sheet pan near the stove.
2. In a small bowl, mix the salt, chili powder, cumin, garlic powder, smoked paprika, and cayenne (if using) and set aside.
3. In a heatproof measuring cup or small bowl, melt the butter in the microwave in 10-second intervals. Whisk in the garlic.
4. Place the fish on the prepared sheet pan and pat dry with a paper towel. Gently massage the garlic butter on both sides of the fish and then sprinkle each side with the spice mixture.
5. Bake for about 12 minutes, until the fish is opaque and easily flakes with a fork. Flake the fish into bite-size pieces and gently toss the fish in the pan juices.

(recipe continues)

1 large fresh jalapeño pepper, stemmed, seeded, and finely chopped

¼ cup chopped fresh cilantro, plus more for garnish

FOR THE TACOS

12 (6-inch) corn tortillas, warmed (see Hot Tips)

Thinly sliced Hass avocado, for garnish

Crema or sour cream, for garnish

Thinly sliced radishes, for garnish

Lime wedges, for serving

Hot sauce, for serving

PERFECT PAIRING

An ice-cold beer, a white Albariño, or the Spicy Watermelon Pine-Aperol Margarita (page 284).

6. **MEANWHILE, MAKE THE CILANTRO CABBAGE SLAW:** In a medium bowl, whisk the lime juice, agave, salt, and black pepper. Add the cabbage, tomatoes, green onions, jalapeño, and cilantro, and using your hands or tongs, toss until thoroughly coated. Set aside to marinate until you're ready to assemble the tacos.
7. **MAKE THE TACOS:** Divide the cilantro cabbage slaw on top of each warm tortilla, and top with the fish. Garnish with the avocado, crema or sour cream, radishes, and cilantro, and serve with lime and hot sauce.

HOT TIPS

Want perfectly warmed tortillas with just the right amount of char? For a gas stove: Ignite a burner to medium-low heat. Use heatproof tongs to rotate a tortilla over the flame until it starts to bubble and develop char marks, about 25 seconds per side. Place the tortilla inside a tortilla warmer or wrap in a kitchen towel and repeat with the remaining tortillas.

For an electric stove: Heat a cast-iron skillet over high heat and add the tortilla, rotating with tongs until char marks develop, 30 to 60 seconds per side. Keep tortillas warm as above.

PERFECT PAIRING
A refreshing red with cherry notes, like a Pinot Noir or Trousseau from France.

One-Pan Chicken Marsala & Orzo

SERVES 4 • **TOTAL TIME** 1 HOUR 10 MINUTES

- 4 (6-ounce) bone-in, skin-on chicken thighs (see Hot Tips)
- 1½ teaspoons kosher salt, divided
- 1 teaspoon freshly ground black pepper, plus more for serving
- 2 tablespoons unsalted butter
- 8 ounces sliced baby bella mushrooms
- 1 shallot, finely chopped
- 4 garlic cloves, finely chopped
- 1¼ cups Marsala wine
- 1 cup dried orzo
- 2 cups chicken stock
- 2 cups coarsely chopped baby spinach (about 4 ounces)
- ½ cup finely grated Parmigiano-Reggiano cheese, plus more for garnish
- ¼ cup heavy cream
- Chopped fresh flat-leaf parsley, for garnish

HOT TIP

For boneless and skinless thighs, heat 2 tablespoons of neutral oil over medium-high heat, add chicken, and let cook undisturbed until golden brown and lightly crisp, 5 to 7 minutes. Flip and cook until its internal temperature is 165°F, about 6 more minutes.

This easy yet elevated weeknight dish brings together my mom's love of chicken Marsala and my obsession with creamy, one-pan comfort. Marsala—a fortified Sicilian wine—adds a nutty sweetness that plays perfectly with savory mushrooms, aromatics, and Parmigiano-Reggiano. It's a date-night favorite but just as good any night of the week. Serve it year-round—pair with Summer Stone Fruit Salad with Basil Mint Vinaigrette (page 60) when it's warm or something heartier, like Burrata Broccolini with Calabrian Chili Romesco (page 221), when the weather cools.

---

1. Pat the chicken thighs completely dry with a paper towel. Evenly sprinkle both sides with 1 teaspoon each of the salt and the black pepper.
2. Place the chicken thighs skin side down in a cold cast-iron skillet or stainless steel pan. Raise the heat to medium and let the chicken cook undisturbed until the skin is golden brown and crispy, and it releases easily from the skillet, about 15 to 20 minutes. Using tongs, flip the chicken and cook undisturbed until it is cooked through with an internal temperature of 165°F, 8 to 10 minutes. Transfer to a plate.
3. Raise the heat to medium-high and melt the butter. Add the mushrooms and cook, stirring occasionally, until most of the liquid released has evaporated and they are golden brown, about 8 minutes. Reduce the heat to medium and add the shallot, garlic, and the remaining ½ teaspoon salt. Cook, stirring constantly, until fragrant, about 1 minute.
4. Add the Marsala wine, raise the heat to medium-high, and simmer until the liquid is reduced by half and slightly thickens, 4 to 5 minutes. Stir in the orzo and chicken stock and bring to a boil over high heat. Reduce the heat to medium and simmer, stirring occasionally, until the orzo is tender and most of the liquid is absorbed, about 8 minutes.
5. Reduce the heat to low, add the spinach, Parmigiano-Reggiano, and cream and cook, stirring frequently, until the greens are wilted, 1 to 2 minutes.
6. **TO SERVE FAMILY STYLE:** Place the chicken and juices on top of the orzo and garnish with fresh parsley, more Parmigiano-Reggiano, and a few twists of black pepper, or divide the orzo mixture among four plates, top with the chicken, and garnish as above.

Foolproof Date-Night Steak

with Creamy Peppercorn Sauce

SERVES 2 • **TOTAL TIME** 35 MINUTES

- 1 tablespoon whole peppercorns (preferably a blend of white, green, and black)
- 2 (6- to 8-ounce) filet mignon steaks
- 1½ teaspoons kosher salt, divided
- 1 tablespoon avocado or other neutral oil
- 2 tablespoons unsalted butter
- 3 garlic cloves, smashed and peeled
- 2 large sprigs fresh rosemary
- 1 medium shallot, finely chopped
- 2 tablespoons brandy or cognac
- ½ cup beef bone broth or stock (see Hot Tips)
- ½ cup heavy cream
- 2 teaspoons Dijon mustard

PERFECT PAIRING

A medium-bodied red wine that's soft but finishes with texture, like a Nebbiolo, Dolcetto, or classic Bordeaux blend.

This is my husband Andrew's favorite meal, and you'll find yourself craving it for date nights, special occasions, or just because. Inspired by a steak au poivre from a tiny Parisian hideaway, it feels fancy, but couldn't be easier to make. If you're new to cooking steak, remember: Pat the meat dry for a perfect sear, use a high-smoke-point oil like avocado oil, and keep a meat thermometer handy (see Hot Tips). While the steak rests, whip up the sauce right in the same skillet—peppercorns for bite, cream for richness, and brandy for a touch of sweetness. Serve with Tuscan Zucchini & Arugula Salad with Parm Crisps (page 72) and Auntie Bug's Shortcut Asparagus Risotto (page 238). Steakhouse perfection right at home!

1. Set a wire rack over a sheet pan (or a grooved wooden cutting board) and have near the stove.
2. Heat a medium stainless steel or cast-iron skillet over medium-high heat. Add the peppercorns and toast, shaking the skillet so they cook evenly, just until fragrant, about 1 minute. Transfer to a mortar and pestle and crush the peppercorns to a mix of finely and coarsely ground, with no pieces larger than a quartered peppercorn (see Hot Tips if you don't have a mortar and pestle). Set aside in a small bowl.
3. Place the steaks on a plate and pat completely dry with a paper towel. Sprinkle 1 teaspoon of the salt all over the steaks.
4. Heat the same skillet over medium-high heat for 2 to 3 minutes, then test for readiness by splashing drops of water on the surface. If the drops dance (versus bubbling and evaporating), the skillet is ready. Add the oil and, once shimmering, add the steaks and cook until a golden-brown crust forms and a meat thermometer reaches 125° to 130°F for medium rare, about 4 minutes per side.

(recipe continues)

HOT TIPS

Don't have a mortar and pestle? Let the toasted peppercorns cool and transfer to a plastic bag. Lightly pound them with a meat mallet, rolling pin, or the bottom of a small heavy pot.

If you prefer a more well-done steak, sear for an extra 1 to 2 minutes per side.

For the most tender bite of steak once served, slice the meat against the grain (opposite the direction the fibers run).

Any stock will work, but bone broth adds great depth of flavor. Taste and adjust the salt as desired.

Don't have time to make the sauce? The steaks are delicious solo, or as a protein to add to salads like the Peach, Kale & Crunchy Quinoa Salad with White Balsamic Vinaigrette (page 79), too!

5. Working quickly, lower the heat to medium and add the butter, smashed garlic cloves, and rosemary sprigs. Using an oven mitt, carefully tilt the pan toward you. Push the steak to the lifted side of the skillet so the butter pools toward the spot that's closest to the heat. Using a large metal spoon, scoop up the butter and pour it over the steaks. Continue basting the steaks with melted butter for 30 to 45 seconds. Transfer the steaks to the wire rack or cutting board to rest while you make the sauce. Cover the steaks loosely with foil and discard the garlic and rosemary.
6. Add the shallot to the pan and cook, stirring constantly, until tender and fragrant, 1 to 2 minutes. Turn off the heat (to avoid flame flare-ups) and add the brandy or cognac. Return the heat to medium and cook, stirring constantly and scraping up any browned bits, until the scent of alcohol has dissipated and the skillet is almost dry, about 1 minute. Add the peppercorns and bone broth, bring to a simmer, and cook, stirring occasionally, until the liquid is reduced by about half, 2 to 3 minutes. Stir in the cream, mustard, and the remaining ½ teaspoon of salt. Bring to a gentle simmer and cook, stirring occasionally, until the sauce thickens enough to coat the back of a spoon, 1 to 2 minutes, and transfer to a small serving bowl.
7. **TO SERVE:** Divide the steaks between two plates and top with the sauce.

The Only Roast Chicken You'll Need

SERVES 4 TO 6 • **TOTAL TIME** 2 HOURS

FOR THE BASIL BUTTER

- 1 stick (8 tablespoons) unsalted butter, at room temperature
- ¼ cup finely chopped fresh basil, plus more for garnish
- 1 teaspoon kosher salt
- ½ teaspoon freshly ground black pepper
- ½ teaspoon garlic powder

FOR THE CHICKEN AND VEGGIES

- 1 (5-pound) whole chicken
- 2½ teaspoons kosher salt, divided
- 1½ teaspoons freshly ground black pepper, divided
- 1 lemon, halved
- 1 head of garlic, top cut off and discarded
- 1 small bunch fresh thyme
- 1 small bunch fresh rosemary
- 1½ pounds baby Yukon Gold potatoes, halved
- 4 cups cherry tomatoes (about 24 ounces)
- 2 tablespoons extra-virgin olive oil
- ½ cup dry white wine
- 1 tablespoon balsamic vinegar

PERFECT PAIRING

Keep it classic with a Pinot Noir or a Chardonnay. For a citrusy contrast, sip on a Limoncello Spritz (page 291).

Nothing is more comforting than the scent of roast chicken filling your home, and with the right method, this recipe delivers every time. A little extra effort—slipping basil (or any herb) butter under the skin—infuses the meat with herbal richness while keeping the breast impossibly moist. This chic, caprese-inspired version is simple yet stunning, with tomatoes and potatoes nestled beneath crispy-skinned, juicy chicken, soaking up the goodness of that fresh basil butter and white wine. Consider swapping this in for your Thanksgiving turkey—it's foolproof and I promise, your guests will thank you! Serve with Burrata Broccolini with Calabrian Chili Romesco (page 221) or Nana's Iconic Crunchy Lemon Parm Salad (page 59).

---

1. Preheat the oven to 425°F.
2. **MAKE THE BASIL BUTTER:** In a small bowl, combine the butter, basil, salt, black pepper, and garlic powder and mix until well combined. Set aside.
3. **MAKE THE CHICKEN AND VEGGIES:** Remove the giblets and neck from the chicken and save for stock or discard. Trim off any excess fat and use paper towels to pat the interior and exterior of the chicken completely dry.
4. Sprinkle the cavity with 1 teaspoon of the salt and ½ teaspoon of the black pepper. Stuff the cavity with the lemon halves, garlic, thyme, and rosemary sprigs.
5. Using your fingers or a large, rounded spoon, carefully loosen the skin from the top of the chicken and separate it from the breast meat, creating a pocket. Being careful not to tear the skin, stuff the basil butter into the pockets under the skin. Using your hands, gently press down on top of the skin to evenly distribute the butter.
6. Tuck the wings underneath the upper back and tie the legs together using kitchen twine. Season the skin all over with 1 teaspoon of the salt and ½ teaspoon of the black pepper.

(recipe continues)

7. Add the potatoes and tomatoes to a large roasting dish in an even layer. Drizzle with oil and toss with the remaining ½ teaspoon salt and ½ teaspoon black pepper. Place the chicken on top of the vegetables.
8. Bake for about 20 minutes, until the chicken skin starts to become crispy and is very lightly browned. Reduce the oven temperature to 375°F and carefully pull out the oven rack to pour the wine into the baking dish. Push the rack back in and bake for about 1 hour 15 minutes (1 hour 35 minutes total), until the chicken is golden brown and reaches an internal temperature of 165°F. (If the skin is getting too brown, loosely tent the chicken with foil.)
9. Let the chicken rest on a large cutting or carving board for at least 10 minutes before carving. Using a slotted spoon, transfer the potatoes and tomatoes to a serving platter. Carefully pour the pan juices into a small serving bowl and whisk in the balsamic vinegar.
10. Carve the chicken and arrange on top of the vegetables. Garnish with basil and serve with the pan sauce on the side.

HOW TO CARVE A CHICKEN

1. Set the chicken breast-side up on a grooved cutting board, or place a sheet pan underneath to catch any juices. Start by pulling one leg away from the body until the joint is exposed. Slice through the skin and joint to remove the leg. Repeat on the other side.
2. Separate the drumstick from the thigh by cutting through the joint where they meet, then set the pieces aside.
3. To remove the breasts, run your knife along one side of the breastbone, following the curve of the rib cage to lift the meat off in one piece. Keep the wing attached if you'd like, or cut it off at the joint and save it for later.
4. Cut the breasts crosswise into thick slices, then carve the meat off the thigh bones and slice it as well.
5. Arrange everything on a platter and serve.

Sheet Pan Veggie Orzo Bowls

with Miso Maple Vinaigrette

SERVES 4 TO 6 • **TOTAL TIME** 40 MINUTES

FOR THE ROASTED VEGGIES

1 large unpeeled sweet potato, cut into ½-inch cubes

1 (15-ounce) can chickpeas, drained, rinsed, and dried

2 tablespoons avocado or other neutral oil

1¼ teaspoons kosher salt

½ teaspoon garlic powder

½ teaspoon paprika

¼ teaspoon freshly ground black pepper

¾ cup chopped walnuts

FOR THE MISO MAPLE VINAIGRETTE

2 tablespoons apple cider vinegar

1 tablespoon fresh lemon juice (about ½ lemon)

1 tablespoon maple syrup

1 tablespoon white miso paste

1 teaspoon Dijon mustard

½ teaspoon freshly ground black pepper, plus more for serving

⅓ cup extra-virgin olive oil

PERFECT PAIRING

A light Grenache from California or France, or a soft but tart Zweigelt from Austria.

This protein-packed, vegetarian dinner-in-a-bowl is a weeknight hero—hearty, vibrant, and endlessly adaptable. Savory-spiced sweet potatoes and chickpeas cozy up with quick-cooking orzo, tender kale, toasted walnuts, and a good-enough-to-drink miso maple vinaigrette. Creamy goat cheese ties it all together. Swap in whatever veggies you've got (chard or spinach work great), and if you're craving extra protein, top with a boiled egg or some shredded chicken.

---

1. **MAKE THE ROASTED VEGGIES:** Preheat the oven to 425°F. Line a sheet pan with parchment paper.
2. To the sheet pan, add the sweet potato and chickpeas and top with the oil, salt, garlic powder, paprika, and black pepper. Using your hands, toss to combine until evenly coated and spread into a single layer.
3. Bake for 20 minutes, until the sweet potato is tender and slightly golden, flipping halfway through. Sprinkle the walnuts over the vegetables and cook until lightly toasted, 3 to 5 minutes. Set aside.
4. **MEANWHILE, MAKE THE MISO MAPLE VINAIGRETTE:** In a large measuring cup, whisk the vinegar, lemon juice, maple syrup, miso, mustard, and black pepper until completely smooth. While whisking, slowly stream in the oil and continue to whisk until slightly thickened.

(recipe continues)

FOR THE BOWLS

1 tablespoon kosher salt for cooking the orzo

1½ cups dried orzo (see Hot Tip)

1 large bunch lacinato kale, stems removed, leaves thinly sliced

Crumbled goat cheese, for garnish

5. **MAKE THE BOWLS:** While the veggies roast, bring a medium pot of water with the salt to a boil. Add the orzo and cook according to the package directions. Strain and return to the pot.
6. To the pot with the cooked orzo, add about half the miso maple vinaigrette and the kale. Use a spoon to combine until the kale is wilted and everything is thoroughly coated.
7. **TO SERVE:** Divide the orzo among serving bowls, and top with the roasted veggies and walnuts. Drizzle with the remaining miso maple vinaigrette and garnish with the crumbled goat cheese and a few twists of black pepper.

HOT TIP

No orzo in the pantry? Swap it out for 3 cups of cooked rice, quinoa, or farro.

Camarones al Mojo de Ajo (Mexican Garlic Shrimp)

SERVES 4 • **TOTAL TIME** 30 MINUTES

1 pound large shrimp, peeled and deveined, tails left on

½ teaspoon baking soda

1 teaspoon kosher salt

½ teaspoon freshly ground black pepper

½ teaspoon garlic powder

½ teaspoon crushed red pepper

½ teaspoon smoked paprika

¼ teaspoon ground cumin

3 tablespoons extra-virgin olive oil, plus more as needed

3 tablespoons blanco tequila (I love LALO)

3 tablespoons unsalted butter

8 garlic cloves, finely chopped

Zest and juice of one lemon

Chopped fresh flat-leaf parsley, for garnish

Lemon wedges, for serving

PERFECT PAIRING

A fun white wine with plenty of acid, fruit, and minerals, like Chenin Blanc from France or South Africa.

This buttery, garlicky plate of shrimp is quick, easy, and downright irresistible. Nana's restaurant, Lupita's La Jolla, closed before I was born, but she made this for me often. It became a childhood favorite, thanks to her signature seasoning blend—garlic, smoked paprika, and cumin—and that unforgettable tequila-garlic-butter sauce. It's traditionally served with lime, but I swear by lemon to bring out the shrimp's natural sweetness. My foolproof fifteen-minute baking soda marinade keeps the shrimp juicy and tender but if you're short on time, skip it. Serve with rice or tortillas.

1. In a large bowl, toss the shrimp and the baking soda. Refrigerate uncovered for 15 minutes.
2. Meanwhile, in a large bowl, combine the salt, black pepper, garlic powder, crushed red pepper, smoked paprika, and cumin and set aside.
3. Rinse the shrimp, drain in a colander, and pat dry. Add to the bowl with the spices and toss to coat thoroughly.
4. Heat the oil in a large cast-iron skillet over medium-high heat. Once shimmering, add the shrimp and cook until opaque and golden brown, 1 to 2 minutes per side (working in batches if necessary, and adding more oil as needed). Transfer the shrimp to a plate. Turn off the heat (to avoid flame flare-ups), add the tequila, and return the heat to medium-low, scraping up any browned bits from the bottom. Stir in the butter until melted, add the garlic, and cook, stirring constantly, until fragrant and lightly brown, 1 to 2 minutes.
5. Turn the heat off and return the shrimp and any juices to the pan. Gently toss to fully coat in the tequila garlic butter.
6. **TO SERVE:** Transfer the shrimp to a serving dish, and spoon the sauce over the top. Top with the lemon juice, lemon zest, and parsley. Serve with lemon wedges.

HOT TIP

For perfectly cooked shrimp, watch as they lose transparency, begin to turn pink, and form a C-shape rather than an O-shape, which signals they're overcooked.

Italian Smash Burger

SERVES 4 • **TOTAL TIME** 25 MINUTES

FOR THE CALABRIAN CHILI AND PARM AIOLI

½ cup mayonnaise

2 tablespoons finely grated Parmigiano-Reggiano cheese

1 tablespoon crushed Calabrian chili peppers

1 tablespoon jarred pepperoncini brine

FOR THE BURGERS

1 pound 80% lean ground beef

4 hamburger buns

2 tablespoons unsalted butter, at room temperature

Kosher salt

Freshly ground black pepper

4 slices fontina or provolone cheese

2 cups baby arugula

1 tomato, thinly sliced

8 slices soppressata or Genoa salami

½ red onion, thinly sliced into rounds

½ cup drained, thinly sliced pepperoncini

PERFECT PAIRING

A bright, light-bodied red wine with balanced acidity, like Frappato or Pinot Noir, or a Blackberry Bourbon Smash (page 292).

Smashing a burger isn't just a technique—it's a little act of delicious destruction. That sizzling, buttery press-down is what creates those lacy, crispy edges and locks in juicy flavor. This version gets an Italian makeover with Calabrian chili and Parm aioli, peppery arugula, melty fontina, tangy pepperoncini, and sweet-spicy soppressata. And because there's no such thing as too much butter, they're served on golden, butter-toasted brioche buns. Pair with Nana's Iconic Crunchy Lemon Parm Salad (page 59) and Spicy Lemon Parm Cauliflower Bites (page 226). Craving a classic? This is your go-to base burger. Now, smash at it!

1. **MAKE THE CALABRIAN CHILI AND PARM AIOLI:** In a small bowl, whisk the mayonnaise, Parmigiano-Reggiano, Calabrian chili peppers, and pepperoncini brine. Set aside.
2. **MAKE THE BURGERS:** Cut two 4-inch squares of parchment paper. Divide the ground beef into four equal portions, form into balls, and transfer to a plate.
3. Heat a large dry cast-iron skillet over medium-high heat. Split the buns, butter each cut side, and toast, buttered side down, until golden, 1 to 2 minutes. Transfer to a plate.
4. In the same skillet over medium-high heat, add 2 ground beef balls, 3 inches apart. Place one piece of parchment paper on top of 1 burger and using a burger press, metal spatula, or pan, smash the first patty down to just under ½ inch thick. Move the parchment to the next burger and repeat. Season the patties with salt and black pepper and cook until a golden-brown crust begins to form on the bottom of each burger, 2 to 3 minutes. Using a metal spatula, flip the burgers and season the other side with salt and black pepper.
5. Immediately add a slice of cheese to each burger, cover with a pot lid or foil, and cook until the cheese is melted, 1 to 2 minutes. Transfer to a plate and cover with foil to keep them warm. Repeat with the remaining patties, changing the parchment paper if needed.
6. Spread both sides of the bun with the aioli. Layer each bottom bun in this order: a handful of the arugula, tomato slice, cheeseburger patty, 2 slices of the soppressata, red onion, and pepperoncini, and close with the top bun.

Nana's Signature Green Enchiladas

SERVES 8 (MAKES 16 ENCHILADAS) • **TOTAL TIME** 1 HOUR 15 MINUTES

FOR THE ENCHILADA SAUCE

2 tablespoons cornstarch

12 medium tomatillos (1 to 1½ pounds), husked and rinsed

3 teaspoons kosher salt, divided

1½ cups coarsely chopped romaine lettuce

1½ cups chicken stock

½ medium bunch fresh cilantro, with 1-inch tender stems

2 medium fresh Anaheim (California) chile or poblano peppers, stemmed, seeded, and coarsely chopped

3 green onions, light and dark green parts only

2 garlic cloves, coarsely chopped

3 tablespoons avocado or other neutral oil

1 cup sour cream

2 tablespoons unsalted butter

½ teaspoon freshly ground black pepper

½ teaspoon garlic powder

¼ teaspoon ground cumin

These enchiladas suizas were a star at Nana's restaurant, Lupita's La Jolla—and they're hands down my favorite way to enchilada. I knew I'd finally nailed the flavors when Nana took one bite and started reminiscing about the good old days at Lupita's. Her secret? A touch of butter for silkiness and romaine lettuce for subtle sweetness, creating a creamy sauce that's richer and more balanced than the usual suiza. Some more Nana wisdom: Flash-fry the corn tortillas to keep them pliable (never soggy!) and always hand-grate the cheese for the ultimate ooey-gooey pull. Serve with Mexican Rice (page 242), the Holy Trinity (page 31), and a pile of crispy tortilla chips. And whatever you do, don't forget the Spicy Watermelon Pine-Aperol Margarita (page 284)!

1. **MAKE THE ENCHILADA SAUCE:** In a small bowl, whisk 3 tablespoons of cold water and the cornstarch to create a slurry and set aside.
2. In a medium pot, add the tomatillos and enough water to just cover them. Season the water with 1 teaspoon of the salt. Bring to a boil over medium-high heat, reduce the heat to medium, and simmer until the tomatillos are fork-tender, 8 to 10 minutes. Using a slotted spoon, remove the tomatillos and transfer to a blender. Discard the water and wipe out the pot.
3. To the blender (with the steam vent in the top open), add the romaine, chicken stock, cilantro, chiles, green onions, and garlic. Blend until smooth, about 1 minute.
4. Heat the oil in the same pot over medium-high heat. Once shimmering, carefully add the tomatillo mixture and cook, whisking constantly until the sauce has thickened slightly and is no longer bright green, 2 to 3 minutes. Reduce the heat to medium. Add the sour cream, butter, the remaining 2 teaspoons salt, the black pepper, garlic powder, and cumin and whisk until thoroughly combined.
5. Stir the cornstarch slurry and, whisking vigorously, slowly pour into the sauce until thoroughly incorporated. Bring the sauce to a boil, stirring occasionally. Once it boils, immediately remove the pot from the heat and set aside.

(recipe continues)

FOR ASSEMBLY

- ¼ cup avocado or other neutral oil, for frying, plus more as needed
- 16 (6-inch) corn tortillas
- 4 cups shredded store-bought rotisserie chicken (or homemade roast chicken)
- 4 cups freshly grated Monterey Jack cheese

FOR SERVING

- Crumbled cotija cheese
- Crema or sour cream
- Chopped fresh cilantro, for garnish
- Pitted black olives, for garnish

PERFECT PAIRING

A sparkling rosé or a soft, creamy white wine like a California Chardonnay, or Spicy Watermelon Pine-Aperol Margarita (page 284).

6. **TO ASSEMBLE:** Preheat the oven to 400°F. Have a paper towel–lined plate, a 9 x 13-inch baking dish, and a 9 x 9-inch baking dish near the stove.
7. Heat the oil in a large skillet over medium-high heat. Once shimmering, check for readiness by dropping a tiny piece of tortilla into the oil: If it bubbles, it's ready! Lightly fry each tortilla one at a time until pliable, about 10 seconds per side. Transfer them to the lined plate, stacking as you go and adding additional oil to the skillet as needed for frying.
8. Spread ⅓ cup of the enchilada sauce evenly over the bottom of both baking dishes.
9. Place a tortilla from the stack on a clean work surface and add 1 tablespoon of the enchilada sauce in the middle of the tortilla and top with a scant ¼ cup of the chicken, and 2 tablespoons of the cheese. Roll the tortilla up tightly into a cigar, and place in the baking dish, seam side down. Repeat with the remaining tortillas, filling up both baking dishes. Pour the remaining enchilada sauce over the enchiladas and sprinkle with the remaining cheese.
10. Place the dishes side by side on the middle rack and bake for 15 to 20 minutes, until bubbling and starting to brown. If desired, turn the broiler on high, and broil both baking dishes for 1 to 2 minutes, until the cheese is golden brown.
11. **TO SERVE:** Sprinkle the cotija cheese over the top of the baking dishes and drizzle with the crema. Garnish with the chopped cilantro and black olives.

HOT TIP

This sauce freezes well, so make a double batch and freeze in a sealable container for up to 3 months or keep extra in the fridge to drizzle over your eggs for breakfast the next morning.

Weeknight Enchilada Casserole

SERVES 6 TO 8 • **TOTAL TIME** 1 HOUR 10 MINUTES

FOR THE ENCHILADA SAUCE

2 tablespoons cornstarch

3 tablespoons avocado or other neutral oil

1 large green bell pepper, seeded and diced

½ white onion, diced

1 Roma (plum) tomato, chopped

1 fresh jalapeño pepper, stemmed, seeded, and chopped

3 garlic cloves, chopped

1 teaspoon kosher salt

½ teaspoon ground cumin

½ teaspoon garlic powder

½ teaspoon freshly ground black pepper

1 (8-ounce) can tomato sauce

2 cups chicken or vegetable stock

When you want all the bold, comforting flavors of enchiladas without the hassle of rolling each tortilla, meet the Weeknight Enchilada Casserole! My mom made this on repeat. The homemade enchilada sauce is a game-changer—worth the effort, and even better when made ahead, double-batched, and frozen for easy dinners on demand. In the mood for meatless? Try the bean and cheese variation, which follows. Serve with Mom's Cheesy Calabacitas (page 229), Mexican Rice (page 242), Mom's Secret Salsa (page 31), and plenty of tortilla chips for scooping.

---

1. **MAKE THE ENCHILADA SAUCE:** In a small bowl, whisk 3 tablespoons cold water and the cornstarch to create a slurry and set aside.
2. Heat the oil in a medium pot over medium-high heat. Once shimmering, add the bell pepper, onion, tomato, and jalapeño and cook, stirring occasionally, until the onions are translucent and the peppers are slightly tender, 5 to 7 minutes. Add the garlic, salt, cumin, garlic powder, and black pepper, and cook, stirring constantly, until the mixture breaks down and becomes saucy and fragrant, 2 to 3 minutes.
3. Stir in the tomato sauce and simmer, stirring occasionally, until slightly thickened, 3 to 5 minutes. Add the stock, raise the heat to high, and bring to a boil. Turn the heat off and using an immersion blender (or a blender with the steam vent in the top open), blend the sauce until mostly smooth, 1 to 2 minutes. If using a blender, return the sauce to the pot and bring to a simmer over medium heat.
4. Stir the cornstarch slurry and slowly whisk into the sauce until thoroughly incorporated. Continue to simmer, stirring occasionally, until the sauce thickens to coat the back of a spoon, 3 to 5 minutes. Set aside off heat.

(recipe continues)

FOR THE ENCHILADAS

4 cups freshly grated Monterey Jack and cheddar cheese

1/3 cup avocado or other neutral oil, for frying, plus more as needed

18 (6-inch) corn tortillas

4 cups shredded store-bought rotisserie chicken (or homemade roast chicken)

1 (15-ounce) can black beans, drained and rinsed

FOR SERVING

Sour cream

Crumbled cotija cheese or queso fresco

Chopped fresh cilantro

Finely chopped white onion

Thinly sliced fresh jalapeño pepper (optional)

5. **MAKE THE ENCHILADAS:** Place one oven rack in the top third of the oven and one in the middle and preheat the oven to 400°F.
6. Add the grated cheeses to a small bowl and mix. Set aside.
7. Heat the oil in a large skillet over medium-high heat. Once shimmering, check for readiness by dropping a tiny piece of tortilla into the oil: If it bubbles, it's ready! Lightly fry each tortilla one at a time until pliable, about 10 seconds per side. Transfer them to a paper towel–lined plate, stacking as you go and adding additional oil to the skillet as needed for frying.
8. Add ½ cup of the enchilada sauce to the bottom of a 9 x 13-inch baking dish and spread evenly to coat. Place 6 tortillas, overlapping each about 2 inches to fit on the bottom of the baking dish, and layer, dividing evenly with 2 cups of the chicken, half of the beans, about 1 cup of the enchilada sauce, and 1½ cups of the cheese. Repeat this process for the next layer. Finish with a final layer of tortillas and the remaining cup of enchilada sauce and 1 cup of cheese.
9. Bake in the middle rack for 15 to 20 minutes, until the enchiladas are bubbling and starting to brown. Move the pan to the top rack, turn the broiler on high, and broil for 1 to 2 minutes, until the cheese is golden brown.
10. **TO SERVE:** Top with a dollop of sour cream, a sprinkle of cotija, cilantro, onion, and jalapeño slices (if using).

PERFECT PAIRING

Summer Berry Sangria (page 287), or a full-bodied red with good acidity like Zinfandel—both great with comfort food.

Bean & Cheese Variation

1. Follow the recipe and method above, replacing the roast chicken with 1 additional (15-ounce) can of whole black beans (drained and rinsed), along with 1 (15-ounce) can of refried beans for a total of 3 cans of beans.
2. In a medium bowl, combine all the beans with ¼ cup of the enchilada sauce, ½ teaspoon kosher salt, ½ teaspoon garlic powder, and ¼ teaspoon ground cumin. Mix until evenly combined and set aside.
3. Follow the same layering process as above (the bean mixture replaces the chicken) but only spread ¼ cup of the enchilada sauce to the base of the baking dish. Bake and serve with all the same toppings!

Sheet Pan Miso Butter Salmon

with Shrooms & Broccolini

SERVES 4 • **TOTAL TIME** 25 MINUTES

FOR THE MISO BUTTER

½ stick (4 tablespoons) unsalted butter, at room temperature

1 tablespoon white miso paste

½ teaspoon grated lemon zest

½ teaspoon honey

½ teaspoon garlic powder

FOR THE SALMON AND VEGGIES

8 ounces sliced shiitake or oyster mushrooms

1 bunch broccolini, thick stalks removed, cut into 1½-inch pieces

3 tablespoons extra-virgin olive oil

1 teaspoon toasted sesame oil

1 teaspoon kosher salt, divided

½ teaspoon garlic powder

½ teaspoon freshly ground black pepper, divided

4 (6- to 8-ounce) salmon fillets with skin

Toasted sesame seeds, for garnish

Lemon wedges, for serving

PERFECT PAIRING

A light- to medium-bodied red wine like Pinot Noir, or have some fun and try Junmai Daiginjo sake!

This sheet pan salmon has it all—nourishing, flavorful, minimal prep, and ready in under 30 minutes. It takes pantry staples and turns them into something seriously delicious. Miso brings umami—a deep, savory richness that makes everything taste more complex and satisfying. Here, it creates a crave-worthy crust on the salmon while broccolini and mushrooms, tossed with toasted sesame oil and spices, roast alongside for the perfect texture. The key to moist, flaky salmon? Broiling, and letting it sit in the oven for a few extra minutes after turning off the heat. Serve over rice and let the miso magic do its thing!

1. Place an oven rack in the top third of the oven and preheat the broiler on high. Line a sheet pan with parchment paper.
2. **MAKE THE MISO BUTTER:** Combine the butter, miso, lemon zest, honey, and garlic powder in a small bowl, mix until well combined, and set aside.
3. **MAKE THE SALMON AND VEGGIES:** Place the mushrooms and broccolini on the lined sheet pan, and drizzle with the olive oil, sesame oil, ½ teaspoon of the salt, the garlic powder, and ¼ teaspoon of the black pepper. Toss with your hands or tongs until coated. Push the veggies to the outer edges of the sheet pan in a single layer.
4. Place the salmon fillets skin side down in the center of the sheet pan and sprinkle with the remaining ½ teaspoon of salt and ¼ teaspoon of black pepper. Using your hands or a small spoon, evenly spread the miso butter on the top of each fillet.
5. Broil on the top rack of the oven for about 8 minutes, until the salmon is golden brown and lightly crisp on top (see Hot Tip). Turn the oven off but keep it closed for 3 to 5 minutes, until the salmon is cooked through and flakes easily with a fork and the veggies are tender.
6. **TO SERVE:** Divide the fish (skin side down) and veggies among four plates. Top with the toasted sesame seeds and serve with lemon wedges.

HOT TIP

If you prefer your salmon rare, check the fish after 6 minutes.

Yellow Chicken Curry & Coconut Rice

SERVES 6 • **TOTAL TIME** 1 HOUR

FOR THE YELLOW CHICKEN CURRY

3 tablespoons avocado or other neutral oil

2 large carrots, peeled and sliced into 1-inch coins

½ large yellow onion, diced

1 teaspoon ground coriander

1 teaspoon ground turmeric

1 teaspoon kosher salt

½ teaspoon freshly ground black pepper

3 garlic cloves, grated or finely chopped

1 tablespoon peeled and grated fresh ginger

¼ cup yellow curry paste (see Hot Tips)

2 large Yukon Gold potatoes, unpeeled and cut into 1-inch cubes

2 cups chicken bone broth or chicken stock (see Hot Tips)

2 (13.5-ounce) cans full-fat coconut milk, divided

1 stalk fresh lemongrass, tough leaves and green top discarded, white bottom bruised with the back of a knife (optional)

2 tablespoons plus 1 teaspoon light brown sugar

1 teaspoon fish sauce

Our family loves celebrating birthdays and milestones at a little Thai spot in Pasadena called Daisy Mint, and no meal is complete without an order of their yellow chicken curry. It's slightly spicy, a touch sweet, deeply savory, and incredibly warming. This brothy at-home version—served over fluffy, coconutty rice—keeps things simple with high-quality store-bought curry paste (see Hot Tips) and rotisserie chicken to cut down on cook time. Fresh ginger, lemongrass, turmeric, and fish sauce add extra depth. For a vegetarian twist, swap in tofu or chickpeas. Pair with the tofu variation of Saucy Chicken Lettuce Cups (page 42) for a full Thai-inspired spread.

---

1. **MAKE THE YELLOW CHICKEN CURRY:** Heat the oil in a large pot over medium heat. Once shimmering, add the carrots, onion, coriander, turmeric, salt, and black pepper and cook, stirring occasionally, until the onions are tender, 5 to 7 minutes. Add the garlic and ginger and cook, stirring constantly until fragrant, about 1 minute. Add the curry paste and cook, stirring constantly, until the paste has evenly coated the veggies and the spices are toasted, about 2 minutes.
2. Add the potatoes, chicken bone broth, 1 can of the coconut milk, the lemongrass (if using), brown sugar, fish sauce, and lime zest. Using a wooden spoon, stir to combine while scraping up any browned bits from the bottom of the pot. Bring the mixture to a boil over high heat, reduce the heat to medium-low and simmer, stirring occasionally, until the potatoes and carrots are tender, about 25 minutes.
3. Raise the heat to medium and add the shredded chicken and the remaining 1 can of coconut milk. Cook, stirring occasionally, until the chicken is warmed through, and the potatoes and carrots are fork-tender, about 5 minutes. Remove from heat, discard the stalk of lemongrass, and stir in the lime juice.

(recipe continues)

- 2 teaspoons grated lime zest (about 1 lime)
- 4 cups shredded store-bought rotisserie chicken (or homemade roast chicken)
- 1 tablespoon fresh lime juice (about ½ lime)

FOR THE COCONUT RICE

- 1½ cups jasmine rice
- 1 (13.5-ounce) can full-fat coconut milk
- 1 cup chicken bone broth or stock
- 1 teaspoon kosher salt
- 2 teaspoons granulated sugar
- Chopped fresh cilantro, for garnish

PERFECT PAIRING

A spiced and aromatic Gewürztraminer that can handle bold curry flavors, or a Chardonnay to cut through the creaminess.

4. **MAKE THE COCONUT RICE:** While the curry simmers, rinse the rice in a fine mesh strainer under cold water until the water runs clear, about 1 minute. Shake the colander to remove excess water. This makes for fluffy rice!
5. In a medium pot over medium-high heat, add the rice, coconut milk, chicken bone broth, salt, and sugar and stir until combined. Bring to a rapid simmer uncovered, and reduce to the lowest possible heat and cook, covered, until the liquid is absorbed, 15 to 20 minutes. Remove from the heat and allow to sit covered for 5 more minutes to steam. Using a fork, gently fluff the rice.
6. **TO SERVE:** Divide the coconut rice among six bowls and top with a few ladles of the curry. Garnish with chopped cilantro.

HOT TIPS

A high-quality yellow curry paste is your BFF here (Mekhala and Mike's Organic Curry Love are both great).

Any stock will work, but bone broth adds great depth of flavor. Taste and adjust the salt as desired.

Nana's Chicken Chile Verde

SERVES 4 TO 6 • **TOTAL TIME** 1 HOUR

FOR THE CHILE VERDE SAUCE

- 10 medium tomatillos (about 1 pound), husked and rinsed
- 2 teaspoons kosher salt, divided
- 2 tablespoons avocado or other neutral oil
- 3 dried chiles de árbol, stemmed
- 2 fresh jalapeño peppers, stemmed, seeded, and cut into 1-inch pieces
- 2 fresh poblano peppers, stemmed, seeded, and cut into 1-inch pieces
- 1 fresh Anaheim (California) or additional poblano pepper, stemmed, seeded, and cut into 1-inch pieces
- 1 small yellow onion, coarsely chopped
- 5 garlic cloves, coarsely chopped
- ½ teaspoon ground cumin
- ½ teaspoon dried oregano
- ½ teaspoon freshly ground black pepper
- 1½ cups chicken stock
- 1 bunch fresh cilantro with 1-inch tender stems

This dish was a legend at Nana's restaurant, Lupita's La Jolla, and now it's ready to earn its place in your kitchen too. The heart of the dish is a silky chile verde sauce—fragrant, slightly spicy, and layered with flavor from tomatillos, fresh poblano, Anaheim, and jalapeño peppers, plus plenty of garlic, onion, and cilantro. While pork is the classic choice, chicken thighs work just as beautifully. Serve it over Steamed Rice (page 244), and alongside No-Mayo Esquites (page 233) and Brothy Frijoles de la Olla (page 241), with plenty of tortilla chips for scooping. And if you're lucky enough to have leftovers, roll them into chicken chile verde burritos!

---

1. **MAKE THE TOMATILLO SAUCE:** In a medium pot, add the tomatillos and enough water to just cover. Season the water with 1 teaspoon of the salt. Bring to a boil over medium-high heat, then lower the heat to medium, and simmer until the tomatillos are fork-tender, 8 to 10 minutes. Using a slotted spoon, transfer the tomatillos to a plate. Discard the water.
2. Meanwhile, heat the oil in a large Dutch oven or stainless steel pot over medium heat. Add the chiles de árbol, jalapeños, poblanos, Anaheim pepper, onion, garlic, cumin, oregano, the remaining 1 teaspoon of salt, and the black pepper. Cook, stirring occasionally, until the vegetables are just tender, about 10 minutes.
3. Transfer the vegetables to a blender along with the boiled tomatillos, chicken stock, and cilantro. Blend (with the steam vent in the blender top open) on medium speed until completely smooth, about 1 minute.

(recipe continues)

FOR THE CHICKEN

- 2 pounds boneless, skinless chicken thighs, cut into 1-inch pieces
- 2 teaspoons garlic powder
- 1 teaspoon kosher salt
- ½ teaspoon freshly ground black pepper
- 2 tablespoons avocado or other neutral oil, plus more as needed

FOR SERVING

- Steamed Rice (page 244)
- Chopped fresh cilantro, for garnish
- Lime wedges

PERFECT PAIRING

A slightly off-dry Riesling from the Mosel in Germany (look for bottles labeled Trocken or Halbtrocken).

4. **MAKE THE CHICKEN:** In a large bowl, generously season the chicken thighs with the garlic powder, salt, and black pepper and toss until coated.
5. Return the pot to medium-high heat with the oil. Once shimmering, add the chicken, working in batches if needed as to not overcrowd the pan, and cook until golden brown, about 3 minutes per side. Transfer the chicken to a plate.
6. Pour the chile verde sauce into the pot and bring to a boil over medium-high heat, stirring occasionally with a wooden spoon to scrape up any browned bits from the bottom of the pot, to meld the flavors, 1 to 2 minutes. Reduce the heat to low, return the chicken and its juices to the pot, cover, and simmer, stirring occasionally, until tender, 20 to 25 minutes. Uncover and continue to simmer until the sauce thickens, 5 to 8 minutes more.
7. Divide the chicken and sauce among bowls over steamed rice and top with the chopped cilantro and lime wedges.

Family Favorite Pot Roast

SERVES 4 • **TOTAL TIME** 4 HOURS 15 MINUTES

- 3 pounds boneless beef chuck roast
- 4 garlic cloves, cut into 12 slivers total
- 1 tablespoon garlic salt seasoning
- 2 teaspoons freshly ground black pepper
- ½ teaspoon kosher salt
- ¼ cup extra-virgin olive oil
- 1 small yellow onion, finely chopped
- 1 Roma (plum) tomato, diced
- 2 tablespoons tomato paste
- ⅓ cup dry red wine (I use Cabernet Sauvignon)
- 6 cups beef stock, plus more as needed
- 6 medium Yukon Gold potatoes, unpeeled and cut into 1-inch cubes
- 1 pound green beans, trimmed and cut into thirds
- Steamed Rice (page 244), for serving (optional)

PERFECT PAIRING

A Merlot-dominant wine like Côtes de Bordeaux or a Sangiovese like Chianti.

This pot roast is a family heirloom—passed down from Nana, perfected by my mom, and fine-tuned in my own kitchen over years of tinkering. To me, this is the taste of home. It's the kind of meal that makes people pause after that first bite, then immediately ask for the recipe. My spin? A splash of wine (no surprise there), a hint of tomato paste for extra depth, and a shift from stovetop to oven for foolproof tenderness every time.

1. Preheat the oven to 350°F.
2. Using a paring knife, make 12 deep cuts all over the meat. Insert one garlic sliver into each cut. Pat the roast dry with a paper towel and season with the garlic salt, black pepper, and salt on all sides.
3. Heat the oil in a large Dutch oven or heavy lidded pot over medium-high heat. Once shimmering, carefully add the meat and cook all sides until evenly browned, 3 to 5 minutes per side. Transfer to a plate.
4. Reduce the heat to medium. Add the onion and cook, stirring occasionally, until translucent, 5 to 7 minutes. Add the tomato and cook, stirring occasionally, until softened, about 3 minutes. Add the tomato paste and cook, stirring constantly to avoid burning, until the mixture darkens and becomes fragrant, 1 to 2 minutes. Add the wine, scraping up the browned bits from the bottom, and cook, stirring occasionally, until the scent of alcohol has dissipated and the mixture begins to thicken, 3 to 4 minutes. Add the beef stock, raise the heat to high, and bring to a simmer. Return the roast back to the pot, along with any juices, cover, and transfer to the oven and bake for 1½ hours.
5. Remove the pot from the oven and, using tongs, flip the roast to ensure even cooking. Nestle the potatoes and green beans around the roast, mostly submerged under the liquid. Return to the oven, covered, and bake for about 2 hours more (about 3½ hours total), until the meat is fork-tender and easily pulls away without resistance.
6. Transfer the roast to a plate to rest for at least 10 minutes. Cut into large chunks and return to the pot along with any juices.
7. Serve family style straight from the pot or divide the meat, veggies, and rice (if using) among four shallow bowls and ladle a generous amount of the sauce over the top.

Kitchen Sink Breakfast-for-Dinner Skillet

SERVES 6 TO 8 • **TOTAL TIME** 1 HOUR

- ¼ cup avocado or other neutral oil, divided
- 1 pound pork breakfast sausage, casings removed (or ground pork breakfast sausage)
- 8 large eggs
- 1¼ cups half-and-half
- 1 teaspoon kosher salt, divided
- 2 cups frozen shredded hash browns, unthawed
- 3 tablespoons unsalted butter
- ½ medium yellow onion, diced
- 1 large bell pepper, diced
- 1 teaspoon garlic powder
- 1 teaspoon Italian seasoning
- ½ teaspoon paprika
- ½ teaspoon freshly ground black pepper, plus more for garnish
- 1 cup chopped baby spinach (about 2 ounces)
- 1½ cups grated sharp yellow cheddar cheese
- ¼ cup finely grated Parmigiano-Reggiano cheese
- Finely chopped fresh chives, for garnish

PERFECT PAIRING

A brunchy spritz like the Slice of Heaven Rossini (page 296), or a Pinot Grigio.

Think of this as a frittata-meets-loaded hash brown mashup—the ultimate one-pan breakfast (or let's be real, anytime meal). A glorious, delicious mess of crispy hash browns, fluffy eggs, savory sausage, melty cheese, and whatever veggies you've got kicking around all come together in a skillet of pure joy. No overthinking required—you literally can't mess this one up. Go vegetarian with vegan sausage or seasoned, cooked mushrooms. Serve with Sweet & Spicy Mexican Fruit Salad with Tajín Vinaigrette (page 67).

1. Preheat the oven to 375°F.
2. Heat 2 tablespoons of the oil in a 10-inch cast-iron skillet over medium-high heat. Add the sausage, using a wooden spoon to break up any large pieces, and cook, stirring occasionally, until browned, 6 to 8 minutes. Using a slotted spoon, transfer to a plate and reserve the skillet off heat.
3. Meanwhile, in a large bowl, whisk the eggs, half-and-half, and ½ teaspoon of the salt until pale yellow and slightly foamy, about 1 minute. Set aside.
4. Heat the remaining 2 tablespoons of oil in the same skillet over medium heat. Spread the hash browns in an even layer and cook, undisturbed, until golden brown, about 4 minutes. Stir in the butter, onion, bell pepper, garlic powder, Italian seasoning, paprika, the remaining ½ teaspoon of salt, and the black pepper, scraping up any browned bits from the bottom of the skillet. Cook until the onion begins to soften, 2 to 3 minutes. Remove from heat and add the sausage and spinach and stir until the spinach is wilted, about 1 minute.
5. Sprinkle half of the cheddar on top, pour the egg mixture over the cheese without stirring, and sprinkle with the remaining cheddar and Parmigiano-Reggiano.
6. Transfer the skillet to the oven and bake until the center is set without jiggling and the top is crispy and golden brown, 35 to 40 minutes. Let cool slightly off heat for about 5 minutes.
7. **TO SERVE:** Run a knife around the edge of the skillet and slice into wedges. Garnish with the chives and a few twists of black pepper.

One-Pan Sicilian Baked Cod
with Roasted Tomatoes & Olives

SERVES 4 • **TOTAL TIME** 45 MINUTES

1½ teaspoons kosher salt, divided

1 teaspoon freshly ground black pepper, divided

1 teaspoon garlic powder

1 teaspoon smoked paprika

½ teaspoon dried oregano

4 (6-ounce) cod fillets, about 1 inch thick (see Hot Tips)

2 cups cherry tomatoes (about 12 ounces), halved

½ small red onion, thinly sliced

½ cup halved kalamata olives

¼ cup dry white wine (I use Sauvignon Blanc)

4 garlic cloves, finely chopped

2 tablespoons extra-virgin olive oil

1 tablespoon drained capers

½ teaspoon crushed red pepper

2 tablespoons fresh lemon juice (about one lemon), for serving

Fresh torn basil, for garnish

Fresh torn mint, for garnish

Lemon wedges, for serving

PERFECT PAIRING

A Sicilian Etna Bianco like Carricante, an Etna Rosato, or a citrusy Sauvignon Blanc!

Chances are you're not reading this from the Sicilian coast (and if you are, lucky you!), but this dish brings all the Taormina vibes straight to your kitchen. This effortlessly elegant one-pan meal features flaky cod nestled among burst cherry tomatoes, briny kalamata olives, herbs, and red onion, all roasting together to create a luscious, built-in sauce—perfect for sopping up with crusty bread or spooning over rice. It's a restaurant-worthy weeknight win that also feels right at home on a dinner party table. Serve with Nana's Iconic Crunchy Lemon Parm Salad (page 59) made with arugula instead of romaine. And I'd be remiss without a quick thank you to Chef Gianluca from Osteria Santa Domenica for the lesson and the inspo!

---

1. Preheat the oven to 400°F.
2. In a small bowl, combine 1 teaspoon of the salt, ½ teaspoon of the black pepper, the garlic powder, smoked paprika, and oregano.
3. Place the fish on a plate and pat dry. Sprinkle the reserved spice mixture all over the fillets and pat to stick to the fish. Set aside.
4. In a 9 x 13-inch baking dish, add the tomatoes, onion, olives, wine, garlic, oil, capers, crushed red pepper, and the remaining ½ teaspoon each of salt and black pepper. Toss to combine. Bake until the tomatoes start to wrinkle and release their juice, 20 minutes.
5. Make a space for the fish in the center of the baking dish and place the fish directly on the bottom of the dish surrounded by the vegetables. Bake for 10 to 12 minutes, until the fish is cooked through and flakes easily with a fork (see Hot Tips).
6. **TO SERVE:** Divide the roasted vegetables among four plates and top with fish. Sprinkle the lemon juice over each plate, garnish with the torn basil and mint, and serve with lemon wedges.

HOT TIPS

When cooking fish, an opaque color signals doneness, along with the flake test: Insert a fork into the thickest part of the fish and pull away at an angle to see if it flakes, indicating a perfect cook. Or use a meat thermometer to check for an internal temperature of 140° to 145°F.

Halibut or sea bass also work great; just adjust bake time depending on the fillet's thickness.

Loaded Twice-Baked Broccoli Cheddar Potatoes

SERVES 4 • **TOTAL TIME** 2 HOURS 15 MINUTES

4 large russet potatoes, unpeeled, scrubbed and dried

1 tablespoon extra-virgin olive oil

2 teaspoons kosher salt, divided

5 slices uncured bacon

1 cup finely chopped broccoli florets

½ cup whole milk

4 ounces cream cheese, at room temperature

¼ cup heavy cream

2 tablespoons unsalted butter, at room temperature

½ teaspoon freshly ground black pepper, plus more for serving

¼ teaspoon crushed red pepper

2 cups freshly grated medium yellow cheddar cheese, divided

¼ cup freshly grated low-moisture mozzarella cheese

Sour cream, for garnish

Finely chopped fresh chives, for garnish

PERFECT PAIRING

A Pinot Noir or creamy Chardonnay from California's Central Coast would be ideal.

Twice-baked potatoes were a childhood staple—fluffy, cheese-smothered pillows of potato with crispy bacon and chives. When my dad was carb-loading for an ultra-marathon (and needed extra greens), the broccoli-cheddar remix was born. My take? Even more indulgent, packed with extra butter, cheddar, and cream cheese, making it hearty enough for a stand-alone meal. Bacon is a must for me, but if you're skipping it, a pinch of smoked paprika or chili adds that smoky hit.

1. Place one oven rack in the top third of the oven and one in the middle and preheat the oven to 400°F. Line a sheet pan with parchment paper. Place an oven-safe wire rack on top of a second sheet pan.
2. Place the potatoes on the parchment-covered sheet pan and pierce each with a fork 5 times. Evenly coat the potatoes with the oil and sprinkle them all over with 1 teaspoon of the salt.
3. Bake on the middle rack until a knife tip can be easily inserted in the center, about 1 hour. Set aside to cool on the sheet pan.
4. Meanwhile, after the potatoes have been in the oven for 30 minutes, lay the bacon strips on top of the wire rack in a single layer and bake on the top rack for about 25 minutes, until golden brown and crispy. Let cool on the wire rack. Once cooled, finely chop and set aside.
5. Slice off the top quarter of the potatoes horizontally and discard (or snack on them!). Using a spoon, carefully scoop out the inside, leaving a ¼-inch border around the potatoes, and place the scooped potato into a large bowl. Leave the hollowed potatoes on the sheet tray.
6. Add the broccoli, milk, cream cheese, cream, butter, the remaining 1 teaspoon of salt, the black pepper, and crushed red pepper to the bowl. Mash everything together, leaving some small chunks of potato. Mix in ½ cup of the chopped bacon, 1 cup of the cheddar, and the mozzarella.
7. Spoon the potato mixture almost to the top of the hollowed potatoes and divide ½ cup of cheddar over the potato mixture. Mound the remaining potato mixture over the cheese. Top with the remaining ½ cup of cheddar and bake for 15 to 20 minutes, until the cheese is melted and bubbly.
8. **TO SERVE:** Top with a generous dollop of sour cream, the remaining bacon bits, a few twists of black pepper, and the chives.

Seared Scallops

with White Wine Butter Sauce & Crispy Pancetta

SERVES 4 • **TOTAL TIME** 30 MINUTES

- 4 ounces pancetta, chopped
- 12 to 14 scallops, muscle removed (about 1 pound)
- 1½ teaspoons kosher salt, divided
- 1 teaspoon freshly ground black pepper, plus more for serving
- 2 tablespoons avocado or other neutral oil, divided
- 2 garlic cloves, finely chopped
- ⅓ cup dry white wine (I use Sauvignon Blanc)
- ½ stick (4 tablespoons) unsalted butter, cut into tablespoons, cold
- Chopped fresh flat-leaf parsley, for garnish
- Lemon wedges, for serving

PERFECT PAIRING

A richer Chardonnay from France or Napa Valley, or a Cucumber Basil Martini (page 288).

HOT TIP

Scallops are easy to overcook. They're ready when they lose translucency, are white inside, and feel firm but not tough or rubbery on the edges. The meat thermometer should read 120°F.

If you've never cooked scallops at home, don't stress—they're quick, easy, and downright impressive. A sizzling hot skillet ensures that golden sear (no sticking!), and cooking them in the same pan after the pancetta adds a subtle smokiness that takes them over the top. Toss some snap peas right into the skillet after the scallops for a quick side with less mess. Or serve with Easy Creamy Parm Polenta (page 218), Auntie Bug's Shortcut Asparagus Risotto (page 238), and Crispy Pecorino Zucchini Fries (page 46) for a next-level meal.

1. Line a plate with paper towels.
2. In a large stainless steel or cast-iron skillet, add the pancetta and cook over medium-high heat, stirring occasionally, until golden brown and crispy, 5 to 7 minutes. Using a slotted spoon, transfer to the lined plate and set aside. Discard the pan fat.
3. Meanwhile, place the scallops on a plate and pat them dry with a paper towel. Season all over with 1 teaspoon each of the salt and black pepper.
4. In the same skillet, heat 1 tablespoon of the oil over medium-high heat. Once shimmering, add the scallops, working in batches if needed as to not overcrowd the pan, and cook, undisturbed, until a golden-brown crust forms and they easily release from the pan, 2 to 3 minutes per side (see Hot Tip). Transfer to a serving plate, loosely cover with foil or parchment, and set aside.
5. Reduce the heat to medium, add the remaining 1 tablespoon of oil and the garlic, and cook, stirring constantly, until fragrant, about 1 minute. Add the wine and stir, scraping up any browned bits from the bottom, and add the remaining ½ teaspoon of salt. Simmer, stirring occasionally, until slightly reduced, 3 to 4 minutes.
6. Reduce the heat to low and quickly whisk in 1 tablespoon of the butter at a time, allowing each tablespoon to melt completely before adding the next. Continue whisking until the sauce thickens slightly, 2 to 4 minutes.
7. **TO SERVE:** Pour the white wine butter sauce over the scallops, sprinkle with the pancetta, and garnish with chopped parsley, a few twists of black pepper, and lemon wedges on the side.

Guinness Irish Beef & Veggie Stew

SERVES 6 TO 8 • **TOTAL TIME** 3 HOURS

- 1/4 cup all-purpose flour
- 1 tablespoon kosher salt, plus more to taste
- 1 tablespoon freshly ground black pepper, plus more to taste
- 1 tablespoon garlic powder
- 1 tablespoon onion powder
- 3 pounds boneless beef chuck roast, cubed into 1½-inch pieces
- 1/4 cup avocado or other neutral oil, divided, plus more as needed
- 1 medium yellow onion, chopped
- 3 tablespoons tomato paste
- 6 garlic cloves, finely chopped
- 1 cup dry red wine (I use Cabernet Sauvignon)
- 1 cup Guinness beer
- 6 cups beef stock
- 2 dried bay leaves
- 1 pound baby Yukon Gold potatoes, unpeeled and cut into 3/4-inch pieces
- 6 medium carrots, peeled and cut into 3/4-inch pieces
- 1½ cups frozen peas, unthawed
- Toasted, buttered ourdough bread, for serving

This rich, saucy meat-and-veggie stew is braised beef at its finest. Inspired by my dad's Irish heritage, I made it one St. Patrick's Day for visiting friends, and we loved it so much we ate it for days—dunking crusty, buttered bread into the Guinness and red wine–infused broth. The chuck roast turns fall-apart tender, while the potatoes, carrots, and peas soak up every bit of flavor. It's even better the next day, so plan for leftovers. Either way, don't forget the bread and butter—you'll want to savor every last drop.

1. In a large bowl, mix the flour, salt, black pepper, garlic powder, and onion powder. Add the chuck roast and toss to thoroughly coat.
2. Heat 2 tablespoons of the oil in a large Dutch oven or stainless steel lidded pot over medium-high heat. Once shimmering, add the meat, working in batches if needed as not to overcrowd the pot, using tongs to turn the meat and cook all sides, until golden brown, 2 to 3 minutes per side. Add more oil as needed. Transfer the meat to a plate and set aside.
3. Reduce the heat to medium and add the remaining 2 tablespoons of oil. Add the onion and cook, stirring frequently, until softened and translucent, 5 to 7 minutes. Add the tomato paste and garlic and cook, stirring frequently until the tomato paste darkens, 2 to 3 minutes.
4. Add the wine, scraping up any browned bits from the bottom. Simmer until the scent of alcohol has dissipated and the sauce thickens, 4 to 6 minutes. Add the meat and any juices, the Guinness, beef stock, and bay leaves and bring to a boil. Reduce the heat to low, cover, and gently simmer until the meat is tender, about 2 hours.
5. Add the potatoes and carrots and simmer until the vegetables are tender but not falling apart, 15 minutes. Remove and discard the bay leaves, stir in the peas, and simmer for 5 minutes.
6. **TO SERVE:** Ladle into bowls and enjoy with toasty buttered bread.

PERFECT PAIRING

A lush fuller-bodied red like Cabernet Sauvignon—not too dry or tannic.

PASTA: MY LOVE LANGUAGE

Pasta, salad, and french fries were basically my entire diet as a kid, and buttered Parmesan noodles felt like peak cuisine (turns out, I was unknowingly eating a variation of Three-Ingredient Authentic Fettuccine Alfredo, page 163). But the real revelation came years later when my husband, Andrew, and I—jet-lagged, hangry, and slightly hungover—sat down to a bowl of pasta al limone at Lil' Frankie's in Manhattan. Just lemon, butter, Parmigiano-Reggiano, and pasta water—so simple, yet completely transformative. That's the beauty of pasta: With the right technique, even the simplest ingredients can become something unforgettable. After every trip to Italy or a visit to our favorite Pasadena pasta spot, I'd rush into the kitchen, eager to re-create our favorite dishes—from Tagliatelle Bolognese (page 154) to Spicy Garlic Shrimp Linguine with Crispy Panko (page 164). Along the way, I picked up invaluable pasta tricks (see Pasta 101, page 150) and can't wait to share them—like why bronze-cut pasta grips sauce better, how cooking al dente creates the perfect bite, and why pasta water (aka liquid gold) is the secret to restaurant-quality results. And the salt? Always two heaping tablespoons per pot.

This chapter is filled with dishes inspired by favorite meals from my favorite bites from all over the map as well as my kitchen—proof that great pasta isn't about complexity, but about mastering the little details.

PASTA 101:

PASTABILITIES FOR SUCCESS

Salt: The first rule of Italian cooking for pasta perfection? Generously salt the water—I use 2 tablespoons. It might sound like a lot, but trust me, it transforms otherwise bland pasta by infusing flavor right from the start.

Bronze-Cut Pasta: If you can find it, always go for bronze-cut (or bronze-die) pasta—it's a game-changer. Extruded through perforated bronze dies, it develops a rough, porous texture that holds on to sauce like a dream. The result? More flavor in every bite and a noticeably better-tasting dish. Worth every penny. Barilla Al Bronzo is my personal fave and is available at most grocery stores!

Al Dente, ALWAYS: Cooking pasta al dente isn't just about the texture—it genuinely improves the dish. A good rule of thumb? Cook it 2 minutes less than the box suggests. In many recipes, pasta finishes in the sauce, soaking up flavor while keeping the perfect bite. An added bonus I picked up in Italy: Al dente pasta is actually easier to digest and has a lower glycemic index than overcooked pasta, meaning it releases glucose more slowly. Better texture, better taste, better for you—what's not to love?

Liquid Gold: Pasta water is the secret weapon of great pasta dishes. That's why I often call for reserving pasta water (aka liquid gold) in recipes. It adds unmistakable glossiness and hydration and helps sauces come together and coat those noodles as perfectly as possible. Even if you're making pasta on the fly, or a recipe that doesn't call for it—do it anyway! A splash or two can rescue a dry or sticky sauce and enhance both texture and flavor.

You Butter Believe It: When in doubt, add butter. Ever wonder why you can't get that restaurant pasta quite right when trying it at home? Butter is the magic touch. A couple dabs will do ya, helping to achieve that glossy sheen and decadence that easily elevates any dish.

Twirl It Up: For pretty plated long cut pasta (spaghetti, fettuccine, tagliatelle, bucatini, etc.), use tongs to twirl while spinning the plate with your other hand—it creates a picture-perfect pasta nest.

Make It Rain: A generous snowfall or mountain of freshly grated Parmigiano-Reggiano and a handful of fresh herbs can really bring a dish to life and make it even more beautiful. And the finer the better. Grab that microplane!

Hidden Flavor Bombs: Anchovies, capers, crushed Calabrian chili peppers, garlic, olives, Parmigiano-Reggiano, Pecorino Romano, sun-dried tomatoes—these staples can transform a simple red sauce or basic pasta into a wonder. It's also a great way to use up those bits and bobs hanging about in your kitchen.

Amalfi-Inspired Spaghetti al Limone

SERVES 6 • **TOTAL TIME** 25 MINUTES

2 tablespoons kosher salt for the pasta water

16 ounces dried spaghetti

1 tablespoon extra-virgin olive oil

1 stick (8 tablespoons) unsalted butter, divided

2 garlic cloves, peeled and smashed

3 lemons, halved, juiced, and squeezed, flesh and rinds reserved

1¾ cups fresh, finely grated Parmigiano-Reggiano cheese, plus more for garnish (see Hot Tips)

⅓ cup torn fresh mint, plus more for garnish (see Hot Tips)

PERFECT PAIRING

An Etna Bianco from Sicily, a juicy red Valpolicella Classico, or a Limoncello Spritz (page 291)—iconic sips for an iconic pasta.

HOT TIPS

You can also use the more traditional basil instead of the mint.

Fresh, finely grated Parm is crucial for this dish.

This dish transformed my love for eating pasta into an obsession with making it. It's a blend of two favorites: the one that started it all—New York's Lil' Frankie's iconic Limone—and the version I tasted along Italy's Amalfi Coast. Amalfi may be a celebrity hideout, but it's also known for its famous oversized, intensely fragrant lemons. Unlike many versions that rely on cream, this silky sauce is made solely with garlic-infused olive oil, butter, Parmigiano-Reggiano, lemons, and pasta water. I use freshly grated cheese for a seamless melt, and finish with a touch of mint. With so few ingredients, the magic is in the method and the balance of flavors. Served alongside My Big Fat Italian Chopped Salad (page 80), it's *la dolce vita* on a plate.

---

1. Bring a large pot of water with the salt to a boil over high heat. Add the pasta and cook until al dente according to the instructions on the package.
2. Meanwhile, heat the oil and 2 tablespoons of the butter in a large pot over medium heat. Once the butter is bubbling, add the garlic and cook, stirring frequently so the butter doesn't burn, until the garlic is lightly golden and fragrant, 2 to 3 minutes. Turn the heat off and discard the garlic.
3. Once the pasta is done cooking, lift the pasta with tongs, shake off some excess water, and carefully transfer it directly into the pot of garlic-infused butter. (Do not drain the pasta; this step is the secret to a creamy sauce!)
4. Reserve 1 cup of the pasta water, and quickly stir ½ cup of the water into the pasta and butter mixture. Add the lemon juice and the reserved juiced lemon halves, the remaining 6 tablespoons of butter, the Parmigiano-Reggiano, and the mint. Using a wooden spoon, immediately begin vigorously and continuously stirring while streaming in the remaining ½ cup of pasta water (pushing and bruising the juiced lemon halves to release their oils), until a loose yet creamy sauce begins to form, 1 to 2 minutes. This should feel like an arm workout!
5. **TO SERVE:** Divide the pasta among six serving bowls. Add a juiced lemon half to each bowl if desired (or discard), and garnish with a mountain of Parmigiano-Reggiano and a few torn mint leaves.

Tagliatelle Bolognese

SERVES 4 TO 6 • **TOTAL TIME** 3 HOURS 45 MINUTES

FOR THE BOLOGNESE

4 ounces pancetta, diced

5 tablespoons unsalted butter, divided

2 celery stalks, finely chopped

1 large carrot, peeled and finely chopped

1 small yellow onion, finely chopped

1½ teaspoons kosher salt, divided

½ teaspoon freshly ground black pepper

2 tablespoons tomato paste

1 pound 80% lean ground beef

1 cup dry red wine (I use Nebbiolo)

1 (24.5-ounce) jar tomato puree

¼ cup beef stock

¼ teaspoon freshly grated nutmeg

½ cup whole milk

¼ cup heavy cream

FOR THE TAGLIATELLE

2 tablespoons kosher salt for the pasta water

14 ounces dried tagliatelle

Freshly grated Parmigiano-Reggiano, for serving

PERFECT PAIRING

A Nebbiolo like Barolo or Barbaresco, or a Bordeaux blend.

Meet the more indulgent, velvety cousin of the classic meat sauce that stole my heart and fed my soul in Bologna. This at-home rendition is a regular in our kitchen, layering the sweetness and tang of tomatoes with the depth of pancetta and ground beef. The secret? Time, patience, and of course, lots of love. A true Bolognese isn't rushed—the longer it simmers, the more its flavors deepen and meld. For extra nuance, swap half the ground beef for ground pork, to add richness and complexity. I love how the sauce clings to tagliatelle's wide ribbons—but it's just as delicious over your favorite pasta, especially with the Tuscan Zucchini & Arugula Salad with Parm Crisps (page 72).

1. Heat a large pot over medium heat. Add the pancetta and cook, stirring occasionally, until golden brown and crispy, 5 to 7 minutes.
2. Melt 3 tablespoons of the butter and add the celery, carrot, onion, 1 teaspoon of the salt, and the black pepper and cook, stirring occasionally, until the onion is translucent and the vegetables are tender, 8 to 10 minutes.
3. Add the tomato paste and cook, stirring frequently, until the color deepens, about 3 minutes. Add the ground beef, using a wooden spoon to break up large pieces, and cook until browned, 6 to 8 minutes. Add the wine, scraping up any browned bits from the bottom of the pot. Simmer until the wine is almost fully evaporated and the scent of alcohol has dissipated, 5 to 7 minutes.
4. Stir in the tomato puree, beef stock, nutmeg, and the remaining ½ teaspoon of the salt. Reduce the heat to low and simmer, uncovered, stirring every 30 minutes and scraping the bottom of the pot to avoid burning, until the sauce has thickened, about 2½ hours.
5. Add the milk and cream and simmer, stirring often, until a thick sauce forms and most of the liquid has evaporated, 20 to 25 minutes.
6. Meanwhile, bring a large pot of water with the salt to a boil. Add the tagliatelle and cook until al dente according to package directions. Reserve 1 generous cup of the pasta water. Using tongs, transfer the pasta directly into the pot with the tomato sauce.
7. Off heat, gently stir in the remaining 2 tablespoons of butter and ¼ cup of the reserved pasta water (if the sauce seems dry), adding more as needed until the pasta is glossy and coated with the sauce.
8. **TO SERVE:** Divide among bowls and top with a mountain of Parmigiano-Reggiano.

PERFECT PAIRING

A Vermentino or Pigato from Liguria is heavenly.

Sweet Pea Pesto Pasta with Crispy Prosciutto

SERVES 6 • **TOTAL TIME** 45 MINUTES

FOR THE SWEET PEA PESTO

- 2 cups fresh basil, plus more for garnish
- 1 cup fresh mint
- 3 tablespoons pine nuts
- 2 garlic cloves, peeled
- 1 cup thawed frozen peas (from a 16-ounce bag, remainder used in a later step, see Hot Tips)
- ¾ cup finely grated Parmigiano-Reggiano
- 3 tablespoons ice water (see Hot Tips)
- 1 teaspoon grated lemon zest, plus more for garnish
- 2 tablespoons fresh lemon juice (about 1 lemon)
- ½ teaspoon crushed red pepper
- ¼ teaspoon kosher salt
- ¼ teaspoon freshly ground black pepper
- ½ cup extra-virgin olive oil, plus more as needed

FOR THE PASTA

- 4 slices prosciutto
- 2 tablespoons kosher salt
- 16 ounces dried fusilli
- 1 tablespoon extra-virgin olive oil
- 2 cups thawed frozen peas (remainder from 16-ounce bag, see Hot Tips)
- 2 tablespoons unsalted butter
- 1 (8-ounce) ball burrata cheese, at room temperature

This is my idea of springtime pasta perfection—made possible year-round with frozen peas. This vibrant pesto combines basil and garlic with sweet peas, fresh mint, and a splash of bright lemon. Crispy, oven-baked prosciutto, more peas, and creamy burrata bring it all together. No burrata? Go for fresh mozzarella instead. Serve with Honey & Chile Roasted Carrots (page 237) for a sweet, smoky, and lightly spiced contrast.

1. **MAKE THE SWEET PEA PESTO:** In a food processor or blender, add the basil, mint, pine nuts, and garlic and pulse until coarse and well combined. Add 1 cup of the peas, the Parmigiano-Reggiano, ice water, lemon zest, lemon juice, crushed red pepper, salt, and black pepper. Stream the oil through the vent while blending until mostly smooth, 1 to 2 minutes.
2. **MAKE THE PASTA:** Preheat the oven to 375°F. Place a wire rack on top of a sheet pan or line a sheet pan with parchment paper.
3. Place the prosciutto on the wire rack or the parchment paper in a single layer and bake for 18 to 20 minutes, until golden brown and crispy. Let the prosciutto cool completely on the wire rack or sheet tray for 6 to 8 minutes before roughly chopping. Set aside.
4. Meanwhile, bring a large pot of water with the salt to a boil. Add the pasta and cook until al dente according to package directions. Reserve ½ cup of the pasta water. Drain the pasta into a colander, discarding the remaining water. Return the pasta to the pot with a drizzle of the oil and toss to coat.
5. Immediately add the sweet pea pesto along with the remaining 2 cups peas, the butter, and 1 tablespoon of the reserved pasta water at a time, stirring quickly to slightly thicken the sauce, until the pesto is a glossy consistency.
6. **TO SERVE:** Divide into six shallow bowls. Tear the burrata into 6 pieces and top each bowl with the cheese, basil, lemon zest, and the crispy prosciutto.

HOT TIPS

This recipe uses 1 (16-ounce) bag of frozen peas in different steps. To quickly thaw frozen peas, empty the bag into a colander and rinse under cold water.

The ice water prevents the herbs from browning and helps to make a smooth sauce.

Bruschetta Pasta

SERVES 4 TO 6 • **TOTAL TIME** 20 MINUTES

- 4 cups cherry tomatoes (about 24 ounces), halved
- 1 cup fresh basil, chopped, plus more for garnish
- ½ cup extra-virgin olive oil
- 3 garlic cloves, finely chopped
- 2 tablespoons plus 1½ teaspoons kosher salt, divided
- 16 ounces dried rigatoni or pasta of choice
- ½ cup finely grated Parmigiano-Reggiano cheese, plus more for garnish
- 2 tablespoons unsalted butter
- ½ teaspoon crushed red pepper

PERFECT PAIRING

A dry Italian Rosato (rosé) with layers of raspberry and currant.

On my first visit to Rome, I didn't just eat—I tasted the city's history, culture, and geography in every bite. While I happily worked my way through bowl after bowl of classic Roman pastas, I also discovered this light yet deeply satisfying summertime dish: pasta alla checca. Made with ingredients reminiscent of bruschetta—sweet cherry tomatoes, fragrant basil, punchy garlic, and rich olive oil and Parmigiano-Reggiano—it's as effortless as it is flavorful. The key? Peak-season tomatoes and real-deal Parmigiano-Reggiano, which melts seamlessly instead of clumping. Aside from boiling the rigatoni, everything comes together in a single bowl. Serve it alongside Famous Brown Butter Lemon Chicken (page 101), and the chicken's nutty, caramelized richness will deepen every bright, fresh bite.

1. In a large bowl, combine the tomatoes, basil, oil, garlic, and 1½ teaspoons of the salt. Set aside at room temperature to marinate while the pasta cooks.
2. Bring a large pot of water with the remaining 2 tablespoons of salt to a boil. Add the rigatoni and cook until al dente according to package directions. Drain the pasta into a colander and add the drained pasta to the marinated tomatoes. Add the Parmigiano-Reggiano, butter, and crushed red pepper and mix until the butter melts and the sauce evenly coats the pasta.
3. **TO SERVE:** Divide into shallow bowls and top with a mountain of Parmigiano-Reggiano and garnish with basil.

Weeknight Sweet Sausage & Fusilli

SERVES 4 TO 6 • **TOTAL TIME** 45 MINUTES

FOR THE SAUCE

3 tablespoons extra-virgin olive oil, divided, plus more for serving

1 pound ground sweet Italian sausage, casings removed

1 small yellow onion, diced

1 tablespoon crushed Calabrian chili peppers

3 garlic cloves, finely chopped

1 teaspoon kosher salt

½ teaspoon freshly ground black pepper

½ teaspoon dried oregano

1 (28-ounce) can whole peeled San Marzano tomatoes, undrained

½ cup fresh basil, plus torn leaves for garnish

1 (4-inch piece) Parmigiano-Reggiano cheese rind or 2 tablespoons finely grated Parmigiano-Reggiano cheese

½ teaspoon granulated sugar

FOR THE PASTA

2 tablespoons kosher salt for the pasta water

16 ounces dried fusilli

2 tablespoons unsalted butter

1 (4-ounce) ball burrata cheese, at room temperature, for serving

Extra-virgin olive oil, for drizzling

Family and friends request this decadent pasta often, and I never tire of making it. While it looks impressive, it comes together with ease—perfect for date night or a last-minute dinner with friends. For a vegetarian twist, swap the sausage for seasoned mushrooms and briny olives. No burrata? Add extra Parmigiano-Reggiano or try a creamy cheese like ricotta.

---

1. **MAKE THE SAUCE:** Heat 2 tablespoons of the oil in a medium pot over medium-high heat. Add the sausage, using a wooden spoon to break up any large pieces, and cook, stirring occasionally, until browned, 6 to 8 minutes. Using a slotted spoon, transfer the sausage to a plate and set aside.
2. Reduce the heat to medium and add the remaining tablespoon of oil. Add the onion and cook, stirring occasionally, until translucent, 5 to 7 minutes. Add the Calabrian chili peppers, garlic, salt, black pepper, and oregano and cook, stirring frequently, until fragrant, about 2 minutes.
3. Stir in the tomatoes, basil, Parmigiano-Reggiano rind, and sugar, and gently break up and crush the whole tomatoes. Bring to a simmer, reduce the heat to medium-low, and cook, stirring occasionally and scraping the bottom of the pot to pick up any remaining sausage bits, until the sauce begins to thicken, 18 to 20 minutes.
4. Off heat, remove the Parmigiano-Reggiano rind and discard. Using an immersion blender (or a blender with the steam vent in the top open), blend until smooth, about 1 minute.
5. If using a blender, return the sauce to the pot along with the sausage and bring to a gentle simmer over medium-low heat.
6. **MAKE THE PASTA:** Meanwhile, bring a large pot of water with the salt to a boil. Add the pasta and cook until al dente according to package directions. Reserve ¼ cup of the pasta water. Drain the pasta into a colander and add the drained pasta to the sauce. Stir in the butter and the reserved pasta water until well combined.
7. **TO SERVE:** Place the pasta on a platter, tear the burrata over the top, and garnish with the torn basil and a drizzle of your favorite extra-virgin olive oil.

PERFECT PAIRING

A medium-bodied Nebbiolo from Barolo, Barbaresco, Alba, or Langhe in Piedmont.

Three-Ingredient Authentic Fettuccine Alfredo

SERVES 4 TO 6 • **TOTAL TIME** 15 MINUTES

- 2 tablespoons kosher salt for the pasta water
- 16 ounces fettuccine pasta, preferably fresh (see Hot Tips)
- 1 stick (8 tablespoons) unsalted European-style butter, cut into ½-inch pieces (see Hot Tips)
- 1¾ cups fresh, finely grated Parmigiano-Reggiano cheese, plus more for garnish (see Hot Tips)

PERFECT PAIRING

A slightly oaked Chardonnay or a Soave Classico, or go red with something light and acidic, like a Barbera.

Believe it or not, authentic Fettuccine Alfredo has just three ingredients—and not a drop of cream! The first time I shared this recipe, I got roasted for calling it traditional, so I went straight to the source in Rome to set the record straight. At Il Vero Alfredo, Andrew and I learned that Alfredo di Lelio first made it in 1908 using only pasta, butter, and Parmigiano-Reggiano. The secret? A deeply flavorful block of real-deal cheese, the high butterfat content of European-style butter (see Hot Tips), and starchy pasta water. Oh, and an intense arm workout while mixing—it might as well be the fourth ingredient. Luckily, you're just fifteen minutes away from silky, saucy perfection. Serve with Perfect Green Bean Salad (page 230).

---

1. Bring a large pot of water with the salt to a boil. Add the pasta and cook until al dente according to package directions. Reserve 1½ cups of pasta water. Using a colander, quickly drain the pasta.
2. Turn off the heat, and, to the same pot, immediately add the butter and about ⅓ cup of the reserved pasta water. Return the fettuccine to the pot and stir to coat with a wooden spoon or tongs. While stirring vigorously, add handfuls of the Parmigiano-Reggiano and small splashes of the reserved pasta water until a thin and creamy sauce forms, about 2 minutes. (I usually use 1 to 1¼ cups of the pasta water but always reserve an extra ¼ cup or so to loosen the sauce as needed.)
3. Using tongs, divide the fettucine among shallow bowls or plates and garnish with as much Parmigiano-Reggiano as your heart desires. Enjoy immediately, as the sauce will thicken quickly.

HOT TIPS

Dry pasta will work great if you can't find fresh fettuccine!

Look for European-style butters that have 82 to 90% butterfat content, like Kerrygold or Plugrà.

Fresh, finely grated Parm is crucial for this dish.

Spicy Garlic Shrimp Linguine
with Crispy Panko

SERVES 6 • **TOTAL TIME** 50 MINUTES

FOR THE SPICY GARLIC SHRIMP AND CRISPY PANKO

1½ pounds large shrimp, peeled and deveined, with tails (see Hot Tips)

¾ teaspoon baking soda

¼ cup extra-virgin olive oil, divided

1 tablespoon unsalted butter

1 cup panko breadcrumbs

2 teaspoons kosher salt, divided

½ teaspoon garlic powder

½ teaspoon dried oregano

1 teaspoon smoked paprika

1 teaspoon crushed red pepper, plus more for garnish

With a sunny hit of lemon and a buttery panko finish, this is a simple dish that delivers big on flavor. It comes together with just a handful of pantry staples: white wine, lemon, juicy tomatoes, and the umami of anchovy and shallots. The game-changer? My quick baking soda marinade trick for ultra-tender shrimp. A final sprinkle of panko toasted in butter with oregano and garlic adds zesty crunch, proving that small details make all the difference. For a date night or girls' wine night, add a platter of Burrata Broccolini with Calabrian Chili Romesco (page 221).

---

1. **MAKE THE SPICY GARLIC SHRIMP AND CRISPY PANKO:** In a large bowl, add the shrimp and baking soda and toss until coated. Refrigerate while you make the crispy panko.
2. In a large skillet, heat 1 tablespoon of the oil and the butter over medium heat and add the panko, ½ teaspoon of the salt, the garlic powder, and oregano. Cook, stirring occasionally, until the panko is a deep golden brown, 3 to 5 minutes. Transfer the breadcrumbs to a plate and set aside. Wipe out the skillet with a paper towel.
3. Rinse the shrimp in cold water and drain in a colander. Pat the shrimp completely dry with paper towels, wipe out the bowl and return the shrimp. Add the remaining 1½ teaspoons of salt, the paprika, and crushed red pepper, and toss until coated.
4. To the same skillet, heat the remaining 2 tablespoons of oil over medium-high heat. Once shimmering, add the shrimp, working in batches if needed as to not overcrowd the pan, and cook, undisturbed, until golden brown and opaque, 1 to 2 minutes per side. Transfer to a plate. Reserve the skillet off heat.

(recipe continues)

FOR THE LINGUINE

2 tablespoons kosher salt for the pasta water

16 ounces dried linguine

3 tablespoons extra-virgin olive oil

¼ cup finely chopped shallots

2 anchovy fillets

½ teaspoon kosher salt

1 cup cherry tomatoes (about 6 ounces), halved

5 garlic cloves, finely chopped

1 cup dry white wine (I use Pinot Grigio)

½ stick (4 tablespoons) unsalted butter

2 tablespoons fresh lemon juice (about 1 lemon)

2 teaspoons grated lemon zest

¼ cup finely grated Parmigiano-Reggiano cheese

¼ cup chopped fresh flat-leaf parsley, plus more for garnish

PERFECT PAIRING

The iconic but often misunderstood Italian white wine: Pinot Grigio!

5. **MAKE THE LINGUINE:** Bring a large pot of water with the salt to a boil.
6. Add the pasta to the boiling water and cook until al dente according to the package directions. Reserve 1 cup of the pasta water, drain the pasta in a colander, and set the pasta aside.
7. Meanwhile, heat the oil in the same skillet over medium heat. Once shimmering, add the shallots, anchovies, and the remaining ½ teaspoon of salt and cook, stirring constantly, until the shallots are translucent and the anchovies have melted into the oil, about 2 minutes. Stir in the tomatoes and cook, stirring occasionally, until the tomatoes soften and begin to wrinkle, 4 to 5 minutes. Add the garlic and cook, stirring constantly, until fragrant, about 1 minute.
8. Stir in the white wine, butter, and lemon juice and zest. Raise the heat to high and bring to a simmer, using a wooden spoon to scrape up any browned bits from the bottom of the skillet. Reduce the heat to medium-low and cook until the wine has reduced by half and the sauce has slightly thickened, about 4 minutes.
9. Reduce the heat to low. Add the shrimp along with the cooked pasta and ½ cup of the reserved pasta water. Using tongs, toss to coat until the sauce becomes glossy and clings to the pasta, about 1 minute.
10. Off heat, add the Parmigiano-Reggiano and ¼ cup more of the reserved pasta water. Toss to combine until the cheese is melted and the sauce slightly thickens, about 1 minute. Mix in the parsley.
11. **TO SERVE:** Divide among six shallow bowls. Top with the crispy panko and garnish with more parsley and red pepper.

HOT TIPS

Two simple cues to make sure you're not overcooking your shrimp:

Cook just until they lose transparency and begin to turn pink, but not beyond.

Check that they are forming a C-shape rather than an O, which signals they are overcooked.

Spaghetti alla Nerano (Fried Zucchini Pasta)

SERVES 4 TO 6 • **TOTAL TIME** 50 MINUTES

- 2 tablespoons plus 1 teaspoon kosher salt, divided
- 2 cups extra-virgin olive oil
- 6 medium zucchini, sliced into ⅛-inch rounds (see Hot Tips)
- 16 ounces dried spaghetti
- ½ teaspoon freshly ground black pepper
- ⅓ cup torn fresh basil, plus sprigs for garnish
- 1 stick (8 tablespoons) unsalted butter, cut into ½-inch pieces
- 1 cup fresh, finely grated Parmigiano-Reggiano cheese, plus more for garnish (see Hot Tips)

PERFECT PAIRING

A white Fiano di Avellino or Costa d'Amalfi Rosato from the region this dish was born, or the Cucumber Basil Martini (page 288).

Stanley Tucci raved about this pasta on *Searching for Italy*—and, come on, who dares to doubt Stanley? The dish has since gained cult status, and the restaurant behind it (the famous Lo Scoglio) generously shared their secret to uniquely tender zucchini: frying it and letting it rest overnight to soften. My time-saving hack? A quick fry, salting the zucchini in layers while it's hot to draw out more moisture, then reserving the infused oil to meld with pasta water for a luxurious sauce. For a decadent Italian dinner, start with Sweet & Savory Balsamic Peach Bruschetta (page 35) and end with the Limoncello Tiramisu (page 268).

1. Bring a large pot of water with 2 tablespoons of the salt to a boil (see Hot Tips).
2. Meanwhile, fry the zucchini: Have a medium bowl near the stove, and heat the oil in a large pot over high heat. Oil temperature is crucial here: Once the oil shimmers, check for readiness by dropping in a piece of zucchini. If it bubbles, it's ready! Or a meat thermometer should read 300°F. Using a spider or slotted spoon, gently place the zucchini rounds into the oil, working in batches as to not overcrowd the pan. Using tongs or a spoon, keep the zucchini moving in a circular motion, to evenly fry, until most of the zucchini rounds are deep golden brown but not burned, 4 to 5 minutes. Color variation is normal.
3. Using a spider or slotted spoon, immediately transfer the fried zucchini rounds to the bowl and sprinkle each batch with a pinch of the salt (about ¼ teaspoon per batch). Repeat with the remaining zucchini.
4. Using a ladle, measure out and pour ½ cup of the zucchini-infused frying oil over the fried zucchini. Discard the remaining oil and wipe out the pot. Return the fried zucchini to the pot, and cover loosely with foil or parchment, and set aside until the pasta is done.

(recipe continues)

HOT TIPS

Here's an occasion to break out your mandoline (and protective glove) if you've got one—you'll slice through those bad boys in no time.

Make sure to fry the zucchini before cooking the pasta. I like to get a head start on boiling the water, but it's better for the zucchini to sit while the pasta cooks, and not have the pasta wait for the zucchini!

This is a recipe where the extra effort for fresh, finely grated Parm really improves the dish.

5. Add the spaghetti to the boiling water and cook until al dente according to the package directions. Reserve 3 cups of the pasta water. Using a colander, drain the pasta and set aside.
6. Add ½ cup of the reserved pasta water, the remaining ¼ teaspoon of salt, and the black pepper to the pot with the zucchini. Bring to a simmer over medium heat and slightly mash the zucchini with a wooden spoon until it is broken down. Continue to cook until the water turns golden brown and the zucchini pieces appear rehydrated, about 2 minutes. Reduce the heat to low, stir in the basil, and cook until fragrant, about 30 seconds.
7. Add the pasta, butter, and 1 cup more of the reserved pasta water and cook, stirring vigorously with a wooden spoon or tongs until the pasta is well coated, the zucchini is evenly distributed, and some of the pasta water has absorbed, about 1 minute.
8. Off heat, add more splashes of the reserved pasta water and handfuls of Parmigiano-Reggiano, stirring vigorously with a wooden spoon or tongs until a creamy sauce forms, about 2 minutes. (I usually use all the pasta water here, but if you don't, that's ok! If the sauce seems too thin, add an extra handful or two of Parmigiano-Reggiano to thicken.)
9. **TO SERVE:** Using tongs, swirl nests of pasta among serving plates. Garnish with a generous handful of Parmigiano-Reggiano, a few twists of black pepper, and sprigs of basil.

Go-To Marinara

MAKES 5 CUPS OF SAUCE • **TOTAL TIME** 50 MINUTES

- ½ cup extra-virgin olive oil, divided
- ½ medium yellow onion, finely chopped
- 6 garlic cloves, finely chopped
- 2 tablespoons tomato paste
- 1 teaspoon dried oregano
- ½ teaspoon crushed red pepper
- 2 (28-ounce) cans whole peeled San Marzano tomatoes, undrained and crushed by hand (see Hot Tip)
- 1 medium bunch fresh basil, stems and leaves
- ½ stick (4 tablespoons) unsalted butter
- 1 teaspoon granulated sugar
- 1 tablespoon kosher salt
- 1 teaspoon freshly ground black pepper

PERFECT PAIRING

A Chianti Classico is the Italian dream wine for any way you enjoy this sauce.

This sauce proves that minimal effort and a few key ingredients can create a powerhouse of deep, robust flavor—an essential for your kitchen. It has a slightly rustic texture from hand-crushed tomatoes, but if you prefer a smoother sauce, a quick blend does the trick (see Hot Tip). Its versatility knows no bounds—whether ladled over Magic Meatballs & Marinara (page 96), layered into Easy Burrata Lasagna (page 172), or served simply with spaghetti and a mountain of Parmigiano-Reggiano. It comes together in under an hour, and I always double the batch so there's a stash waiting in the freezer.

---

1. In a large pot, heat ¼ cup of the oil over medium heat. Once shimmering, add the onion and cook, stirring occasionally, until translucent, 5 to 7 minutes. Add the garlic and cook, stirring constantly, until fragrant but not browning, 1 to 2 minutes. Add the tomato paste, oregano, and crushed red pepper and cook, stirring occasionally, until the tomato paste deepens in color, 4 to 5 minutes. Add the crushed tomatoes, the remaining ¼ cup of oil, basil, butter, sugar, salt, and black pepper and stir to combine.
2. Raise the heat to medium-high and bring to a gentle boil. Immediately reduce the heat to medium-low to maintain a gentle simmer. Cook, uncovered, stirring occasionally, until the sauce thickens slightly, 25 to 30 minutes. Remove the basil and discard.
3. Use immediately or transfer to an airtight container, cool, and refrigerate. The sauce will keep in the fridge for 3 to 5 days, and in the freezer in a tightly sealed container for up to 2 months.

HOT TIP

I prefer to crush whole tomatoes by hand in a large bowl. For a super-smooth sauce, use an immersion or standing blender after the basil is removed to blitz the marinara to your desired consistency.

Easy Burrata Lasagna

SERVES 8 TO 10 • **TOTAL TIME** 1 HOUR 15 MINUTES

- 16 ounces lasagna noodles
- 3 tablespoons extra-virgin olive oil
- ½ medium yellow onion, finely chopped
- 1 pound 90% lean ground beef
- 2½ teaspoons kosher salt, divided
- ⅔ cup dry white wine (I like Sauvignon Blanc)
- ¾ cup whole milk
- 4 cups Go-To Marinara (page 171) or store-bought marinara sauce
- ½ teaspoon freshly ground black pepper
- ¼ teaspoon freshly ground nutmeg
- 4 (8-ounce) balls burrata cheese, at room temperature
- 1½ cups finely grated Parmigiano-Reggiano cheese

PERFECT PAIRING

A Sangiovese from Tuscany (whether Chianti or Montalcino) is lasagna's BFF: It's the perfect grape for this dish.

Let's be real, who really wants to make béchamel? This lasagna was inspired by one of the best lessons I've ever had in the kitchen—and the revelation of using burrata instead of béchamel. One bite, and I was in lasagna heaven. This version is simplified but stays true to the essence of the original. To mimic the texture of fresh, semi-dry pasta, I took a cue from Ina Garten and soak dry lasagna noodles in hot water, cutting down on both time and effort. You can also prep it up to a day ahead and bake it just before dinner. For a vegetarian version, simply omit the beef. It's a lasagna I know you'll love.

---

1. Place an oven rack in the top third of the oven and a second in the middle and preheat the oven to 375°F. Place a parchment-lined sheet pan on the middle rack to catch any lasagna overflow.
2. Fill a large baking dish or heatproof bowl with the hottest tap water. Add the lasagna noodles one by one, completely submerging each. Let them soak while you make the sauce, until slightly tender and pliable, about 30 minutes.
3. Meanwhile, in a medium pot, heat the oil over medium-high heat. Once shimmering, add the onion and cook, stirring occasionally, until the onion is translucent, 5 to 7 minutes. Add the ground beef and 1½ teaspoons of the salt and cook, breaking up any large pieces with a wooden spoon, until no longer pink, 3 to 5 minutes. Add the wine, scrape up any browned bits from the bottom of the pot, and bring to a boil.
4. Reduce the heat to medium to maintain a rapid simmer. Cook, stirring occasionally, until the wine has almost evaporated, about 5 minutes. Add the milk and bring the sauce to a boil over high heat. Reduce the heat to medium to maintain a rapid simmer and cook, stirring occasionally, until most of the liquid has evaporated, 8 to 10 minutes.

(recipe continues)

HOT TIP

If you're like me and love a little spice, add 1 tablespoon of crushed Calabrian chili peppers to the marinara sauce.

5. Add the marinara, the remaining 1 teaspoon of salt, the black pepper, and nutmeg and bring to a boil over high heat. Reduce the heat to medium and simmer, stirring often and scraping the bottom of the pot, until the sauce thickens slightly and the flavors meld together, about 10 minutes.
6. Drain the water from the lasagna noodles. To assemble the lasagna, evenly spread 1 heaping cup of the meat sauce to the bottom of a 9 x 13-inch baking dish. Layer ⅓ of the lasagna noodles (overlapping as needed), followed by another heaping cup of the meat sauce, ⅓ of the burrata, and finally ⅓ of the Parmigiano-Reggiano. Repeat two more layers of the noodles, meat sauce, burrata, and Parmigiano-Reggiano. Cover tightly with foil.
7. Bake on the top rack in the oven for 30 to 35 minutes, until bubbling. Carefully remove the foil and discard. Raise the heat to 425°F and cook for about 15 minutes longer, until the top and edges begin to brown. If you want a little more color, turn the oven to broil on high and broil for 1 to 2 minutes, until the cheese is golden brown.
8. Allow to rest for at least 10 minutes before serving.

Green Mac & Cheese

SERVES 6 TO 8 • **TOTAL TIME** 1 HOUR

FOR THE PANKO RITZ TOPPING

- 1 (3.4-ounce) sleeve Ritz crackers (32 crackers)
- 1 cup panko breadcrumbs
- ½ stick (4 tablespoons) unsalted butter, melted
- 1 teaspoon kosher salt
- ½ teaspoon freshly ground black pepper

FOR THE GREEN MAC AND CHEESE

- 1 stick (8 tablespoons) unsalted butter, plus more for greasing
- Ice
- 2 tablespoons plus 1¼ teaspoons kosher salt, divided
- 1 (5-ounce) container baby spinach (about 5 cups)
- 2 small bunches fresh chives, divided
- 2 garlic cloves, peeled
- 16 ounces dried cellentani or cavatappi pasta
- ½ cup all-purpose flour
- 2 cups whole milk
- 2 cups heavy cream
- 1 teaspoon garlic powder
- ½ teaspoon freshly ground black pepper
- ¼ teaspoon ground nutmeg

This veggie-packed, emerald-hued macaroni and cheese might just outshine the classic—trust me, it won't disappoint! It's a delicious way to (not-so-subtly) sneak in extra greens for kids of all ages while still delivering on that rich, nostalgic comfort. Spinach, chives, and garlic blend seamlessly into a velvety cheddar, fontina, and Gruyère cheese sauce, while the panko Ritz cracker topping ensures the ultimate crispy, buttery bite. Still not sold on the greens? I've got you—see Hot Tips for a straight-up classic mac and cheese version. Try it with Spicy Lemon Parm Cauliflower Bites (page 226) or Honey & Chile Roasted Carrots (page 237) for a full veg meal.

---

1. Preheat the oven to 425°F.
2. **MAKE THE PANKO RITZ TOPPING:** In a blender or food processor, blitz the crackers until the consistency of rough sand (alternatively, seal them in a gallon-size resealable bag and crush them with a rolling pin or meat mallet). Transfer to a medium bowl. Stir in the panko, butter, salt, and black pepper and mix well.
3. **MAKE THE GREEN MAC AND CHEESE:** Grease a 9 x 13-inch baking dish with butter and set aside.
4. Prepare an ice bath by filling a medium bowl with ice and water. Put a colander inside the bowl, on top of the ice, and place near the stove.
5. Bring a large pot of water with 2 tablespoons of the salt to a boil. Add the spinach and 1 bunch of the chives and cook, completely submerged, just until their color turns vibrant green, about 30 seconds. Using a pasta spider or slotted spoon, transfer the spinach and chives to the prepared ice bath until cool, about 30 seconds. Keep the boiling water on the stove.
6. Transfer the spinach and chives to the same blender or food processor you used for the crackers; discard the ice bath. Add the garlic and 1 tablespoon of the boiling water and blend on high until completely smooth, about 1 minute. The sauce should be thick enough to coat the back of a spoon. If it's too thick, add hot water, a tablespoon at a time, until the mixture thins. Set aside.

(recipe continues)

1 (8-ounce) block sharp white cheddar cheese, grated (see Hot Tips)

1 (8-ounce) block fontina cheese, grated (see Hot Tips)

1 (6-ounce) block Gruyère cheese, grated (see Hot Tips)

PERFECT PAIRING

A Sauvignon Blanc from the Loire Valley or a glass of Prosecco will counter the sharpness of cheese and spinach with a soft, round nuttiness.

7. Add the pasta to the boiling water and cook until al dente according to package directions. Reserve 1/4 cup of the pasta water. Using a colander, drain the pasta and set aside.
8. Melt the butter over medium-high heat in the pasta pot. When the butter foams, slowly add in the flour and cook, whisking constantly until the mixture is smooth and turns a deep beige, about 2 minutes. Slowly pour in the milk and cream, whisking until smooth, about 1 minute. Add the remaining 1 1/4 teaspoons of salt, the garlic powder, black pepper, and nutmeg and stir to combine. Bring to a rolling simmer and cook, stirring occasionally, until the mixture has thickened, 3 to 4 minutes.
9. Mix the three cheeses together in a large bowl, reserving 2 cups. Off heat, slowly whisk in all but the reserved cheese until completely melted and smooth.
10. Add the spinach puree and whisk until the mixture is uniform in color. Stir in the pasta, adding splashes of the reserved pasta water to loosen the sauce, if needed.
11. Pour the mac and cheese into the prepared baking dish. Sprinkle the remaining 2 cups of cheese over the top, followed by the panko Ritz topping.
12. Bake for 10 to 12 minutes, until the sauce is bubbling, and the top is crispy and golden brown.
13. Meanwhile, finely chop the remaining 1 bunch of chives. Sprinkle over the mac and cheese and serve family style.

HOT TIPS

Not feeling the greens? Skip the spinach, chives, and garlic cloves and you've got yourself a traditional mac and cheese!

If you can't find fontina, low-moisture mozzarella is a great swap that will give a similar ooey-gooeyness. And if you're in a pinch and only have pre-grated cheese, you'll need about 6 1/2 cups total.

Broccoli Orecchiette
with Garlicky Anchovy-Toasted Breadcrumbs

SERVES 6 • **TOTAL TIME** 45 MINUTES

FOR THE ANCHOVY-TOASTED BREADCRUMBS

1½ cups cubed stale white or sourdough bread (from about 3 slices, see Hot Tips)

2 tablespoons extra-virgin olive oil

1 tablespoon unsalted butter

3 anchovy fillets

½ teaspoon kosher salt

½ teaspoon crushed red pepper

2 garlic cloves, finely chopped

1 teaspoon grated lemon zest (about ½ lemon)

FOR THE BROCCOLI ORECCHIETTE

2 tablespoons kosher salt for the pasta water

16 ounces dried orecchiette (see Hot Tips)

2 tablespoons extra-virgin olive oil, plus more for serving

2 garlic cloves, finely chopped

If you think you're not an anchovy person, this dish just might change your mind. In Puglia, on Italy's southeastern coast, a bowl of broccoli rabe orecchiette convinced me—they don't overpower; in fact, they add an irreplaceable savory depth. This version keeps things bold yet approachable, swapping in broccoli for broccoli rabe, brightening things up with lemon zest and juice, and layering in plenty of crushed garlic. The result? A seriously exciting way to eat broccoli. Keep the coastal vibe going and serve with Seared Scallops with White Wine Butter Sauce & Crispy Pancetta (page 144).

---

1. **MAKE THE ANCHOVY-TOASTED BREADCRUMBS:** In a food processor or a blender, add the stale bread and blend until the texture of coarse sand, about 1 minute.
2. In a large skillet over medium heat, add the oil, butter, and anchovies and cook, stirring constantly, until the anchovies completely dissolve into the oil and butter, about 2 minutes. Add the breadcrumbs, salt, and crushed red pepper and cook, stirring occasionally, just until the breadcrumbs turn a light golden brown, about 3 minutes. Add the garlic and cook, stirring constantly, until fragrant and the breadcrumbs turn a deep golden brown, 1 to 2 minutes.
3. Off heat, stir in the lemon zest until combined. Transfer the breadcrumbs to a plate and set aside. Wipe out the skillet with a paper towel.

(recipe continues)

1 large head of broccoli, thick stems removed (or 12-ounce bag broccoli florets), chopped into ¼-inch pieces

1 cup fresh, finely grated Pecorino Romano cheese

½ stick (4 tablespoons) unsalted butter

1 tablespoon fresh lemon juice (about ½ lemon)

Kosher salt and freshly ground black pepper

PERFECT PAIRING

An herby Grüner Veltliner or a new world Chardonnay from the US, Australia, or New Zealand.

4. **MAKE THE BROCCOLI ORECCHIETTE:** Bring a large pot of water with the salt to a boil. Add the pasta and cook until al dente according to package directions. Reserve 1 cup of the pasta water. Using a colander, drain the pasta and set aside.
5. Heat the oil in the same skillet over medium-high heat. Once shimmering, add the garlic and cook, stirring constantly, until fragrant but not brown, about 1 minute. Add the broccoli and the salt, stir to combine, and cook until the broccoli turns a vibrant green, 2 to 3 minutes. Add ¾ cup of the reserved pasta water and stir until combined. Cover, reduce the heat to medium-low, and cook, undisturbed, until the broccoli is fork-tender, 3 to 4 minutes. Add the pasta and stir to combine.
6. Off heat, add the Pecorino Romano, the remaining ¼ cup of reserved pasta water, butter, and lemon juice. Vigorously stir to combine until the butter is melted, a slightly thickened sauce begins to form, and the broccoli disintegrates further, 1 to 2 minutes. Season with salt and a few twists of black pepper.
7. Immediately, divide among six bowls and top with an extra drizzle of olive oil and the anchovy-toasted breadcrumbs.

HOT TIPS

If you don't have stale bread on hand or want a shortcut, use 1 cup of store-bought panko breadcrumbs, and follow the same method (minus blending the breadcrumbs).

While orecchiette is typically used in this dish, it also works well with conchiglie or cavatelli.

Carbone-at-Home Spicy (No) Vodka Rigatoni

SERVES 6 • **TOTAL TIME** 30 MINUTES

- 2 tablespoons plus 1 teaspoon kosher salt, divided
- 16 ounces dried rigatoni
- 2 tablespoons extra-virgin olive oil
- 1 small yellow onion, finely chopped
- 3 tablespoons crushed Calabrian chili peppers (see Hot Tips)
- 4 garlic cloves, finely chopped
- ½ teaspoon freshly ground black pepper, plus more for serving
- ¼ teaspoon granulated sugar
- 8 ounces tomato paste (just under ¾ cup)
- ¾ cup heavy cream, at room temperature
- 1 cup fresh, finely grated Parmigiano-Reggiano cheese, plus more for garnish (see Hot Tips)
- ½ stick (4 tablespoons) unsalted butter

PERFECT PAIRING

A jammy Gamay will counter the heat or try a full-bodied Montepulciano or Sangiovese.

I once unexpectedly scored a table at the famed Carbone in New York City and instantly fell for their ultra-spicy vodka rigatoni. While trying to crack their pasta code, the waiter let me in on a secret—there's no vodka in the recipe, just liquid gold: starchy pasta water. I'm excited to share my highly spiced dupe. Calabrian chili peppers steal the show here, so dial in the heat to your liking (see Hot Tips). Keep it classy and classic with the Little Gem Caesar Wedge (page 84).

1. Bring a large pot of water with 2 tablespoons of the salt to a boil. Add the pasta and cook until al dente according to package directions. Reserve 1 cup of the pasta water. Using a colander, drain the pasta and set aside.
2. Meanwhile, heat the oil in a large skillet over medium heat. Once shimmering, add the onion and cook, stirring frequently, until translucent, 5 to 7 minutes. Add the Calabrian chili peppers, garlic, the remaining 1 teaspoon salt, the black pepper, and sugar and cook, stirring often to avoid burning, until fragrant, about 2 minutes. Add the tomato paste and cook, stirring often, until the tomato paste darkens, about 3 minutes. Stir in ¼ cup of the reserved pasta water until combined. Reduce the heat to medium-low and stir in the cream until fully incorporated.
3. Off heat, add another splash of the reserved pasta water, a handful of Parmigiano-Reggiano, and 1 tablespoon of the butter, stirring quickly to combine the ingredients. Repeat this process three more times until you have used all the cheese and butter.
4. Add the pasta to the pan and toss to combine. Add more splashes of the reserved pasta water until the sauce is glossy, silky, and thick enough to coat the back of a spoon.
5. Immediately, divide among six plates and top with generous amounts of Parmigiano-Reggiano and a few twists of black pepper.

HOT TIPS

For less spice, use 1 to 2 tablespoons of Calabrian chili peppers. For even less heat, try 1½ teaspoons of crushed red pepper or omit the pepper.

The extra effort for fresh, finely grated Parm really improves the dish.

Silky Sesame Midnight Noodles
with Chili Crisp

SERVES 6 • **TOTAL TIME** 15 MINUTES

FOR THE SAUCE

- 4 green onions (white and green parts), thinly sliced, divided
- 3 tablespoons reduced-sodium soy sauce
- 4 garlic cloves, grated
- 3 tablespoons toasted sesame oil
- 2 to 3 tablespoons chili crisp
- 1 tablespoon avocado or other neutral oil
- 1 teaspoon rice wine vinegar
- ¾ teaspoon granulated sugar

FOR THE PASTA

- 2 tablespoons kosher salt, for the pasta water
- 16 ounces dried fettuccine
- ¼ cup freshly grated Parmigiano-Reggiano
- 3 tablespoons unsalted butter

FOR SERVING

- Chopped salted roasted peanuts
- Chopped fresh cilantro
- Toasted sesame seeds

Can a bowl of noodles have a big personality? These saucy sesame noodles certainly do—bringing heat, crunch, and bold flavor with chili crisp, roasted peanuts, and a flurry of green onions and cilantro. They hit all the late-night takeout cravings but come together in just fifteen minutes with whatever pasta you have on hand. I used fettuccine, which does a great impression of hand-pulled noodles. The sauce? A punchy mix of pasta water, garlic, chili crisp, soy, and toasted sesame oil—with one unexpected twist. You guessed it: Parmigiano-Reggiano. If you're not up for joining the midnight noodle club and manage to eat this at a normal hour, be sure to pair it with My Favorite Chinese Chicken Salad (page 63).

---

1. **MAKE THE SAUCE:** In a large bowl, whisk half of the green onions, the soy sauce, garlic, sesame oil, chili crisp, oil, vinegar, and sugar. Set aside.
2. **MAKE THE PASTA:** Bring a large pot of water with the salt to a boil over high heat. Add the pasta and cook until al dente according to package directions. Reserve ½ cup of the pasta water. Using a colander, drain the pasta and add into the green onion mixture.
3. Into the bowl with the pasta, add the Parmigiano-Reggiano, ¼ cup of the reserved pasta water, and the butter. Using tongs, vigorously toss until combined and the butter is melted, the sauce thickens, and the noodles are thoroughly coated. If the sauce is too thick, add small splashes of pasta water to thin. Taste to adjust with salt as needed.
4. **TO SERVE:** Divide between six bowls. Top with the remaining green onions and loads of the peanuts, cilantro, and sesame seeds.

PERFECT PAIRING

Nothing says late-night snack fest like popping a bottle of sparkling rosé.

ALWAYS SOUP SEASON

There's not much that's more comforting than a big bowl of soup. Soup feeds the soul, making it one of my favorite ways to care for the people I love. Maybe you had a go-to sick day soup growing up. For me, nothing felt more nurturing than Mom's pot of Nana's Cure-All Fideo (Mexican Noodle Soup, page 191), which never failed to deliver the soothing I craved. Whether you're making soup for a friend who's under the weather, a neighbor going through a tough time, or to give yourself some extra TLC, trust me—it's always soup season.

Even better, soup is versatile and often hands-off once in the pot. It can be the start of the meal, like the Sweet Potato Poblano Soup with Lime Crema (page 202) or the whole event, like Mom's Modern Pozole Rojo (Mexican Pork & Hominy Soup, page 199), White Bean, Corn & Chicken Chili (page 196), or Roasted Carrot Tomato Soup with Garlicky Grilled Cheese (page 211). Go for the Creamy Chicken Tortilla Soup (page 188), a comforting favorite like Cozy Tortellini Soup (page 195), or something deeply satisfying like Hearty Kale & Lentil Soup with Parm Crostini (page 205) or Roasted Potato Leek Soup (page 206). Whatever you're craving, there's a soup for it—and a good reason to make it. These bowls are guaranteed to warm your soul and fill your heart.

Creamy Chicken Tortilla Soup

SERVES 6 TO 8 • **TOTAL TIME** 45 MINUTES

2 teaspoons chili powder
2 teaspoons paprika
1½ teaspoons dried oregano
1½ teaspoons ground coriander
1 teaspoon ground cumin
¾ teaspoon cayenne pepper (adjust for heat as desired)
½ teaspoon freshly ground black pepper
¼ cup avocado or other neutral oil
1 yellow onion, finely chopped
2 carrots, peeled and finely diced
1 red bell pepper, seeded and finely diced
4 garlic cloves, finely chopped
1 tablespoon plus 1 teaspoon kosher salt
1 (14-ounce) can crushed tomatoes
6 cups chicken stock
2 cups heavy cream
12 (6-inch) corn tortillas, roughly torn into 2-inch pieces
4 cups shredded store-bought rotisserie chicken (or homemade roast chicken)

FOR SERVING

Freshly grated Colby Jack cheese
Sour cream
Sliced Hass avocado
Chopped fresh cilantro
Tortilla strips or crushed tortilla chips

I'm not kidding when I say this is the best chicken tortilla soup around—and I've tried my fair share. Everyone who tastes it raves about its creaminess and bold flavor. My version is rich, velvety, and packed with flavor, thanks to layers of spices, veggies, and a little trick—tortillas blended right into the broth (plus a good pour of cream) to create a luscious soup. Rotisserie chicken makes it weeknight-easy, and the toppings? Load it up with sour cream, cheese, avocado, cilantro, and plenty of crunchy tortilla strips! One pot, big flavor and pure comfort in a bowl.

1. In a small bowl, combine the chili powder, paprika, oregano, coriander, cumin, cayenne, and black pepper. Set aside.
2. Heat the oil in a large pot over medium heat. Once shimmering, add the onion and cook, stirring occasionally, until translucent, 5 to 7 minutes. Add the carrots, bell pepper, garlic, and salt and cook, stirring occasionally, until the carrots are slightly tender and the garlic is fragrant, 5 to 8 minutes. Add the reserved spice mixture and cook, stirring constantly, until fragrant, 30 seconds to 1 minute.
3. Add the crushed tomatoes and cook, stirring occasionally, until the mixture begins to simmer, 3 to 5 minutes. Add the chicken stock, raise the heat to high, and bring to a simmer. Cook until the carrots are completely tender, 10 to 12 minutes.
4. Add the cream and torn tortillas and return to a strong simmer, then reduce the heat to low to maintain a gentle simmer, stirring occasionally, until slightly thickened, 8 to 10 minutes. Off heat, using an immersion blender (or a blender with the steam vent in the top open), blend until smooth, 1 to 2 minutes.
5. If using a blender, pour the soup back into the pot. Stir in the shredded chicken.
6. **TO SERVE:** Ladle into bowls and top with generous sprinkles of cheese, dollops of sour cream, avocado, chopped cilantro, and tortilla strips.

PERFECT PAIRING

A medium- to full-bodied red wine with a tiny bit of pepper, like Tempranillo from Rioja, or Mencía.

Nana's Cure-All Fideo (Mexican Noodle Soup)

SERVES 6 TO 8 • **TOTAL TIME** 35 MINUTES

¼ cup avocado or other neutral oil, divided, plus more as needed

2 cups cut fideo pasta (see Hot Tips)

½ medium white onion, coarsely chopped

1 celery stalk, diced

1 carrot, peeled and diced

½ teaspoon kosher salt

3 garlic cloves, chopped

3 Roma (plum) tomatoes, chopped

3 tablespoons chicken bouillon powder

½ teaspoon ground cumin

1 (8-ounce) can tomato sauce

4 cups shredded or diced store-bought rotisserie chicken (or homemade roast chicken)

Fideo is often called "Mexican Penicillin" and, similar to pozole, everyone has their favorite version. My grandma's recipe—a comforting cup she used to give out for free at Lupita's La Jolla—is her take on a tomato-based chicken noodle soup. She would even hand-fry and mail angel hair noodle nests to my mom and me so we'd never run out! Over long nights in the kitchen, I finally re-created the recipe with Nana and my mom. Though I still fry the noodles for the signature flavor and texture, you can use cut fideo pasta for a literal shortcut to Nana's OG version. In our family—and maybe soon in yours—fideo is what we make when someone's had a rough day, is under the weather, or just needs a little extra love. Scoop up the brothy goodness with tortilla chips and if you're short on time, check out the Hot Tips!

1. Line a large plate with paper towels.
2. Heat 2 tablespoons of the oil in a large pot over medium-high heat. Once shimmering, check for readiness by dropping one piece of fideo in: If it bubbles, it's ready! Reduce the heat to just above medium and, working in batches as to not overcrowd the pot, add the fideo in a thin layer across the bottom of the pot. Fry, stirring constantly with a wooden spoon, until the fideo is golden brown, about 3 minutes. Using a slotted spoon, remove the fideo and spread it out evenly on the lined plate. Repeat with the remaining fideo, adding more oil, if needed. Discard the remaining oil and wipe out the pot.
3. In the same pot, heat 2 tablespoons of the oil over medium-high heat. Once shimmering, add the onion, celery, carrot, and salt and cook, stirring occasionally, until nearly tender, about 7 minutes. Add the garlic and cook, stirring constantly, until fragrant, 1 minute. Add the tomatoes and cook, stirring occasionally, until slightly broken down, 2 to 3 minutes.
4. Transfer the vegetables to a blender. Add 2 cups of water along with the bouillon powder and cumin and, with the steam vent open in the top, blend until completely smooth, 1 to 2 minutes.

(recipe continues)

FOR SERVING

Chopped fresh cilantro

Lime or lemon wedges

Hot sauce

Tortilla chips or warmed tortillas

PERFECT PAIRING

A comforting wine like Cabernet Sauvignon, Syrah, or Tempranillo complement this "Mexican Penicillin" beautifully.

5. Return the blended mixture to the pot, add 7 cups of water and the tomato sauce, and bring to a boil over high heat. Stir in the fried fideo, then return to a boil. Reduce the heat to medium and simmer, uncovered, stirring occasionally and skimming off any foam that rises to the surface, until the fideo is tender, about 15 minutes.
6. Stir in the chicken, and simmer until heated through, about 3 minutes.
7. **TO SERVE:** Ladle into bowls, top with chopped cilantro, and serve with lime wedges, hot sauce, and chips.

HOT TIPS

For an even faster version, omit the celery and carrot and blend the raw onion, garlic, and tomatoes with salt, bouillon, cumin, and 2 cups of water. Add the mixture to the pot and follow the recipe as directed above. It won't be quite as flavorful and the veggies won't be as pronounced, but it will still be delicious.

If you can't find cut fideo, use 9 ounces of angel hair pasta, broken into 1-inch pieces (add the pasta to a resealable plastic bag and smack with a rolling pin or meat mallet).

Cozy Tortellini Soup

SERVES 6 TO 8 • **TOTAL TIME** 45 MINUTES

- 2 tablespoons extra-virgin olive oil
- 1 pound mild Italian pork sausage, casings removed
- ½ yellow onion, finely chopped
- 3 garlic cloves, finely chopped
- 2 tablespoons crushed Calabrian chili peppers
- 1 tablespoon Italian seasoning herb blend (see Hot Tip)
- 1 (28-ounce) can crushed tomatoes
- 6 cups chicken stock
- 1 (4-inch piece) Parmigiano-Reggiano rind (optional)
- 1½ teaspoons kosher salt
- ½ teaspoon freshly ground black pepper, plus more for serving
- 9 ounces cheese tortellini
- 1 large bunch lacinato kale, stems removed, leaves coarsely chopped
- 1 cup heavy cream
- 1 cup finely grated Parmigiano-Reggiano cheese, plus more for garnish
- 2 tablespoons unsalted butter

PERFECT PAIRING

A deep, velvety, and rich Valpolicella, or a Primitivo, Tempranillo, or Cabernet Sauvignon!

Good old store-bought, cheese-stuffed tortellini are pure nostalgia for me—plus they're a freezer staple for quick and, yes, cozy meals like this. Herby Italian sausage gets browned and simmered in a creamy, tomatoey broth infused with garlic, Calabrian chili peppers, and Italian herbs. A generous dose of Parmigiano-Reggiano (and the rind, if you have it) deepens the flavor, while tender kale and pillowy tortellini bring it all together in forty-five minutes. You'll crave it year-round, and it's especially perfect for crisp fall and winter months. Want a veggie twist? Swap the sausage for chickpeas or cannellini beans.

1. Heat the oil in a large pot over medium-high heat. Once shimmering, add the sausage and cook, using a wooden spoon to break it apart, until browned, 6 to 8 minutes. Add the onion and garlic and cook, stirring occasionally, until the onion is translucent and starting to brown, about 5 minutes. Add the Calabrian chili peppers and Italian seasoning and cook, stirring constantly, until fragrant, about 1 minute.
2. Add the crushed tomatoes and cook, stirring often and scraping up any browned bits from the bottom, until the liquid reduces slightly, about 8 minutes. Add the chicken stock, Parmigiano-Reggiano rind (if using), salt, and black pepper. Bring to a boil over high heat, then reduce the heat to medium and simmer, partially covered, stirring occasionally until the flavors meld, about 15 minutes.
3. Add the tortellini and kale, bring to a boil over high heat, then reduce the heat to medium and maintain a simmer. Cook, partially covered, until the tortellini are cooked and the kale is wilted and tender, 2 to 3 minutes. Stir in the cream. Off heat, stir in the cheese and butter.
4. **TO SERVE:** Ladle into bowls and top with a generous amount of cheese and a few twists of black pepper.

HOT TIP

No Italian seasoning? Make your own with 1 teaspoon each of dried basil, dried oregano, and dried thyme.

White Bean, Corn & Chicken Chili

SERVES 6 TO 8 • **TOTAL TIME** 45 MINUTES

- ¼ cup avocado or other neutral oil
- 1 yellow onion, chopped
- 4 garlic cloves, finely chopped
- 2 teaspoons kosher salt, divided
- 1½ teaspoons dried oregano
- 1 teaspoon ground coriander
- ½ teaspoon ground cumin
- 3 (15-ounce) cans cannellini beans, strained and rinsed (see Hot Tips), divided
- 8 cups chicken stock
- 4 cups shredded store-bought rotisserie chicken (or homemade roast chicken)
- 1 cup frozen corn, thawed
- 1 (7-ounce) can chopped fire-roasted green chiles
- 1 large bunch Swiss chard, stemmed and coarsely chopped (see Hot Tips)

FOR SERVING

- Freshly grated Colby or Monterey Jack cheese
- Sour cream or full-fat Greek yogurt
- Diced Hass avocado
- Chopped fresh cilantro
- Thinly sliced fresh jalapeño pepper (optional)
- Tortilla chips
- Lime wedges

It's chili time! This white bean and corn chicken chili is so easy, comes together in under an hour, and bursts with flavor. It's lighter and brothier than a traditional chili, but still incredibly nourishing and satisfying. Smashing some of the beans thickens the broth, creating a slightly creamy base with no dairy or blender required. Fire-roasted green chiles add smokiness, frozen corn brings a touch of sweetness, and Swiss chard melts right in. Folding in store-bought chicken toward the end makes this a lifesaver on busy weeknights. And of course chili isn't complete without toppings. Pile them high! Serve with Jalapeño Cornbread with Maple Butter (page 234).

1. Heat the oil in a large pot over medium-high heat. Once shimmering, add the onion and cook, stirring occasionally, until translucent, 5 to 8 minutes. Add the garlic and cook, stirring constantly, until fragrant, about 1 minute. Add 1 teaspoon of the salt, the oregano, coriander, and cumin and cook, stirring, until fragrant, about 1 minute.
2. Add 2 cans of the beans to the pot and, using a potato masher or fork, smash the beans until they're mostly broken down. Add the remaining can of beans, the chicken stock, and the remaining 1 teaspoon of salt. Raise the heat to high and bring to a boil, then reduce the heat to medium and simmer, stirring occasionally, until the liquid begins to thicken, 6 to 8 minutes.
3. Add the chicken, corn, and chiles, bring to a boil, and cook, stirring occasionally, until the soup thickens slightly, about 10 minutes. Stir in the chard and cook until the leaves turn bright green and silky, about 3 minutes.
4. **TO SERVE:** Ladle into bowls and top with generous sprinkles of cheese, hefty dollops of sour cream, avocado, cilantro, and jalapeño slices (if using). Serve with tortilla chips and lime wedges.

PERFECT PAIRING

A California Chardonnay from a cooler climate like the Sonoma Coast or Mendocino.

HOT TIPS

No cannellini beans on hand? Try white navy beans or Great Northern beans.

Chopped kale or spinach are great swaps for Swiss chard.

Mom's Modern Pozole Rojo (Mexican Pork & Hominy Soup)

SERVES 8 • **TOTAL TIME** 3 HOURS

FOR THE CHILE PASTE

3 dried ancho chiles, stemmed and seeded

3 dried guajillo chiles, stemmed and seeded

3 to 5 small dried chiles de árbol (depending on heat preference), stemmed

¼ teaspoon kosher salt

½ cup chicken stock

FOR THE POZOLE

3½ teaspoons kosher salt, divided, plus more to taste

1 tablespoon all-purpose flour

1 teaspoon freshly ground black pepper, plus more to taste

1 teaspoon garlic powder

1½ pounds boneless pork shoulder, cut into 2-inch chunks

1 pound pre-cut pork neck bone or 1 additional pound boneless pork shoulder, cut into 2-inch chunks

3 tablespoons avocado or other neutral oil

1 large white onion, peeled and halved

There are as many opinions about pozole as there are varieties of maíz, which I wholeheartedly respect. Even Nana doesn't like watching my mom and me make this nourishing, slightly modernized version—but she sure does love eating it! You slowly simmer a brothy base with homemade chile paste, fall-apart tender seared pork, and chewy hominy until every spoonful is packed with flavor. I love to set up a topping bar with piles of shredded cabbage, cilantro, white onion, radishes, and lots of lime to finish. It's a labor of love, but the payoff is huge—one bite, and you'll experience a hug in a bowl. It's so good that I've shared my chicken version (page 201), too!

---

1. **MAKE THE CHILE PASTE:** In a small saucepan, combine the ancho, guajillo, and de árbol chiles, salt, and 1½ cups of water. Cover and bring to a boil over medium-high heat. Reduce the heat to medium and cook, partially covered, until the chiles are rehydrated and softened, 7 to 9 minutes. Set the pot aside to cool for 5 minutes, uncovered.
2. Using tongs, transfer the chiles to a blender and add the chile-infused water and chicken stock. With the steam vent in the top open, blend until smooth, about 1 minute. Set aside.
3. **MAKE THE POZOLE:** In a small bowl, combine 2½ teaspoons of the salt, the flour, black pepper, and garlic powder.
4. Pat the pork shoulder chunks and pork neck bone dry with a paper towel. Place in a large bowl and toss with the seasoning mixture to coat.
5. Heat the oil in a large Dutch oven or stainless steel lidded pot over medium-high heat until shimmering. Place the bones and meat in the pot, working in batches, if necessary, to avoid overcrowding the pan. Cook until golden brown on all sides, 3 to 4 minutes per side, adding more oil as needed.

(recipe continues)

- 1 large head of garlic, top cut off and discarded
- 2 teaspoons dried oregano, preferably Mexican (see Hot Tips)
- ½ teaspoon ground cumin
- 2 dried bay leaves
- 8 cups chicken stock
- 2 (25-ounce) cans white hominy, drained and rinsed (see Hot Tips)
- 2 tablespoons fresh lime juice (about 1 lime)

FOR SERVING

- Thinly sliced green cabbage
- Chopped fresh cilantro
- Finely chopped white onion
- Thinly sliced radishes
- Lime wedges

PERFECT PAIRING

A robust Cabernet Sauvignon from California, or a silky Grenache from Paso Robles.

6. Add the onion halves, head of garlic, oregano, cumin, and bay leaves, stir to combine, and cook until the spices are fragrant, about 1 minute. Stir in the chicken stock, scraping up any browned bits from the bottom of the pot.
7. Add the blended chile paste, the hominy, and the remaining 1 teaspoon of salt to the pot and stir to combine. Raise the heat to high and bring to a boil. Cover, reduce to medium-low heat, and simmer. Cook, stirring occasionally, skimming off any foam that rises to the top, until the pork is falling off the bone and fork-tender, about 2 hours.
8. Using tongs, remove and discard the onion, garlic, and bay leaves. Transfer the pork bones and chunks to a plate or cutting board. Using two forks, shred the pork shoulder and any meat from the neck bones; discard the bones and any unwanted fatty bits. Return the meat and its juices to the pot. Add the lime juice, stir to combine, and taste to adjust the salt and black pepper as desired.
9. **TO SERVE:** Ladle into bowls and garnish with loads of cabbage, cilantro, onion, and radishes, and serve with lime wedges.

HOT TIPS

I prefer Mexican oregano because of its pronounced floral and zingy flavor, brightness, and notes of citrus and anise, but use the best you can find. I like to crumble it between my fingers before adding to release the fragrance.

Pozole is a traditional Mexican stew or soup. It's typically made with hominy, which is corn that has gone through a soaking process, resulting in large, tender kernels. It's sold both dried and canned. We use canned to save time!

Chicken Variation

1. Replace the pork with 2½ pounds of bone-in, skin-on chicken thighs. Pat them completely dry with a paper towel and season both sides of the chicken thighs with the salt, flour, black pepper, and garlic powder mixture.
2. Heat the oil in a large Dutch oven or stainless steel lidded pot over medium-high heat. Once shimmering, cook the chicken, working in batches, starting skin side down, until golden brown, about 4 minutes per side. Transfer the chicken to a large plate and add the onion, head of garlic, oregano, cumin, and bay leaves to the pot, and stir to combine until spices are fragrant, about 1 minute. Add the stock, scraping up any browned bits from the bottom of the pot. Add the chicken, blended chile paste, hominy, the remaining 1 teaspoon of salt, and 1 teaspoon chicken bouillon powder.
3. Bring to a boil, skimming off the fat and foam. Cover, reduce the heat to medium-low, and simmer, stirring occasionally and skimming off any foam that rises to the top, until the chicken is tender, 45 minutes. Using tongs, discard the onion, garlic, and bay leaves.
4. Transfer the chicken to a large plate, discard the skin and bones, and, using two forks, shred the chicken. Return the chicken and its juices to the pot. Add the lime juice, season to taste, and garnish as instructed.

Sweet Potato Poblano Soup
with Lime Crema

SERVES 8 • **TOTAL TIME** 1 HOUR 25 MINUTES

FOR THE LIME CREMA

½ cup sour cream

1 teaspoon grated lime zest

2 tablespoons fresh lime juice (about 1 lime)

3 tablespoons whole milk

1 teaspoon ground cumin

¼ teaspoon kosher salt

FOR THE SWEET POTATO POBLANO SOUP

3 medium sweet potatoes, peeled and cut into 1½-inch pieces (see Hot Tip)

2 large poblano peppers, stemmed, seeded, and cut into 2-inch pieces

1 yellow onion, cut into eighths

1 head of garlic, top cut off and discarded

¼ cup avocado or other neutral oil

1 tablespoon kosher salt, divided

2 teaspoons chili powder

1 teaspoon freshly ground black pepper

1 teaspoon garlic powder

¼ teaspoon cayenne pepper

8 cups vegetable stock

1½ cups heavy cream

1 cup salted roasted pepitas (pumpkin seeds), for garnish

You just might become a sweet potato fanatic after one bowl of this spiced, creamy soup with zesty lime crema. Roasting brings out sweet potatoes' natural caramelization while blending creates a smooth, satiny texture. Roasted poblano peppers and a whole head of garlic add an earthy smokiness without the heat. It's warming, generously seasoned, savory, and deeply satisfying, especially with Jalapeño Cornbread with Maple Butter (page 234).

1. **MAKE THE LIME CREMA:** In a small bowl, combine the sour cream, lime zest, lime juice, milk, cumin, and salt. Set aside. If making ahead, store in an airtight container in the refrigerator, then bring to room temperature while making the soup.
2. **MAKE THE SWEET POTATO POBLANO SOUP:** Preheat the oven to 425°F. Line 2 sheet pans with parchment paper.
3. In a large bowl, combine the sweet potatoes, poblano peppers, onion, and the garlic head. Drizzle with the oil and season with 2 teaspoons of the salt and the chili powder, black pepper, garlic powder, and cayenne. Toss to coat well. Divide the vegetables between the sheet pans and place the head of garlic cut side down on one pan. Bake until the edges of the vegetables are crispy and golden brown, 25 to 30 minutes.
4. In a large pot, using tongs or a kitchen towel, squeeze the head of garlic to release the cloves and discard the skin. Add the roasted vegetables, vegetable stock, and the remaining 1 teaspoon of salt. Bring to a boil over high heat, then reduce the heat to medium and simmer until the vegetables are fork-tender, about 15 minutes.
5. Off heat, using an immersion blender (or a blender with the steam vent in the top open), blend until completely smooth, 1 to 2 minutes. If using a blender, return the soup to the pot.
6. Stirring constantly, slowly pour in the cream until incorporated.
7. **TO SERVE:** Ladle into bowls and top with a generous drizzle of the lime crema and a handful of the pepitas.

PERFECT PAIRING

A rich but zippy Zinfandel from California or a Blaufränkisch from Austria.

HOT TIP

No sweet potatoes on hand? This soup will be just as delicious with the same amount of winter squash (especially honeynut or butternut)!

PERFECT PAIRING

A peppery and juicy Syrah from Paso Robles or a more floral version from the Northern Rhône in France.

Hearty Kale & Lentil Soup with Parm Crostini

SERVES 6 • **TOTAL TIME** 1 HOUR

FOR THE KALE AND LENTIL SOUP

2 tablespoons extra-virgin olive oil

½ yellow onion, chopped

2 carrots, peeled and diced

2 celery stalks, chopped

2 teaspoons kosher salt

½ teaspoon freshly ground black pepper

½ teaspoon ground cumin

½ teaspoon crushed red pepper

3 garlic cloves, grated

1½ cups dried green or brown lentils, rinsed and drained

8 cups vegetable stock

2 dried bay leaves

1 large bunch lacinato kale, stems removed, leaves coarsely chopped

1 cup finely grated Parmigiano-Reggiano

2 tablespoons unsalted butter

Chopped fresh parsley

FOR THE PARM CROSTINI

½ stick (4 tablespoons) unsalted butter, at room temperature

½ cup finely grated Parmigiano-Reggiano cheese

1 garlic clove, grated

¾ teaspoon garlic powder

½ teaspoon kosher salt

1 baguette, cut into ½-inch slices

Lentils have always been a serious comfort food for me—nutty, creamy, and nourishing. This hearty veggie-based soup is easy, deeply flavorful, and reminds me of the lentil dishes my mom used to make. A simple base of onion, carrots, and celery is infused with cumin, crushed red pepper, garlic, and bay leaves and gets a glow-up with a whole cup of Parmigiano-Reggiano, plus butter and kale for richness and texture. And the best part? A garlicky Parm crostini on the side. Just slather a quick garlic and Parm butter onto baguette slices, bake until crisp, and get dipping! My idea of balance!

---

1. **MAKE THE KALE AND LENTIL SOUP:** Heat the oil in a large Dutch oven or stainless steel lidded pot over medium heat. Once shimmering, add the onion, carrots, celery, salt, and black pepper and cook, stirring occasionally, until the onion is translucent and the vegetables are tender, 8 to 10 minutes. Add the cumin, crushed red pepper, and garlic, and cook, stirring constantly until fragrant, 1 to 2 minutes.
2. Stir in the lentils, vegetable stock, and bay leaves, raise the heat to high, and bring to a boil. Reduce the heat to medium-low and maintain a gentle simmer. Cook, partially covered, until the lentils soften, about 35 minutes.
3. **MAKE THE PARM CROSTINI:** Meanwhile, preheat the oven to 375°F. Line a sheet pan with parchment paper.
4. In a medium bowl, combine the butter, Parmigiano-Reggiano, garlic, garlic powder, and salt until well incorporated.
5. Using a butter knife, spread the cheesy garlic butter evenly on one side of each slice of baguette. Place the slices buttered side up on the lined sheet pan and bake until the cheese melts and the crostini turn light golden brown, about 15 minutes.
6. **FINISH THE SOUP:** Once the lentils are softened, discard the bay leaves. Stir in the kale, fully submerging the leaves, and cook until wilted and tender, 2 to 3 minutes.
7. Off heat, stir in the Parmigiano-Reggiano and butter. Taste and adjust the salt and black pepper as desired.
8. **TO SERVE:** Ladle into six bowls and top with more Parmigiano-Reggiano and chopped parsley with the Parm crostini on the side or rim of the bowl.

Roasted Potato Leek Soup
with Lemony Crème Fraîche

SERVES 6 TO 8 • **TOTAL TIME** 1 HOUR 15 MINUTES

As you cook your way through this book, you'll probably notice I have a thing for potatoes. Maybe it's my Irish heritage or maybe the comfort they brought me growing up. There weren't many heart-broken or sick days that an order of fries couldn't fix! This potato soup delivers that same kind of soothing but with an elevated twist. Roasting the potatoes and slow-cooking the leeks in plenty of butter creates complex caramelized flavor that blends seamlessly with cream, veggie stock, and herbs. Potatoes and leeks are a match made in heaven, and the lemon-zested crème fraîche knocks it out of the park. Perfect for a chilly day, or any time you're craving some potato comfort.

FOR THE LEMONY CRÈME FRAÎCHE

- ½ cup crème fraiche or sour cream
- 2 tablespoons heavy cream
- 1 teaspoon grated lemon zest
- ¼ teaspoon kosher salt

FOR THE POTATO LEEK SOUP

- 4 medium Yukon Gold potatoes, peeled and cut into 1½-inch pieces
- 3 medium russet potatoes, peeled and cut into 1½-inch pieces
- 2 tablespoons extra-virgin olive oil
- 2 teaspoons kosher salt, divided
- 6 tablespoons unsalted butter
- 4 medium leeks (white and light green parts only), halved lengthwise, washed, and thinly sliced
- 1 teaspoon dried thyme
- ½ teaspoon freshly ground black pepper, plus more for serving
- 8 cups vegetable stock
- 1 cup heavy cream
- Chopped fresh chives
- Flaky sea salt, for garnish

1. **MAKE THE LEMONY CRÈME FRAÎCHE:** In a small bowl, whisk the crème fraîche, heavy cream, lemon zest, and salt. Set aside.
2. **MAKE THE POTATO AND LEEK SOUP:** Preheat the oven to 425°F. Line a sheet pan with parchment paper.
3. Toss all the potatoes with the oil and 1 teaspoon of the salt on the sheet pan until well coated. Layer them evenly and roast, undisturbed, until tender and starting to brown on the edges, 30 to 35 minutes.
4. Meanwhile, melt the butter in a large Dutch oven or stainless steel lidded pot over medium heat. Add the leeks, the remaining 1 teaspoon of salt, the thyme, and black pepper and cook, partially covered, stirring occasionally, until the leeks are very tender and starting to brown, 18 to 20 minutes. If the leeks are browning too quickly, reduce the heat to medium-low.
5. Transfer the roasted potatoes to the pot along with the vegetable stock and bring to a boil over high heat. Reduce the heat to medium and simmer. Cook, uncovered, until the soup cooks down and the flavors meld, about 15 minutes.
6. Reduce the heat to low and, using an immersion blender (or a blender with the steam vent in the top open), blend until mostly smooth with a little texture remaining, 1 to 2 minutes. If using a blender, return the soup to the pot over low heat. While constantly stirring, slowly add the cream. Add some additional warm broth if the soup is a bit thick.
7. **TO SERVE:** Ladle into bowls and top with a drizzle of the lemony crème fraîche, chives, flaky salt, and a few twists of black pepper.

PERFECT PAIRING

A Côtes du Rhône Blanc or a Chardonnay from France or Argentina.

Family Favorite Albondigas (Mexican Meatball Soup)

SERVES 6 TO 8 • **TOTAL TIME** 1 HOUR 20 MINUTES (PLUS OVERNIGHT SOAK TIME)

Nana served this soup for over a decade at Lupita's La Jolla, and over the years, my mom and I made little changes like upping the seasonings and adding mint. It's loaded with veggies swimming in a savory broth with tender beef and rice meatballs. Soaking the rice ahead is a family secret that keeps the albondigas light and pillowy. Garlic, oregano, cumin, celery hearts and leaves, and fresh mint add layers of flavor, while a squeeze of lime juice makes it all pop. The best part? This hearty soup comes together in just over an hour but tastes like it has been simmering all day long. You can also swap in chicken or turkey for the meatballs and adjust the stock to match.

FOR THE SOUP

- 2 tablespoons extra-virgin olive oil
- ½ yellow onion, chopped
- 1 Roma (plum) tomato, diced
- 1 celery heart, leaves reserved and stalks cut into ½-inch pieces
- 3 garlic cloves, finely chopped
- 1½ teaspoons dried oregano
- 1 teaspoon kosher salt, plus more to taste
- ¼ teaspoon ground cumin
- 8 cups beef stock
- 3 medium carrots, peeled and cut into 1-inch cubes
- 2 medium zucchini, peeled and cut into 1-inch cubes
- 1 medium chayote, peeled and cut into 1-inch cubes (see Hot Tip)
- 1 large Yukon Gold potato, peeled and cut into 1-inch cubes
- 4 sprigs fresh mint, plus leaves for garnish

1. **MAKE THE SOUP:** Heat the oil in a large Dutch oven or stainless steel lidded pot over medium heat. Once shimmering, add the onion, tomato, celery leaves, garlic, oregano, salt, and cumin and cook, stirring frequently, until the onion is softened and translucent, 3 to 5 minutes.
2. Add the beef stock and bring to a boil over high heat. Add the celery heart stalks, carrots, zucchini, chayote, and potato. Cover and bring back up to a boil.
3. Reduce the heat to medium, cover, and simmer, stirring occasionally, until the vegetables are fork-tender, 15 to 20 minutes.

(recipe continues)

FOR THE ALBONDIGAS

- 1/4 cup long grain white rice, soaked in water overnight and strained
- 1 pound 85% lean ground beef
- 1 large egg
- 2 tablespoons all-purpose flour
- 2 tablespoons finely chopped fresh mint, plus more for garnish
- 2 teaspoons kosher salt
- 1½ teaspoons dried oregano
- 3/4 teaspoon garlic powder
- 1/4 teaspoon freshly ground black pepper, plus more to taste
- 2 tablespoons fresh lime juice (about 1 lime)

FOR SERVING

- Fresh oregano leaves
- Lime wedges

PERFECT PAIRING

A velvety, plummy Grenache like one from Châteauneuf-du-Pape in France, or a Côtes du Rhône or Cabernet Sauvignon.

4. **MAKE THE ALBONDIGAS:** Meanwhile, in a large bowl, combine the strained soaked rice, ground beef, egg, flour, mint, salt, oregano, garlic powder, and black pepper until a uniform mixture forms.
5. Using a 1-ounce cookie scoop or large spoon, make 20 heaping 2 tablespoon-sized meatballs and place directly onto a large plate or unlined sheet pan. Lightly drizzle your hands with water and roll the meatballs between your palms until they're smooth and return them to the sheet pan, about 1 inch apart.
6. Once the vegetables in the soup are fork-tender, submerge the meatballs in the broth, raise the heat to high and bring to a boil, and add the mint sprigs. Reduce the heat to medium and simmer, covered, until the meatballs begin to float, 8 to 10 minutes.
7. Reduce the heat to low and continue to simmer, covered, until the meatballs are cooked through and the rice grains inside the meatballs are tender, about 20 minutes.
8. Finish and serve the soup: Discard the mint sprigs. Add the lime juice, taste, and adjust the salt and black pepper as desired. Ladle into bowls and garnish with the fresh mint and oregano leaves. Serve with lime wedges.

HOT TIP

If you can't find chayote, a Mexican squash, use an extra zucchini or potato.

Roasted Carrot Tomato Soup
with Garlicky Grilled Cheese

SERVES 8 • **TOTAL TIME** 1 HOUR 25 MINUTES

FOR THE ROASTED CARROT AND TOMATO SOUP

4 carrots, peeled and cut into 2-inch pieces

1 large red bell pepper, seeded and coarsely chopped

1 yellow onion, peeled and cut into eighths

2 small heads of garlic, tops cut off and discarded

¼ cup extra-virgin olive oil, divided

2½ teaspoons kosher salt, divided

1 teaspoon freshly ground black pepper, divided

1 teaspoon paprika

2 garlic cloves, finely chopped

2 tablespoons tomato paste

1 teaspoon crushed Calabrian chili peppers

2 (28-ounce) cans whole peeled San Marzano tomatoes, undrained

8 cups vegetable stock

1½ cups heavy cream

1 cup finely grated Parmigiano-Reggiano cheese, plus more for serving

Fresh basil leaves, for garnish

This twist on traditional tomato soup gets a boost from roasted carrots, red bell pepper, and garlic with Calabrian chili for a spiced-sweet-and-savory kick. Blended with cream and Parmigiano-Reggiano, the soup turns silky and the flavors bloom. This wouldn't be a proper tomato soup moment without a garlicky fontina grilled cheese. Fontina's melt-factor and nutty richness make it the perfect choice, and using the oven to "grill" the sandwiches means you can make them while the soup cooks. Enjoy that cheese pull!

---

1. **MAKE THE ROASTED CARROT AND TOMATO SOUP:** Preheat the oven to 400°F. Line a sheet pan with parchment paper.
2. In a large bowl, add the carrots, bell pepper, onion, and the garlic heads. Drizzle with 2 tablespoons of the oil and season with 1½ teaspoons of the salt, ½ teaspoon of the black pepper, and the paprika and toss to coat. Evenly distribute the vegetables onto the prepared sheet pan, with the garlic heads cut side down.
3. Bake for 25 to 30 minutes, until the veggies are golden brown. Let cool on the sheet pan. Keep the oven on for the garlicky grilled cheese sandwiches.
4. Meanwhile, heat the remaining 2 tablespoons of oil in a Dutch oven or large stainless steel lidded pot over medium heat. Once shimmering, add the chopped garlic and cook, stirring constantly, until fragrant, 1 minute. Add the tomato paste and Calabrian chili peppers and cook, stirring constantly, until the mixture darkens and becomes fragrant, 1 to 2 minutes. Add the tomatoes, stir to combine, and bring to a simmer over medium heat.
5. Using tongs or a kitchen towel, squeeze the roasted garlic cloves from each head into the pot. Discard the skins. Add the roasted veggies, vegetable stock, the remaining 1 teaspoon of salt and remaining ½ teaspoon black pepper. Stir to combine and bring to a simmer over medium heat.

(recipe continues)

FOR THE GARLICKY GRILLED CHEESE (SEE HOT TIP)

1 stick (8 tablespoons) unsalted butter, at room temperature

½ cup finely grated Parmigiano-Reggiano cheese

½ teaspoon garlic powder

¼ teaspoon kosher salt

8 slices sourdough or bread of choice

2 cups freshly grated fontina cheese

PERFECT PAIRING

A rustic Italian Dolcetto or Barbera, or a Sangiovese or Montepulciano.

6. Reduce the heat to low and, using an immersion blender (or a blender with the steam vent in the top open), blend until completely smooth. If using a blender, return the soup to the pot over low heat. Stirring constantly, slowly add the cream and Parmigiano-Reggiano until incorporated. Keep warm over low heat until ready to serve.
7. **MAKE THE GARLICKY GRILLED CHEESE:** While the tomatoes are simmering and the veggies are roasting, line a sheet pan with parchment paper.
8. In a medium bowl, stir together the butter, Parmigiano-Reggiano, garlic powder, and salt. Spread the mixture onto both sides of the bread slices. Transfer 4 bread slices to the sheet pan 1 inch apart. Top each with ½ cup of the fontina and the remaining slices of bread.
9. Bake until golden brown and the cheese melts, flipping halfway through, about 12 minutes total. If you want the crust extra toasty, turn the broiler on high for the last 1 to 2 minutes.
10. **TO SERVE:** Ladle the soup into eight bowls, top with cheese and basil, and serve a sandwich half alongside.

HOT TIP

This recipe makes 8 sandwich halves—so if everyone wants a full sandwich to themselves, double the recipe.

Smoky Ham & Split Pea Soup

SERVES 8 • **TOTAL TIME** 1 HOUR 30 MINUTES

- 3 tablespoons extra-virgin olive oil
- ½ medium yellow onion, diced
- 2 medium carrots, peeled and diced
- 2 celery stalks, diced
- 1 teaspoon light brown sugar
- ½ teaspoon kosher salt
- ½ teaspoon ground thyme
- ½ teaspoon allspice
- 8 ounces diced ham (1 heaping cup)
- 1½ pounds smoked ham hock, or leftover bone-in ham shank
- 5 cups chicken stock
- 2 dried bay leaves
- 1 pound split peas, rinsed and drained
- Whole fresh flat-leaf parsley, for garnish
- Toasted buttered sourdough bread, for serving

PERFECT PAIRING

A unique Italian white wine like Falanghina or a Chenin Blanc from South Africa.

My mom, Lupe, is the queen of cooking with whatever's in the kitchen and turning leftovers into something special so that nothing goes to waste. Every Thanksgiving and Christmas, we'd order a brown sugar–crusted ham from the Honey Baked Ham Company in Pasadena, and this split pea soup was her way of giving leftovers new life. It's delicious, comforting, and practically made for a slab of warm, buttered, sourdough bread. My version is packed with veggies and leans on a smoked ham hock (or ham bone), a bit of brown sugar, and a touch of allspice to capture that signature Honey Baked flavor. In Lupe's honor, toss in whatever veggies you have waiting in your fridge—she wouldn't have it any other way!

---

1. Heat the oil in a Dutch oven or large stainless steel lidded pot over medium heat. Once shimmering, add the onion and cook, stirring, until translucent, 5 to 7 minutes. Add the carrots, celery, brown sugar, salt, thyme, and allspice and cook, stirring occasionally, until the vegetables are just tender, about 5 minutes.
2. Add the diced ham and cook, stirring occasionally, until the bottom of the pot starts to develop browned bits, 4 to 6 minutes. Add the ham hock and stir in the chicken stock, 4 cups water, and bay leaves. Bring to a boil over high heat and skim any foam that rises to the top.
3. Add the split peas, stir to combine, and bring to a boil. Reduce the heat to medium-low and simmer, covered, stirring occasionally, until the split peas are tender, the soup thickens, and the meat on the ham hock easily pulls away from the bone, 90 minutes for the ham hock, 60 if using the bone.
4. Simmer, uncovered, while transferring the ham hock to a cutting board or plate. Using two forks, shred the meat and return it to the pot. Discard the bone and any skin and bay leaves.
5. **TO SERVE:** Ladle into eight bowls, top with the parsley, and enjoy with the toast.

ALL ABOUT THE SIDES

I'm a Sides Girl on Thanksgiving and, honestly, most other days of the year. Sure, side dishes can play the supporting role, adding brightness to rich mains, cutting through decadence with a hit of acidity, or soaking up all the best parts of a sauce. But let's be real: Sides don't have to be the backup singers. They can, and often should, take center stage.

I mean—Crispy Garlic Butter Smashed Potatoes with Feta (page 222)? Swoon. Honey & Chile Roasted Carrots with Labneh (page 237)? A master class in sweet, smoky, and tangy balance. Burrata Broccolini with Calabrian Chili Romesco (page 221)? Try not to fall in love.

This chapter is packed with vibrant, flavor-forward veggie dishes that don't just complement the main event—they might just steal the spotlight. Whether you're assembling a spread or making a few and calling it dinner (highly recommended), there's something here for every craving. Think family favorites like Auntie Bug's Shortcut Asparagus Risotto (page 238) and Mom's Cheesy Calabacitas (page 229), or comfort-driven essentials like Brothy Frijoles de la Olla (page 241), Jalapeño Cornbread with Maple Butter (page 234), Easy Creamy Parm Polenta (page 218), and No-Mayo Esquites (page 233) are just sooo good.

Sides may be the accessories, but in the right hands, they're the whole outfit.

Easy Creamy Parm Polenta

SERVES 6 TO 8 • **TOTAL TIME** 35 MINUTES

¼ teaspoon baking soda

1½ cups medium-grind polenta (not instant)

1¾ teaspoons kosher salt

½ stick (4 tablespoons) unsalted butter

1 cup heavy cream

1½ cups finely grated Parmigiano-Reggiano cheese, plus more for garnish

Only a few ingredients, and this polenta earns its place at the table alongside just about anything in this book. A Northern Italian staple, polenta is beloved for its humble origins—simple, hearty, nourishing, endlessly adaptable, and affordable. Its naturally nutty, subtly sweet corn flavor makes it the ideal foundation for bold, saucy mains or a star in its own right. A little butter, a splash of cream, and the right hit of Parmigiano-Reggiano transforms stone-ground cornmeal into a perfectly creamy, cheesy dream—made even smoother with a pinch of baking soda to keep it clump-free and foolproof. I swear by traditional stone-ground cornmeal (sometimes labeled as corn grits) over instant—it delivers a depth of flavor and satisfying texture that's worth the extra minutes on the stove. This is the carb-panion I crave with Red Wine–Braised Short Ribs (page 90).

---

1. In a large Dutch oven or stainless steel lidded pot, bring 6 cups of water and the baking soda to a boil over high heat. Reduce the heat to medium and slowly add the polenta, whisking constantly until fully incorporated. Stir in the salt, reduce the heat to low, and maintain a gentle simmer. Cook, partially covered, stirring often with a wooden spoon and scraping the bottom of the pot to prevent it from sticking, until very thick and smooth, about 25 minutes.
2. Off heat, stir in the butter until melted. Stir in the cream, and fold in the cheese (see Hot Tip).
3. **TO SERVE:** Transfer to a large serving bowl or dish and garnish with more cheese.

HOT TIP

If your polenta is a bit too thick, stir in a little extra water along with the heavy cream at the end.

Burrata Broccolini with Calabrian Chili Romesco

SERVES 4 TO 6 • **TOTAL TIME** 35 MINUTES

FOR THE BROCCOLINI

1 pound baby broccolini, tough ends trimmed, thick stalks halved lengthwise

3 tablespoons extra-virgin olive oil

1 teaspoon kosher salt

1 teaspoon garlic powder

½ teaspoon freshly ground black pepper

1 tablespoon honey

¼ cup finely grated Parmigiano-Reggiano cheese

FOR THE CALABRIAN CHILI ROMESCO

1 (16-ounce) jar roasted red bell peppers, drained

4 garlic cloves, peeled

1 small shallot, coarsely chopped

1 cup chopped toasted walnuts, plus more for garnish (see Hot Tip)

½ cup fresh flat-leaf parsley

⅓ cup extra-virgin olive oil

1 tablespoon crushed Calabrian chili peppers

2 teaspoons grated lemon zest

2 tablespoons fresh lemon juice (about 1 lemon)

1 tablespoon honey

½ teaspoon smoked paprika

½ teaspoon kosher salt

1 (4-ounce) ball burrata cheese, at room temperature, for serving

This dish brings bold Spanish flavors (plus a touch of Italian heat!) with smoky, garlicky romesco—a luscious blend of roasted red peppers, nuts, and olive oil—layered under crisp, honey-glazed broccolini topped with cool, creamy burrata. The contrast of textures and layers of flavor make it downright irresistible. This recipe intentionally yields extra romesco, because trust me—you'll want it. Spoon it over eggs, swipe it onto sandwiches, or pair it with roasted vegetables and grilled steak in the days ahead. Elegant yet effortless, this is the kind of recipe that makes you look like you tried harder than you did—the ideal dish for entertaining.

1. **MAKE THE BROCCOLINI:** Preheat the oven to 425°F. Line a sheet pan with parchment paper.
2. Arrange the broccolini in a single layer on the parchment and drizzle with the oil. Using your hands, massage the oil into the broccolini. Season with the salt, garlic powder, and black pepper, toss to combine, and spread into an even layer.
3. Roast until crisp and charred in spots, about 15 minutes. Drizzle with the honey and sprinkle with the cheese. Return the sheet pan to the oven and cook until the cheese becomes golden brown and crisp, 2 to 3 minutes. The honey can burn quickly, so watch closely.
4. **MAKE THE CALABRIAN CHILI ROMESCO:** Meanwhile, in a food processor or blender, add the roasted red peppers, garlic, shallot, walnuts, and parsley and pulse until the mixture is well mixed. Add the oil, Calabrian chili peppers, lemon zest, lemon juice, honey, smoked paprika, and salt and blend on low, slowly increasing the speed to medium, until the mixture is smooth, 30 seconds to 1 minute.
5. **TO SERVE:** Cover the bottom of a large serving platter with ½ cup of the sauce and pile the broccolini on top. Tear pieces of the burrata and dollop over the broccolini. Drizzle with extra sauce, and garnish with the walnuts.

HOT TIP

To toast walnuts, warm in a small dry skillet over medium heat until fragrant and golden brown, 3 to 5 minutes.

Crispy Garlic Butter Smashed Potatoes
with Feta

SERVES 4 • **TOTAL TIME** 1 HOUR 10 MINUTES

FOR THE SMASHED POTATOES

- 2 pounds baby Yukon Gold potatoes, unpeeled
- 1 tablespoon kosher salt, for cooking the potatoes
- ¾ teaspoon baking soda
- 3 tablespoons extra-virgin olive oil
- 2 teaspoons garlic powder
- 1 teaspoon kosher salt
- ½ teaspoon freshly ground black pepper

FOR THE CRISPY GARLIC BUTTER SAUCE

- ½ stick (4 tablespoons) unsalted butter
- 3 garlic cloves, thinly sliced lengthwise
- 2 teaspoons grated lemon zest
- ¾ teaspoon crushed red pepper

FOR SERVING

- 1 cup crumbled feta (from feta in brine)
- 1 tablespoon fresh lemon juice (about ½ lemon)
- Chopped fresh flat-leaf parsley or fresh dill, for garnish
- Flaky sea salt, for garnish
- Lemon wedges

Crispy smashed potatoes have a way of disappearing fast—golden, crunchy, and made for soaking up flavor. This version channels the garlic feta fries I couldn't get enough of at the Mediterranean spot where I worked in my teens (and that I still order from religiously). They're drenched in a heavenly garlic butter infused with lemon zest and red pepper, loaded with creamy crumbles of feta, and showered with fresh parsley or dill. Don't skip my trick for the crispiest potatoes—parboil them with baking soda.

---

1. **MAKE THE SMASHED POTATOES:** Place a baking rack at least 3 inches from the broiler and preheat the oven to 450°F. Line a sheet pan with parchment paper.
2. In a large pot, add the potatoes and fill with enough cold water to cover by about 1 inch. Add the salt and baking soda and bring to a boil over high heat. Reduce the heat to medium and simmer until the potatoes are fork-tender, about 20 minutes. Drain, pat dry, and transfer to the prepared sheet pan to cool slightly.
3. Once cool, using the bottom of a lightly oiled cup or jar, flatten each potato into ½-inch-thick rounds.
4. Drizzle the potatoes with the oil and sprinkle with the garlic powder, the remaining 1 teaspoon of salt, and the black pepper on both sides. Roast, flipping halfway through, for about 35 minutes total, until the potatoes are golden and crispy on the edges. To get them extra crispy, turn the broiler on high for an additional 2 to 3 minutes, watching carefully to avoid burning.
5. **MAKE THE CRISPY GARLIC BUTTER SAUCE:** While the potatoes roast, in a medium saucepan, melt the butter over medium heat until just beginning to foam. Reduce the heat to medium-low, and add the garlic, lemon zest, and crushed red pepper and cook, stirring constantly, until the garlic slices turn golden, 1 to 2 minutes. Immediately pour into a small bowl.
6. **TO SERVE:** Place half of the smashed potatoes onto a serving platter. Drizzle with half of the garlic butter sauce and sprinkle with half of the feta. Top with the remaining potatoes, crispy garlic butter sauce, the remaining feta, and the lemon juice. Garnish with the parsley, flaky salt, and serve with lemon wedges.

Colcannon

SERVES 6 TO 8 • **TOTAL TIME** 40 MINUTES

- 3 large Yukon Gold potatoes, peeled and cut into 1-inch pieces
- 2 large russet potatoes, peeled and cut into 1-inch pieces
- 3 garlic cloves, peeled
- 1 tablespoon plus 1½ teaspoons kosher salt, divided
- 1 stick (8 tablespoons) unsalted butter, divided
- 1 medium leek (white and light green parts only), halved lengthwise, washed, and thinly sliced
- ½ medium bunch curly kale, ribs removed and roughly chopped (about 2 cups firmly packed)
- ¼ small head green cabbage, thinly sliced then roughly chopped (about 2 cups)
- ½ teaspoon freshly ground black pepper
- 1¼ cups heavy cream
- Finely chopped chives, for garnish (optional)

As an O'Brien, it felt only right to honor a traditional Irish dish—though I couldn't help weaving in a few touches of my own. This version of colcannon keeps its roots: tender cabbage, hearty kale, and creamy potatoes, with softened leeks swapped for the usual green onions along with a shower of fresh chives. A blend of Yukon Gold and russet potatoes deepens the flavor with buttery notes and gentle sweetness, or use whatever you have—it'll still mash up something that could charm a leprechaun.

---

1. In a large lidded pot, add the potatoes and garlic and fill with enough cold water to cover the potatoes by about 1 inch. Add 1 tablespoon of the salt and bring to a boil over high heat. Reduce the heat to medium and simmer until the potatoes are fork-tender, about 20 minutes.
2. Meanwhile, melt 6 tablespoons of the butter in a Dutch oven or stainless steel pot over medium heat. Add the leeks and cook, stirring frequently, until tender, 3 to 5 minutes. Stir in the kale, cabbage, the remaining 1½ teaspoons salt, and the black pepper. Cook, continuing to stir often, until the vegetables have softened and let off some of their liquid, 3 to 5 minutes. Add the heavy cream and bring to a simmer. Remove from heat and cover while the potatoes finish cooking.
3. Drain the cooked potatoes and garlic and using a potato ricer, rice them into a pot with the greens (see Hot Tip). Mix well.
4. Transfer to a serving dish and with a spoon, make a small well in the center. Place the remaining 2 tablespoons of butter in the well, and garnish with chives, if desired.

HOT TIP

No ricer? Drain the potatoes and garlic cloves and add to the greens. Gently mash them with a potato masher until mostly smooth. Don't over mash or mix, as they will become gummy.

Spicy Lemon Parm Cauliflower Bites

SERVES 4 • **TOTAL TIME** 45 MINUTES

- 2 tablespoons unsalted butter, melted
- 2 tablespoons extra-virgin olive oil
- 2 teaspoons grated lemon zest
- ½ teaspoon kosher salt
- ½ teaspoon crushed red pepper
- ¼ teaspoon garlic powder
- ¼ teaspoon paprika
- ¼ teaspoon freshly ground black pepper, plus more for garnish
- 1 medium head cauliflower (or 24-ounce bag cauliflower florets), cut into florets (see Hot Tip)
- 1 cup finely grated Parmigiano-Reggiano cheese, divided
- Chopped fresh flat-leaf parsley, for garnish
- Flaky sea salt, for garnish
- Lemon wedges, for serving

I love a whole roasted cauliflower, but these bites are quicker, easier, and packed with flavor in every nook and cranny—perfect for entertaining. Roasted with olive oil, herbs, spices, Parmigiano-Reggiano, and citrus, they hit that ideal balance of crisp edges and tender centers. Each floret gets a golden, lemony Parm crust that delivers just the right mix of brightness and depth. Even the cauliflower skeptics won't stand a chance.

---

1. Place an oven rack in the middle and another about 3 inches from the broiler and preheat the oven to 450°F. Line a sheet pan with parchment paper.
2. In a large bowl, whisk the butter, oil, lemon zest, salt, crushed red pepper, garlic powder, paprika, and black pepper. Add the cauliflower florets to the bowl and toss until coated. Add ¾ cup of the Parmigiano-Reggiano and mix well.
3. Transfer the cauliflower to the prepared sheet pan, making sure each piece is about ½ inch apart. Bake on the middle rack for 15 minutes, use a spatula to flip them, and continue to cook for 10 more minutes, until golden brown and crispy. To make them crispier, turn the broiler on high and broil for 1 to 2 minutes, until the edges of the florets become deeper golden brown.
4. **TO SERVE:** Transfer to a serving platter. Sprinkle with the remaining ¼ cup of Parmigiano-Reggiano. Garnish with parsley, a few twists of black pepper, and flaky salt. Serve with lemon wedges.

HOT TIP

In an ideal world, your cauliflower florets are equal in size—if not, halve the large florets for crispier results.

Mom's Cheesy Calabacitas (Mexican Squash)

SERVES 4 TO 6 • **TOTAL TIME** 25 MINUTES

- 2 tablespoons avocado or other neutral oil
- ½ medium sweet onion (such as Vidalia), finely chopped
- 3 medium zucchini, halved lengthwise and cut into ¾-inch chunks
- 1 (7-ounce) can corn kernels, drained, or 1 cup fresh or frozen, thawed corn kernels
- 1 Roma (plum) tomato, finely chopped
- ½ teaspoon chicken bouillon powder (see Hot Tips)
- ½ teaspoon kosher salt
- 1 tablespoon unsalted butter
- ½ cup crumbled queso fresco
- ¼ cup crumbled cotija cheese, plus more for garnish

My mom's calabacitas (zucchini cooked with sweet onion, tomato, and corn and showered with cheese) were a signature childhood dish. We ate it on busy school nights, special occasions, and every moment in between. She swears by Vidalia onion and a pinch of chicken bouillon powder for that perfect balance of savory and sweet, coaxing out the zucchini's natural sugars while the tomatoes add just the right hit of brightness. The key? Cooking it until perfectly tender, never mushy. I hope this dish finds its way into your kitchen the same way it always had a place in ours!

1. Heat the oil in a large stainless steel lidded skillet over medium-high heat. Once shimmering, add the onion and cook, stirring frequently, until softened and slightly translucent, 3 to 4 minutes. Stir in the zucchini and cook until vibrant green, 2 to 3 minutes. Stir in the corn, tomato, bouillon powder, and salt and cook, stirring occasionally, until the tomato starts to soften, about 1 minute. Spread into an even layer in the pan, cover, and cook, stirring halfway through, until the squash is tender but not mushy, 6 to 8 minutes. Uncover, add the butter, and stir until melted.
2. Off heat, sprinkle with the queso fresco and cotija, cover, and let the cheese melt, about 3 minutes.
3. Serve directly out of the skillet or transfer to a serving dish and garnish with more cotija.

HOT TIPS

If you don't have any bouillon powder on hand, add 2 generous pinches of salt.

If you can't find queso fresco or cotija, swap in crumbled feta cheese.

Perfect Green Bean Salad

SERVES 4 TO 6 • **TOTAL TIME** 20 MINUTES

Ice

2 tablespoons plus ¾ teaspoon kosher salt, divided

1½ pounds green beans, trimmed and cut into 2½-inch pieces

¼ cup extra-virgin olive oil

1 teaspoon grated lemon zest

3 tablespoons fresh lemon juice (about 1½ lemons)

¼ cup finely grated Parmigiano-Reggiano cheese, plus more for garnish

¼ cup chopped salted roasted almonds, plus more for garnish

My parents have an amazing love story woven with memories of the restaurants they discovered while traveling for my dad's ultra-marathon races. One of their favorites? Tommaso's Ristorante Italiano in San Francisco—famous for brick oven pizzas, lasagna, and ravioli . . . but also, unexpectedly, a green bean salad. In their honor (and with a healthy dose of skepticism), I set out to make the best version possible. Crisp-tender green beans are doused with olive oil, lemon zest and juice, freshly grated Parm, and a shower of crunchy, salted roasted almonds. Just be sure to dress it right before serving to keep the beans vibrant and snappy.

1. Prepare an ice bath by filling a large bowl with ice and water and setting it aside in the sink.
2. Bring a medium pot of water with 2 tablespoons of the salt to a boil. Add the green beans and cook, stirring occasionally, until crisp-tender, 6 to 7 minutes.
3. Using a colander, immediately strain the green beans and transfer them to the prepared ice bath. Once completely cool, strain the green beans and dry them.
4. Dry the ice bath bowl and add the green beans, oil, lemon zest, lemon juice, and the remaining ¾ teaspoon salt and, using your hands or tongs, toss to combine until well coated. Add the cheese and almonds and toss well.
5. **TO SERVE:** Transfer to a serving bowl and top with extra cheese and almonds.

HOT TIP

This recipe is so flexible and delicious. Experiment with different nuts, cheeses, or dried fruit, like tart dried cherries.

No-Mayo Esquites (Mexican Street Corn Salad)

SERVES 4 TO 6 • **TOTAL TIME** 20 MINUTES

- ¼ cup plus 1 tablespoon extra-virgin olive oil, divided
- 4 cups fresh corn kernels (from 4 medium ears of corn), or frozen, unthawed
- 2 garlic cloves, finely chopped
- 1 teaspoon kosher salt, divided
- 1½ teaspoons chili powder
- 1 teaspoon garlic powder
- ½ teaspoon freshly ground black pepper
- 2 teaspoons grated lime zest
- ¼ cup fresh lime juice (about 2 limes)
- ½ cup crumbled cotija cheese, plus more for garnish
- 1 teaspoon Tajín seasoning, plus more for garnish (see Hot Tip)
- 4 green onions (white and green parts), thinly sliced
- 1 cup chopped fresh cilantro, plus more for garnish
- ½ medium red onion, chopped
- 1 large fresh jalapeño pepper, stemmed, seeded, and chopped (deveined for less heat)
- ¼ cup salted roasted pepitas (pumpkin seeds)

I've always loved the garlicky, cheesy tang of esquites, but the mayo-heavy versions never quite did it for me. This no-mayo take lets crumbled cotija bring the creaminess, and the classic Tajín, garlic, lime, jalapeño, and cilantro deliver the punchy flavors that make esquites so good. Tajín is nonnegotiable here—you'll find it at most grocery stores, but if not, see the Hot Tip. These disappear wherever I serve them, whether as a side or a standout appetizer. Set them out with some tortilla chips and I dare you to stop at just one bite!

1. Heat 2 tablespoons of the oil in a large skillet over medium-high heat. Once shimmering, add the corn, spread into an even layer in the pan, and cook, undisturbed, until the corn is light golden brown on the bottom, about 4 minutes. Flip the corn and cook until golden brown, about 2 minutes more. Add the garlic, ½ teaspoon of the salt, the chili powder, garlic powder, and black pepper and cook, stirring frequently so the garlic doesn't burn, until the garlic has softened, 1 to 2 minutes. Set aside.
2. In a medium bowl, whisk the remaining 3 tablespoons of oil, the remaining ½ teaspoon of salt, the lime zest, lime juice, cotija, and Tajín. Add the corn mixture along with the green onions, cilantro, onion, jalapeño pepper, and pepitas and toss to combine.
3. **TO SERVE:** Transfer to a serving dish and garnish with more cotija, cilantro, and a sprinkle of Tajín.

HOT TIP

No Tajín? Use a chile lime seasoning (with salt) or make your own using 1 tablespoon fine chile flakes, ¾ teaspoon kosher salt, and 1 teaspoon lime zest.

Jalapeño Cornbread with Maple Butter

SERVES 8 • **TOTAL TIME** 40 MINUTES

FOR THE JALAPEÑO CORNBREAD

- 1¼ cups medium-grind cornmeal
- ¾ cup all-purpose flour
- 2 teaspoons baking powder
- 1 teaspoon kosher salt
- ½ teaspoon baking soda
- 1¼ cups shaken buttermilk, at room temperature
- ⅓ cup honey
- 2 large eggs, at room temperature
- ¼ cup avocado or other neutral oil
- 2 medium fresh jalapeño peppers, stemmed, seeded, and deveined, 1 diced and 1 thinly sliced
- 5 tablespoons unsalted butter, melted, divided

FOR THE MAPLE BUTTER

- 1 stick (8 tablespoons) unsalted butter, at room temperature
- ½ cup maple syrup
- ½ teaspoon kosher salt
- Flaky sea salt, for serving

There's nothing like warm homemade cornbread alongside a bowl of chili or stew on a cold day. This version walks the perfect line between sweet and savory, with jalapeños bringing just enough heat to balance the maple-kissed corn flavor—in less than twenty-five minutes! The secret? A screaming-hot preheated cast-iron skillet slicked with butter before the batter goes in to instantly form that chewy, golden crust that crisps to perfection as it bakes. Slather on some whipped maple butter and you're in business. Want to dial back the heat? Skip the sliced jalapeño on top or leave it out entirely. Either way, it's cornbread at its best.

---

1. **MAKE THE JALAPEÑO CORNBREAD:** Place an 8-inch cast-iron skillet (see Hot Tip) in the oven. Preheat the oven to 425°F.
2. In a large bowl, whisk the cornmeal, flour, baking powder, salt, and baking soda. In a separate medium bowl, whisk the buttermilk, honey, eggs, oil, and the diced jalapeño until well combined.
3. Pour the wet ingredients into the dry ingredients and, using a wooden spoon, stir until just a few floury streaks remain. Stir in 4 tablespoons of the melted butter until the mixture is smooth.
4. Remove the hot skillet from the oven, add the remaining 1 tablespoon of melted butter, and carefully tilt the skillet to evenly coat the bottom and sides. Immediately pour the batter into the pan, smooth with a spatula, and top with the jalapeño slices.
5. Bake for 20 to 22 minutes, until the edges are deep golden brown and a toothpick inserted in the center comes out clean. Allow to cool in the pan for at least 15 minutes before cutting.
6. **MAKE THE MAPLE BUTTER:** Meanwhile, in a medium bowl, add the butter, maple syrup, and salt. Using a whisk or an electric handheld mixer, beat until pale yellow and very fluffy, 1 to 3 minutes.
7. **TO SERVE:** Slice the cornbread into eight wedges. Generously spread the maple butter onto each slice and finish with a generous pinch of flaky salt.

HOT TIP

Cast iron works best for this cornbread, but an 8 x 8-inch pan will also work—you just won't get quite the same thick and buttery crust.

Honey & Chile Roasted Carrots with Labneh

SERVES 4 • **TOTAL TIME** 40 MINUTES

FOR THE CALABRIAN CHILI HONEY DRIZZLE

2 tablespoons honey

1 tablespoon white balsamic vinegar

½ teaspoon crushed Calabrian chili peppers

FOR THE HONEY ROASTED CARROTS

2 tablespoons extra-virgin olive oil

¾ teaspoon kosher salt

½ teaspoon garlic powder

½ teaspoon freshly ground black pepper

1 pound baby rainbow carrots, peeled, ends trimmed (or full-size carrots, halved lengthwise)

FOR THE LABNEH

1 cup labneh (see Hot Tips)

1 tablespoon extra-virgin olive oil

¼ teaspoon kosher salt

FOR SERVING

Pomegranate seeds

Salted roasted pepitas (pumpkin seeds)

Chopped fresh flat-leaf parsley (or fresh herb of choice)

These gorgeous roasted carrots, coated in a Calabrian chili honey drizzle, piled on top of creamy labneh (strained Middle Eastern yogurt), and sprinkled with pomegranate seeds, pepitas, and fresh herbs, are proof that even a humble vegetable can become a standout side. Destined to become your go-to method for transforming everyday carrots into something exceptional, this dish is layered with savory, sweet, spicy, and tangy flavors, plus plenty of texture. Perfect for spring gatherings and holiday tables.

---

1. **MAKE THE CALABRIAN CHILI HONEY DRIZZLE:** In a measuring cup or small bowl, whisk the honey, vinegar, and chiles until combined. Set aside.
2. **MAKE THE HONEY ROASTED CARROTS:** Preheat the oven to 425°F. Line a sheet pan with parchment paper.
3. In a medium bowl, whisk 1 tablespoon of the Calabrian chili honey drizzle, the oil, salt, garlic powder, and black pepper. Add the carrots to the bowl and, using your hands or tongs, toss until coated. Transfer the carrots to the prepared sheet pan in an even layer, spacing them at least ½ inch apart. Roast for 25 to 30 minutes, until slightly charred on the edges and tender (see Hot Tips). Allow to cool on the baking sheet for at least 5 minutes.
4. **MAKE THE LABNEH:** Meanwhile, in a medium bowl, stir together the labneh, oil, and salt until smooth.
5. **TO SERVE:** Spread the labneh into a thick layer covering the bottom of a large serving plate. Using tongs, pile the roasted carrots on top, leaving some labneh peeking out around the edges. Drizzle with the remaining Calabrian chili honey drizzle and garnish with the pomegranate seeds, pepitas, and chopped parsley.

HOT TIPS

If you can't find labneh, sub the thickest full-fat Greek yogurt you can find or try Skyr brand.

To add more char to the carrots, turn the broiler on high and broil on the top rack for 1 to 2 minutes.

Auntie Bug's Shortcut Asparagus Risotto

SERVES 4 TO 6 • **TOTAL TIME** 20 MINUTES

- 2 (10-ounce) bags frozen brown rice (see Hot Tips)
- ½ stick (4 tablespoons) unsalted butter, divided
- 1 shallot, finely chopped
- 5 garlic cloves, finely chopped
- 1 teaspoon kosher salt
- 1 bunch asparagus, bottoms trimmed, cut into 1-inch pieces
- ¼ cup dry white wine (I use Sauvignon Blanc)
- 1½ cups chicken stock
- 2 cups finely grated Pecorino Romano cheese, plus more for garnish (see Hot Tips)
- 1 teaspoon freshly ground black pepper, plus more for garnish
- Chopped fresh flat-leaf parsley, for garnish

The first time I tried my Auntie Bug's shortcut risotto, I got it—her obsession made perfect sense. Traditional risotto is high maintenance—demanding patience, constant stirring, and perfect timing—but this version? It's all the comfort and creaminess without the hassle. The secret weapon: frozen brown rice instead of the usual dry arborio! I prefer brown rice for its nutty flavor and hearty texture. Add buttery shallots, bright asparagus, a splash of crisp white wine, and nutty Pecorino Romano, and you've got a dish that feels far fancier than the effort it takes. Want to switch it up? Toss in frozen peas or any veggie you love—it's endlessly adaptable.

1. Remove the rice from the freezer and set on the counter to slightly thaw.
2. In a Dutch oven or stainless steel lidded pot, melt 2 tablespoons of the butter over medium heat. Add the shallot and cook, stirring occasionally, until translucent and starting to brown, about 3 minutes. Add the garlic and salt and cook, stirring constantly, until fragrant, about 1 minute.
3. Stir in the asparagus and the wine. Raise the heat to medium-high, cover, and cook until the asparagus is just tender, about 5 minutes.
4. Add the slightly thawed rice and stir to combine, breaking up any large chunks with the bottom of a wooden spoon. Cook, stirring constantly, until most of the liquid is absorbed, 2 to 3 minutes.
5. Stir in the chicken stock and cook, stirring often, until the liquid thickens slightly, 3 to 5 minutes.
6. Off heat, add the remaining 2 tablespoons of butter. Stirring quickly and continuously, add the Pecorino Romano and black pepper and cook until the sauce thickens, and the rice absorbs most of the liquid, 3 to 4 minutes.
7. **TO SERVE:** Spoon into serving bowls and garnish with the Pecorino Romano, chopped parsley, and a few twists of black pepper.

HOT TIPS

You can substitute frozen long-grain basmati or jasmine rice.

I love the salty bite of Pecorino Romano, but Parmigiano-Reggiano is a great sub, too.

Brothy Frijoles de la Olla (Mexican Beans)

SERVES 6 TO 8 • **TOTAL TIME** 3 HOURS (PLUS SOAK TIME)

FOR THE BEANS

- 3 cups dried Peruano (Mayocoba) or pinto beans, sorted and rinsed
- 1½ tablespoons kosher salt, divided
- ½ yellow onion, peeled
- 1 fresh jalapeño pepper, stemmed and slit lengthwise (optional)
- ¾ teaspoon ground cumin
- 1 dried bay leaf

FOR SERVING

- Crumbled queso fresco (see Hot Tips)
- Crumbled cotija cheese (see Hot Tips)
- Finely chopped white onion
- Chopped fresh cilantro
- Mom's Secret Salsa (page 31)
- Tortilla chips or tortillas

Beans are a staple in many Mexican households, and our family's version is simple, healthy, and wildly satisfying—especially when piled high with toppings. While frijoles de la olla are traditionally made with pinto beans, my mom and I swear by extra-creamy Peruano beans. This recipe is as low-maintenance as it gets, relying on just a few key ingredients (see Hot Tips) to build deep, rich flavor as the beans simmer. Time and toppings are the trick here, along with quality dried beans—check out a local Mexican market or order online from our favorite, Rancho Gordo. Soaking isn't a must, but it speeds up cooking and improves digestibility. If you're in a hurry, follow your pressure cooker directions to get the job done beautifully.

---

1. **MAKE THE BEANS:** Place the rinsed beans and ½ tablespoon of the salt into a large bowl or pot and cover with 4 inches of water. Cover with a lid or kitchen towel and leave to soak at room temperature for a minimum of 4 hours and preferably overnight. If you can't soak your beans, don't worry—just increase your cooking time by an additional 25 to 30 minutes.
2. Drain the soaked beans and place them into a large Dutch oven or stainless lidded pot along with 7 cups of cold water, the onion, jalapeño (if using), the remaining 1 tablespoon of salt, the cumin, and bay leaf. Stir to combine and bring to a boil over high heat.
3. Reduce the heat to medium-low, cover, and simmer, stirring occasionally, until the beans are completely tender, 1½ to 2½ hours. Remove the onion and bay leaf and discard.
4. **TO SERVE:** Ladle into serving bowls and garnish with the queso fresco, cotija, onion, cilantro, and salsa. Serve with the tortilla chips and/or warmed tortillas for dipping.

HOT TIPS

To build flavor, throw in a leftover rind of Parmigiano-Reggiano, a ham hock, or a few stems of fresh oregano.

If you can't find queso fresco or cotija, swap in crumbled feta cheese.

Mexican Rice

SERVES 6 • **TOTAL TIME** 40 MINUTES

- 1 tablespoon chicken bouillon powder (see Hot Tip)
- 3 tablespoons extra-virgin olive oil
- ½ medium white onion, finely chopped
- ½ teaspoon kosher salt
- 1½ cups long grain white rice
- 2 garlic cloves, finely chopped
- 1 (4-ounce) can tomato sauce
- Chopped fresh cilantro, for garnish

One of my earliest kitchen memories with my mom and grandma is of a group of their friends devouring this rice and pleading with them for the recipe. It's that kind of dish—the one everyone wants a scoop of, then a second, and then the secret to making it. Our take on classic Mexican-style or Spanish rice comes together quickly with just a few ingredients and the right method. It's packed with flavor, thanks to the perfect balance of toasted rice, warm spices, onion, garlic, tomato, and a hint of chicken bouillon powder. It's a staple in our house, always served alongside beans, tacos, enchiladas, or chilaquiles—but honestly, it's just as good straight from the pot with a spoon.

1. In a measuring cup, whisk 3 cups of warm water and the bouillon powder until completely dissolved. Set aside.
2. Heat the oil in a medium lidded pot over medium-high heat. Once shimmering, add the onion and salt and cook, stirring often, until slightly softened and translucent, 3 to 4 minutes.
3. Add the rice and cook, stirring almost constantly, until toasted and light golden brown, 5 to 8 minutes. Add the garlic and cook, stirring constantly, until fragrant, 1 minute. Add the tomato sauce and stir until combined. Stir in the bouillon and bring to a boil, then reduce the heat to low, cover, and gently simmer until most of the liquid has evaporated and the rice is tender, about 20 minutes.
4. Remove from heat, covered, so the rice continues to steam, about 8 minutes. Using a fork, gently fluff the rice.
5. **TO SERVE:** Transfer to a serving dish and garnish with the cilantro.

HOT TIP

Swap in 3 cups of chicken stock for the bouillon powder, or veggie bouillon or broth, if desired.

Steamed Rice

SERVES 6 • **TOTAL TIME** 35 MINUTES

- 1½ cups long grain white rice
- 1 tablespoon chicken bouillon powder (see Hot Tip)
- 1 tablespoon unsalted butter

This is my go-to simple recipe for foolproof, fluffy rice. I use it for countless recipes, and it's a great staple to have in your back pocket.

1. Rinse the rice in a fine mesh strainer under cold water until the water runs clear, about 1 minute. Shake the colander to remove excess water. This makes for fluffy rice!
2. Bring 3 cups of water to a boil in a medium lidded pot over high heat. Stir in the chicken bouillon, butter, and rice and return to a boil. Reduce the heat to medium-low and simmer, covered, until the liquid is absorbed, 15 to 20 minutes. Remove from heat, covered, so the rice continues to steam, about 8 minutes. Using a fork, gently fluff the rice.

HOT TIP

Butter makes everything better, and the chicken bouillon deepens the flavor. You can skip or if you're vegetarian, try veggie bouillon.

CHERRY ON TOP

Before I fell in love with cooking, I specialized in transforming boxed cupcake mixes into something that tasted straight out of a pastry chef's kitchen. A silky swap of butter for oil, creamy milk instead of water, a whisper of vanilla or almond extract for depth, an extra pinch of salt to tease out the sweetness—and cream cheese in the frosting for that irresistible tang. I proudly shared my sugary twists with friends and boyfriends. The funny thing is, over the years, I realized my cravings lean more savory than sweet, and this is exactly why I'm the perfect guide to usher you into the land of sugar. Stay with me here! If I'm going to eat dessert, it's going to be unforgettable and never cloyingly sweet, indulgent, balanced, and worth every bite.

This chapter is filled with my all-time favorite recipes—the ones that prove dessert isn't just the final course, it's the grand finale. The cherry on top? It's the details: the addition of pecans in a graham cracker crust for Key Lime Pie with Pecan Graham Cracker Crust (page 267), the deep nuttiness of brown butter folded into cookie dough for the Loaded Brown Butter Chocolate Chip Cookies (page 255), the way mascarpone melts into the citrusy, boozy syrup in Limoncello Tiramisu (page 268). It's the twist that turns a classic cannoli into No-Churn Cannoli Ice Cream (page 258), all the rich, chocolate-flecked goodness, spun into something creamy and effortless. I'm sharing globally approved treats like the Sisterhood of the Traveling Zucchini Carrot Cake (page 261) and, as promised, cream cheese for Toasted Coconut Cupcakes with Brown Butter Cream Cheese Frosting (page 263). These are recipes for celebrations, whether it's a milestone moment or just a Wednesday night that deserves a little extra joy.

Because when dessert is this good, there's always room for one more bite.

Raspberry Lemon Drop Cheesecake Bars

SERVES 12 • **TOTAL TIME** 2 HOURS (PLUS CHILL TIME)

FOR THE GRAHAM CRACKER CRUST

1 stick (8 tablespoons) unsalted butter, melted, plus more for the baking dish

18 graham cracker sheets, pulsed or blended into fine crumbs (about 2¼ cups)

2 tablespoons turbinado (raw) or granulated sugar

1 teaspoon kosher salt

FOR THE LEMON FILLING

⅔ cup granulated sugar

1 tablespoon grated lemon zest (about 2 lemons)

24 ounces cream cheese, at room temperature

2 teaspoons pure vanilla bean paste or extract

½ teaspoon kosher salt

3 large eggs, at room temperature

2 tablespoons fresh lemon juice (about 1 lemon)

FOR THE RASPBERRY TOPPING

3 cups sour cream, at room temperature

1 (13-ounce) jar raspberry preserves (seeds are ok!)

2 tablespoons granulated sugar

1 tablespoon fresh lemon juice (about ½ lemon)

Whipped cream, for topping

Fresh raspberries, for garnish

When I set out to dream up a cheesecake recipe just for you, my mind drifted to my Aunt Adri's signature version—always topped with a cloud of lightly sweetened sour cream. What if that topping became its own layer, infused with the deep berry flavor of sweet raspberry preserves? The result? A dessert that's as stunning as it is nostalgic, channeling those cream-cheese-and-jam-on-a-toasted-bagel vibes—that is, if the bagel were a buttery graham cracker crust. This decadent dessert is easy to make and light, bright, and tangy. Just be gentle with the mixing—overwhipping the filling can lead to cracks, and we want that smooth, dreamy finish.

1. Place one rack in the middle of the oven and one rack in the bottom third and preheat the oven to 350°F.
2. Butter a 9 x 13-inch baking dish and line with parchment paper, leaving a 2-inch overhang on the long sides of the dish. Fill a second large baking dish with hot tap water and place on the bottom third oven rack. This isn't your typical water bath—the baking dish isn't submerged. Instead, the bottom pan creates steam, ensuring the filling cooks evenly.
3. **MAKE THE GRAHAM CRACKER CRUST:** In a medium bowl, combine the melted butter, graham cracker crumbs, sugar, and salt. Stir until the mixture is the texture of damp sand. Pour into the prepared pan and, using the bottom of a measuring cup, press the mixture evenly across the bottom and a little more than halfway up the sides, ensuring there are no cracks.
4. Bake for 10 minutes, until the sides of the crust are light golden. Set on a wire rack to cool completely before adding the filling.
5. **MEANWHILE, MAKE THE LEMON FILLING:** In the bowl of a stand mixer fitted with the paddle attachment (or in a bowl using a handheld mixer), add the sugar and lemon zest. Using your fingers, rub the zest into the sugar until pale yellow, about 1 minute. Add the cream cheese, vanilla, and salt and beat on medium speed until the mixture is mostly smooth, about 3 minutes. Add one egg at a time, fully incorporating each before adding the next and scraping down the sides of the bowl as needed. Add the lemon juice and beat on medium-low until thoroughly combined and silky smooth, 1 to 2 minutes.

(recipe continues)

PERFECT PAIRING

A demi-sec or doux (sweeter style) Champagne, or Prosecco sweetened with a touch of fruit juice.

HOT TIP

To get smooth slices and clean edges on your cheesecake bars, have a tall glass with hot water and a kitchen towel standing by. Dip the knife in the water and wipe clean and repeat for clean slices.

6. Pour the filling into the cooled crust and, using a silicone spatula, smooth the top. Bake on the middle rack for 45 to 48 minutes, until the outer corners of the cheesecake are set and the center jiggles slightly when you touch the dish. Set on a wire rack to cool for 8 to 10 minutes before topping with the raspberry layer. Leave the oven on.
7. **MAKE THE RASPBERRY TOPPING:** Meanwhile, in a medium bowl, combine the sour cream, preserves, sugar, and lemon juice. Using a whisk or a handheld mixer, mix until smooth and the preserves are incorporated, 30 seconds to 1 minute. Pour the raspberry topping over the cooled cream cheese layer and, using a silicone spatula, smooth it evenly over the top.
8. Bake for 15 to 18 minutes, until the top layer is a deeper pink, beginning to set, and appears jellylike. Set on a wire rack to cool for at least 30 minutes then transfer to the fridge, uncovered, for a minimum of 4 hours or overnight. Wait to cover the dish with plastic wrap or foil until it's cooled completely to prevent condensation from dripping on the top layer.
9. **TO SERVE:** Slide a sharp knife around the edges of the cheesecake that are touching the dish, and use the parchment overhang to transfer to a cutting board. Slice the cheesecake into even squares (see Hot Tip). Evenly divide among serving plates and top with the whipped cream and fresh raspberries.

Far Niente
Vietti
2020
BAROLO
CASTIGLIONE
EnRoute
2021
MISE EN BOUTEILLES D'ORIGINE
FAMILLE PERRIN
Coudoulet de Beaucastel
COTES-DU-RHONE
APPELLATION D'ORIGINE CONTROLÉE
Mauro Sebaste
Centobricchi
2022
Barbera d'Alba
2022
GAMBINO
ALBINO
ROSATO TOSCANO
TENUTA DI ARCENO
CHIANTI CLASSICO
2021
Mauro Sebaste
Parigi
2022
Nebbiolo d'Alba
PRESQU'ILE

Ultimate Chocolate Cupcakes

MAKES 24 CUPCAKES • **TOTAL TIME** 1 HOUR

FOR THE CHOCOLATE CUPCAKES

1¾ cups all-purpose flour

¾ cup Dutch-processed cocoa powder

2 teaspoons instant espresso powder (see Hot Tips)

2 teaspoons baking soda

1 teaspoon baking powder

¾ teaspoon kosher salt

1¼ cups granulated sugar

¾ cup lightly packed light brown sugar

1 cup shaken buttermilk, at room temperature

½ cup avocado or other neutral oil

2 large eggs, at room temperature

2 teaspoons pure vanilla bean paste or extract

1 cup very strong or cold brew coffee, warm

When Andrew and I first started dating, I discovered something unexpected: His unwavering commitment to chocolate cake for breakfast. A red flag? Maybe. A reason to keep dating—and eventually marry him? Absolutely. In his honor, I give you Ultimate Chocolate Cupcakes, perfect for celebrations, birthdays, entertaining, and simply embracing the undeniable joy of cake at noon. These beauties are the best I've ever had—chocolatey, rich with a touch of coffee to boost the chocolate flavor and keep the crumb uncommonly crumbly. The chocolate buttercream gets a lift with a swirl of cream cheese, adding just the right amount of tang to balance the lush dark chocolate. Bake them for the people you love, and don't be surprised when they become a forever request.

---

1. **MAKE THE CHOCOLATE CUPCAKES:** Place two racks in the center of the oven and preheat the oven to 375°F. Line 2 muffin pans with paper baking cups.
2. In a medium bowl, whisk the flour, cocoa powder, espresso powder, baking soda, baking powder, and salt until there are no clumps. Set aside.
3. In the bowl of a stand mixer fitted with the whisk attachment (or in a bowl using a handheld mixer), add the sugars, buttermilk, oil, eggs, and vanilla and mix on low speed until combined, 1 to 2 minutes.
4. Slowly begin adding the dry ingredients to the wet, mixing just until combined and scraping down the sides with a silicone spatula as needed. Turn off the mixer and pour in the coffee, then mix on low speed just until combined—don't overmix!
5. With a ⅓ cup measuring cup, scoop the batter and add to each baking cup, filling them about ⅔ of the way. Bake with one tray on each rack for about 12 minutes, then rotate the pans, switching the pans from the lower rack to the higher and rotating them from front to back.

(recipe continues)

FOR THE CHOCOLATE BUTTERCREAM FROSTING (SEE HOT TIPS)

- ¾ cup chopped semisweet chocolate (4 ounces)
- 4 cups powdered sugar
- ¾ cup Dutch-processed cocoa powder
- ½ teaspoon kosher salt
- 2 sticks (16 tablespoons) unsalted butter, at room temperature
- 8 ounces cream cheese, at room temperature
- 2 teaspoons pure vanilla bean paste or extract
- ⅓ cup whole milk

PERFECT PAIRING

A sweet wine like Banyuls is a classic pairing with anything chocolate, or sip with a Cabernet Sauvignon carried over from dinner.

6. Bake for 9 to 12 minutes more (21 to 24 minutes total), until a toothpick inserted in the center comes out clean. Let cool for at least 10 minutes in the pan before transferring to a wire rack to cool completely before frosting.
7. **MAKE THE CHOCOLATE BUTTERCREAM FROSTING:** In a small, microwave-safe bowl, add the chocolate and microwave in 30-second increments, scraping down the sides of the bowl and stirring after each round, until the chocolate is melted and glossy, about 2 minutes total. Allow to cool slightly in the bowl.
8. In a sieve set over a large bowl, sift the powdered sugar, cocoa powder, and salt.
9. In the bowl of a stand mixer fitted with the whisk attachment (or in a bowl using a handheld mixer), add the butter, cream cheese, and vanilla and beat on low until combined. Raise the speed to medium, and beat until the mixture is fluffy and smooth, about 2 minutes.
10. Reduce the speed to low and slowly add the powdered sugar mixture, scraping down the sides of the bowl as needed. Once the mixture is mostly combined, increase the speed to medium and mix until fluffy and smooth, scraping the bowl as needed, about 2 minutes.
11. Reduce the speed to low and pour in the melted chocolate until completely incorporated. Slowly stream in the milk, mixing until the frosting is silky smooth. Set aside at room temperature until the cupcakes have cooled.
12. To frost, place 2 heaping tablespoons of frosting onto each cupcake. Using an offset spatula or a butter knife, swirl the frosting across the surface of the cupcake. Store the cupcakes covered at room temperature for 1 to 2 days or covered in the fridge for 3 to 5 days.

HOT TIPS

No espresso powder? Try instant coffee powder!

The frosting can be made up to 5 days in advance. Refrigerate in an airtight container and bring to room temperature before frosting.

Loaded Brown Butter Chocolate Chip Cookies

MAKES 24 COOKIES • **TOTAL TIME** 45 MINUTES (PLUS CHILL TIME)

- 2 cups all-purpose flour
- 1 teaspoon baking soda
- 1 teaspoon kosher salt
- 2 sticks (16 tablespoons) unsalted butter, divided
- 1 cup lightly packed light brown sugar
- ¼ cup granulated sugar
- 2 teaspoons pure vanilla bean paste or extract
- 1 large egg plus 2 large egg yolks, at room temperature
- Scant ¾ cup chopped 70 to 80% dark chocolate (or your favorite)
- 2 (1.4-ounce) Heath candy bars, chopped
- ½ cup chopped pretzel sticks
- Flaky sea salt, for garnish

PERFECT PAIRING

Got milk?

I set out to create the most definitively delicious chocolate chip cookie for you—and somewhere between the late-night baking sessions and a dozen test batches, I became completely obsessed. Five variations? Of course. Three actual 2:00 a.m. breakthroughs with over fifteen hours of testing? Absolutely. The result? A cookie that nails the sweet-salty balance, packed with deep brown butter flavor, crisp edges, and a perfectly chewy center. But I didn't stop there. These are loaded—stuffed with melty chocolate chunks, nostalgic Heath bar bits, and just the right amount of salty pretzel pieces for that extra crunchiness. The hardest part? Waiting an hour for the dough to chill (but trust me, it's worth it for the texture). And did I mention there's no mixer required? They freeze beautifully (see Hot Tip), so stash some dough for future cravings—you'll thank yourself later.

1. Line 2 sheet pans (that will fit in your fridge, or a few plates) with parchment paper and set aside.
2. In a medium bowl, whisk the flour, baking soda, and salt.
3. Cut 1 stick of butter into small cubes and place in a large, heatproof bowl. Set in the fridge to chill.
4. In a small saucepan over medium heat, melt the remaining 1 stick of butter. Stir constantly with a wooden spoon until the butter begins to foam, then turns golden brown and smells nutty, about 4 minutes. Immediately remove from the heat. Pour the browned butter, scraping up all the browned bits from the bottom of the saucepan, over the chilled cubed butter. Whisk until the butter melts completely, 1 to 2 minutes.
5. Add the sugars and vanilla and whisk until well combined. Add the egg and egg yolks one at a time, whisking to fully incorporate each before adding the next.

(recipe continues)

HOT TIP

This dough was made for the freezer! Once the dough balls are frozen, transfer them to a gallon-size resealable bag, seal, and store for up to one month in the freezer. To bake frozen cookies, thaw to room temperature, and increase the baking time by 1 to 2 minutes.

6. Using a silicone spatula, fold in the dry ingredients in small batches, scraping down the sides as needed, until no streaks of flour remain. Don't overmix! Fold in the chopped chocolate, Heath bars, and pretzels until evenly distributed.
7. Using a 1-ounce cookie scoop or large spoon, evenly portion the dough into 24 (2 tablespoon-sized) balls and place them on one of the prepared sheet pans. Cover with plastic wrap and transfer to the fridge to chill for about 1 hour.
8. Place racks in the upper and lower thirds of the oven and pre-heat the oven to 350°F.
9. Place 12 cookies per sheet pan, leaving at least 2 inches between each cookie.
10. Bake one pan on each rack for 4 minutes, then rotate the pans, switching the pans from the lower rack to the higher and rotating them from front to back. Bake for 4 to 6 more minutes (8 to 10 minutes total), until the cookies are golden at the edges and slightly gooey in the middle.
11. Sprinkle with the flaky salt and set the pans on wire racks to cool for about 5 minutes. Transfer the cookies from the tray directly onto the wire rack for another 10 minutes—if you can wait that long!

No-Churn Cannoli Ice Cream

SERVES 6 TO 8 • **TOTAL TIME** 15 MINUTES (PLUS CHILL TIME)

- 2 cups heavy cream, chilled
- 1 (14-ounce) can sweetened condensed milk
- 1 teaspoon pure vanilla bean paste or extract
- ¾ teaspoon almond extract
- ¼ teaspoon kosher salt
- ½ cup semisweet mini chocolate chips, plus more for garnish
- ½ cup chopped butter crisps, such as Jules Destrooper (see Hot Tips), plus more for garnish
- ⅓ cup chopped salted roasted pistachios, plus more for garnish
- 2 teaspoons grated orange zest, plus more for garnish
- Flaky sea salt, for garnish

PERFECT PAIRING

A chilled and sweet Sauternes, Vin Santo, or Moscato d'Asti would be amazing!

When cannoli dips were all the rage online, I took inspiration from my time at Pasticceria Minotauro, a family-owned pastry shop in Taormina, where I learned the art of crafting cannoli. Traditionally, the crisp shells are filled with a sweet ricotta mixture, often accented with pistachios, orange zest, and chocolate—flavors that instantly transport me back to that Sicilian bakery. One sweltering summer day, I had a thought: What if that luscious filling became ice cream? Meet this no-churn masterpiece, where almond, heavy cream, and sweetened condensed milk come together in a ridiculously simple, ultra-creamy frozen treat. Speckled with crunchy pops of pistachio, orange, chocolate chips, and crushed butter crisp cookies (my take on the shell), it delivers all the charm of a cannoli with none of the fuss. Just mix, freeze, and *andiamo*!

1. Place a 9 x 5-inch loaf pan in the freezer to chill while you prepare the ice cream.
2. In the bowl of a stand mixer fitted with the whisk attachment (or in a bowl using a handheld mixer), add the cream and whip on low speed, slowly increasing the speed to medium-high until medium stiff peaks form, 3 to 5 minutes. Watch carefully and don't overwhip.
3. Using a wooden spoon or silicone spatula, gently fold in the sweetened condensed milk, vanilla, almond extract, and salt until just combined. Fold in the chocolate chips, butter crisps, pistachios, and orange zest.
4. Immediately pour the mixture into the chilled loaf pan and, using a silicone spatula or spoon, smooth over the top. Sprinkle with generous spoonfuls of chocolate chips, butter crisps, and pistachios.
5. Cover tightly with plastic wrap and freeze until firm, about 6 hours.
6. **TO SERVE:** Using an ice cream scoop (see Hot Tips), scoop into glasses or bowls and top with the orange zest and flaky salt.

HOT TIPS

If you can't find butter crisps, try chopped waffle cones.

To easily scoop ice cream, dip the scoop into a cup of hot water in between each scoop.

Sisterhood of the Traveling Zucchini Carrot Cake

SERVES 10 TO 12 • **TOTAL TIME** 1 HOUR 10 MINUTES

FOR THE ZUCCHINI CARROT CAKE

- Softened unsalted butter, for the pans
- 2 cups all-purpose flour
- 2 teaspoons baking soda
- 1 teaspoon ground cinnamon
- ½ teaspoon ground allspice
- ½ teaspoon kosher salt
- 4 large eggs, at room temperature
- 1¼ cups granulated sugar
- 1 cup virgin unrefined coconut oil, melted and cooled to room temperature
- ¼ cup shaken buttermilk, at room temperature
- 2 teaspoons pure vanilla bean paste or extract
- 2 cups packed shredded carrots
- 1 cup shredded zucchini
- 1 (8-ounce) can crushed pineapple, drained
- ¾ cup chopped toasted walnuts (see Hot Tips)

I may be biased (ok, I am!), but I believe with all my heart that this is the best carrot cake around. It's moist, richly textured, and addictively balanced in sweetness, spice, and tang. This family heirloom has been passed down through generations of carrot cake fans, each one improving and personalizing it like a well-loved playlist—tweaking, remixing, and fine-tuning until it hit all the right notes. The recipe started with my mom's best friend's mother, who shared it with Auntie Bug, who passed it to my mom, and eventually, to me. My contributions? Crushed pineapple for extra moisture, shredded zucchini for tender texture, coconut oil for richness, a touch of allspice for warmth, and of course, an irresistible cream cheese frosting (see Hot Tips). If you miraculously have leftovers, store them covered in the fridge—but don't forget to bring the cake to room temp before serving for that just-baked taste.

---

1. **MAKE THE ZUCCHINI CARROT CAKE:** Preheat the oven to 350°F. Butter 2 (9-inch round) cake pans and line the bottoms with rounds of parchment paper (see Hot Tips).
2. In a large bowl, whisk the flour, baking soda, cinnamon, allspice, and salt until combined.
3. In a separate large bowl, beat the eggs with a handheld mixer or whisk until the yolks and whites are one uniform color, about 30 seconds. Add the sugar, oil, buttermilk, and vanilla and whisk or beat until incorporated.
4. While whisking, slowly add the dry ingredients. Once only a few streaks of flour remain, use a silicone spatula to fold in the carrots, zucchini, pineapple, and walnuts until just combined.
5. Divide the batter between the prepared baking pans and, using a spatula, smooth the top. Bake for 25 to 30 minutes, until a toothpick inserted in the center comes out clean. Allow the cakes to cool in the pans on a wire rack for at least 10 minutes. Run a knife around the edge of the pans and invert the cakes

(recipe continues)

FOR THE CREAM CHEESE FROSTING

16 ounces cream cheese, at room temperature

1 stick (8 tablespoons) unsalted butter, at room temperature

1½ teaspoons pure vanilla bean paste or extract

½ teaspoon kosher salt

3½ cups powdered sugar

Ground cinnamon, to garnish

PERFECT PAIRING

A sweet sparkling wine with notes of pear and Meyer lemon, like Moscato d'Asti or Asti Spumante.

onto the wire rack (removing the parchment if it sticks to the cakes). Turn them right side up and let cool completely.

6. **MAKE THE CREAM CHEESE FROSTING:** In the bowl of a stand mixer fitted with the whisk attachment, (or in a large bowl if using a handheld mixer), beat the cream cheese and butter on medium-high speed until smooth and fluffy, about 2 minutes. Reduce the speed to medium-low, add the vanilla and salt, and mix to incorporate. Add the powdered sugar and beat until smooth, 2 to 3 minutes more.
7. Once the cakes are completely cooled, place one cake on a large plate or cake stand and use a spatula to spread about ¾ cup of the frosting in an even layer over the top. Place the second cake on top and frost the top and sides of the cakes evenly with the remainder of the frosting. Garnish with a dusting of cinnamon.

HOT TIPS

To line a circular pan with parchment paper, trace the outline of the bottom of the pan with a pencil and cut the parchment accordingly. Flip the parchment over so the side with markings faces the bottom of the pan.

To easily toast nuts, warm in a small skillet over medium heat until fragrant and golden brown, 3 to 5 minutes. No walnuts? Try toasted pecans.

If you're a frosting fanatic, make 1½ times the recipe for a thicker coating.

Toasted Coconut Cupcakes
with Brown Butter Cream Cheese Frosting

SERVES 24 • **TOTAL TIME** 1 HOUR 30 MINUTES

FOR THE COCONUT CUPCAKES

3 cups all-purpose flour

2 teaspoons baking powder

¾ teaspoon kosher salt

½ teaspoon baking soda

1½ sticks (12 tablespoons) unsalted butter, at room temperature

½ cup virgin unrefined coconut oil, melted and cooled to room temperature

1⅔ cups granulated sugar

5 large eggs, at room temperature

1 tablespoon pure vanilla bean paste or extract

½ teaspoon coconut extract

½ cup sour cream

1¼ cups shaken buttermilk, at room temperature

½ cup sweetened shredded coconut

These light and fluffy coconut cupcakes are inspired by our wedding cakes—yes, there were two!—a coconut cream masterpiece and a lemon lavender layer cake. (Andrew lobbied for cookies and cream, but let's say he learned an early lesson in marital compromise!) The coconut cream was a huge hit, and I've been dreaming of re-creating it for everyday cravings ever since. This cupcake version goes all in on coconut flavor without going overboard: coconut oil, shredded coconut, and coconut extract in the batter, plus a generous sprinkle of toasted coconut on top. The brown butter cream cheese frosting is bliss and brings a layer of everlasting happiness!

---

1. **MAKE THE COCONUT CUPCAKES:** Place two racks close to the center of the oven and preheat the oven to 375°F. Line 2 muffin pans with paper baking cups.
2. In a medium bowl, whisk the flour, baking powder, salt, and baking soda.
3. In the bowl of a stand mixer fitted with the whisk attachment (or in a bowl using a handheld mixer), add the butter and oil and beat on medium-low until combined, 2 to 3 minutes. Add the sugar and beat on medium-high until pale yellow and fluffy, scraping down the sides as needed, about 2 minutes.
4. With the mixer on low, add the eggs one at a time, fully incorporating each before adding the next, then add the vanilla and coconut extract. Raise the speed to medium-high and beat until smooth and fluffy, scraping down the sides as needed, about 3 minutes. Reduce the speed to medium-low, add the sour cream, and mix until just combined.
5. Reduce the speed to low, add half of the dry ingredients, mix until just combined, add half of the buttermilk, and mix until just combined. Repeat the process and mix until smooth, about 1 minute—don't overmix! Using a silicone spatula, gently fold in the shredded coconut.

(recipe continues)

FOR THE BROWN BUTTER CREAM CHEESE FROSTING

1½ sticks (12 tablespoons) unsalted butter, divided, at room temperature

8 ounces cream cheese, at room temperature

1 tablespoon pure vanilla bean paste or extract

½ teaspoon kosher salt

4 cups powdered sugar

FOR THE TOASTED COCONUT TOPPING

2½ cups sweetened shredded coconut

PERFECT PAIRING

A white Vermouth from Italy or France on the rocks, with an orange twist.

HOT TIP

Muffin pans can vary slightly in size—if you have any leftover batter, just bake off a few more!

6. Fill each baking cup about ¾ of the way full (see Hot Tip).
7. Bake for 10 minutes, then rotate the pans, switching the pans from the lower rack to the higher and rotating them from front to back. Continue to bake for 7 to 10 minutes more (17 to 20 minutes total), until golden around the edges and a toothpick inserted in the center comes out clean. Transfer to a wire rack to cool completely in the pan before frosting. Clean the batter bowl while the cupcakes cool.
8. **MAKE THE BROWN BUTTER CREAM CHEESE FROSTING:** Add 4 tablespoons of the butter in a small saucepan over medium heat, stirring constantly with a wooden spoon, until golden brown and the aroma is nutty, 2 to 3 minutes. Immediately pour the brown butter into the clean batter bowl and let cool to room temperature.
9. Add the remaining 8 tablespoons of butter, cream cheese, vanilla, and salt and beat on medium speed until smooth, about 1 minute. Reduce the speed to low and slowly add the powdered sugar, scraping down the sides as needed, until just combined. Raise the speed to medium, and beat until fluffy, 1 to 2 minutes.
10. **MAKE THE TOASTED COCONUT TOPPING:** Preheat the oven to 375°F.
11. On a sheet pan, spread 1 cup of the shredded coconut into an even layer. Bake, stirring halfway through, for 6 to 8 minutes, until deep golden brown. Immediately transfer to a wide shallow bowl along with the remaining 1½ cups shredded coconut and combine. Let cool completely.
12. To assemble, using an offset spatula or butter knife, evenly spread about 1½ tablespoons of frosting over each cupcake. Dip the top of each frosted cupcake into the toasted coconut, pressing lightly to fully coat.
13. Store the frosted cupcakes covered at room temperature for 1 day or in a resealable container in the fridge for up to 3 days.

PERFECT PAIRING

A glass of Prosecco or a zippy French Jurançon Sec.

Key Lime Pie with Pecan Graham Cracker Crust

SERVES 10 TO 12 • **TOTAL TIME** 50 MINUTES (PLUS CHILL TIME)

For our five-year wedding anniversary, Andrew surprised me with a key lime pie, squeezing dozens of tiny limes by hand, as quickly and quietly as he could before I woke up. True love as far as I'm concerned! That anniversary pie sent me on a mission (almost) impossible to improve on one of my favorite desserts: I added pecans to the graham cracker crust for crunch, folded in sour cream and lime zest to the filling for creaminess and zing, and topped it with a heavenly sweet vanilla bean whipped cream to tie it all together. I hope you'll agree it's the best key lime pie out there!

FOR THE PECAN GRAHAM CRACKER CRUST

- 12 graham cracker sheets
- ½ cup pecan halves
- 1 stick (8 tablespoons) unsalted butter, melted
- 1 tablespoon turbinado (raw) or granulated sugar
- ½ teaspoon kosher salt

FOR THE FILLING

- 4 large egg yolks, at room temperature
- 1 tablespoon grated lime zest, plus more for garnish
- 2 (14-ounce) cans sweetened condensed milk
- ¾ cup key lime juice (about 6 limes) (see Hot Tip)
- ½ cup sour cream or full-fat Greek yogurt
- ½ teaspoon pure vanilla bean paste or extract
- ½ teaspoon kosher salt

FOR THE WHIPPED CREAM

- 1 cup heavy cream
- ¼ cup powdered sugar, sifted
- 2 teaspoons pure vanilla bean paste or extract
- ¼ teaspoon kosher salt

1. **MAKE THE PECAN GRAHAM CRACKER CRUST:** Preheat the oven to 350°F.
2. In a food processor or blender, blend the graham crackers and pecans until the texture of coarse sand, 10 to 15 seconds. Add the melted butter, sugar, and salt, and pulse a few times until the mixture resembles coarse wet sand. Don't over-blend!
3. Transfer the mixture to a deep 9- or 10-inch pie plate and pack the mixture down to evenly coat the bottom and the sides of the pan. Bake for 8 to 10 minutes, until light golden brown on the edges. Allow to cool completely in the pan at room temperature.
4. **MAKE THE FILLING:** In a large bowl, whisk the egg yolks and lime zest until well combined. Whisk in the sweetened condensed milk, lime juice, sour cream, vanilla, and salt until well incorporated.
5. Pour the mixture into the cooled pie crust and, using a silicone spatula, smooth the top. Bake for 18 to 20 minutes, until the filling is mostly set but jiggles slightly. Allow to cool completely in the pan at room temperature, then cover and refrigerate for a minimum of 3 hours or overnight.
6. **MAKE THE WHIPPED CREAM:** In the bowl of a stand mixer fitted with the whisk attachment (or in a large bowl if using a handheld mixer), combine the cream, powdered sugar, vanilla, and salt on low speed, slowly increasing the speed to medium-high until medium stiff peaks form, 3 to 5 minutes. Watch carefully, as it's easy to overwhip the cream. Cover and refrigerate until ready to serve.
7. **TO SERVE:** Slice the pie and transfer to serving plates. Top with a generous dollop of whipped cream and lime zest.

HOT TIP

If you can't find Nellie & Joe's (or key limes), use a fresh mix of ½ cup lime juice and ¼ cup lemon juice.

Limoncello Tiramisu

SERVES 12 • **TOTAL TIME** 40 MINUTES (PLUS CHILL TIME)

FOR THE LIMONCELLO SYRUP

1 cup limoncello

½ cup granulated sugar

¼ cup grated lemon zest (about 2 lemons)

⅓ cup fresh lemon juice (about 3 lemons)

FOR THE MASCARPONE CREAM AND ASSEMBLY

4 large eggs, separated, divided, at room temperature

⅔ cup granulated sugar, divided

16 ounces mascarpone cheese, at room temperature

2 cups heavy cream, cold

2 teaspoons grated lemon zest, plus more for garnish

2 tablespoons fresh lemon juice (about 1 lemon)

2 (7-ounce) packs of ladyfinger biscuits (48 biscuits)

Fresh mint leaves, for garnish

PERFECT PAIRING

A Moscato d'Asti would be incredible and, of course, so would more limoncello!

Some desserts are too good to keep to yourself—like this limoncello tiramisu. We first tasted it in a cooking class at Latteria, a family-owned grocery store in Positano, and after a dozen rounds of testing, I found limoncello tiramisu perfection. It's a little slice of sunny Italy right at home.

1. **MAKE THE LIMONCELLO SYRUP:** In a medium saucepan, combine 1½ cups water, the limoncello, sugar, lemon zest, and lemon juice and bring to a boil over high heat. Reduce to medium heat and simmer, stirring occasionally, until the sugar dissolves and the mixture thickens slightly, 6 to 8 minutes. Pour into a large, shallow dish and let cool.
2. **MAKE THE MASCARPONE CREAM:** In a large bowl with a handheld mixer (see Hot Tip), add the egg yolks and ⅓ cup of the sugar and beat on medium-high until pale yellow, scraping down the sides as needed, 2 to 3 minutes. Gently fold in the mascarpone until just incorporated.
3. In a second large bowl, add the egg whites and beat on medium-high speed until soft peaks form, about 2 minutes. Gradually add in the remaining ⅓ cup of sugar and beat until stiff and glossy peaks form, 2 to 4 minutes.
4. In a third large bowl, whip the cream on low, slowly raising to medium-high until medium stiff peaks form, 4 to 5 minutes. Don't overwhip the cream.
5. Gently fold the cream into the mascarpone mixture until mostly incorporated. Fold in the lemon zest, lemon juice, and whipped egg whites until mostly incorporated—don't overmix!
6. **TO ASSEMBLE:** Dip each ladyfinger into the cooled limoncello simple syrup for 1 to 2 seconds, and arrange in an even layer on the bottom of a deep 9 x 13-inch baking dish. Spread ⅓ of the mascarpone cream over the ladyfingers. Repeat to create 3 layers and end with the mascarpone cream. Cover and refrigerate for at least 4 hours, or overnight.
7. **TO SERVE:** Cut into squares and evenly divide among serving plates. Garnish with the mint leaves and more lemon zest.

Orange Blossom Olive Oil Cake

with Honey Mascarpone Cream

SERVES 8 TO 10 • **TOTAL TIME** 1 HOUR 15 MINUTES

FOR THE ORANGE BLOSSOM OLIVE OIL CAKE

1 cup extra-virgin olive oil, plus more for the pan

1¾ cups all-purpose flour

½ cup medium grind cornmeal

1 teaspoon baking soda

1 teaspoon baking powder

½ teaspoon kosher salt

1 cup granulated sugar, plus more for topping

1 tablespoon grated orange zest (about 1 orange), plus more for garnish

4 large eggs, at room temperature

3 tablespoons fresh orange juice (about ½ orange)

1 teaspoon orange blossom water (see Hot Tip)

FOR THE HONEY MASCARPONE CREAM

8 ounces mascarpone cheese

½ cup heavy cream

¼ cup honey

1 teaspoon pure vanilla bean paste or extract

FOR GARNISH

Chopped salted roasted pistachios

Flaky sea salt

This olive oil cake is pure alchemy—the kind of dessert that feels effortless but delivers unexpected depth. It's fruity, lightly floral, and rich, with a bright cornmeal and citrus crumb thanks to a simple trick: massaging orange zest into the sugar to release its natural oils. High-quality olive oil is the not-so-secret key here, delivering a perfectly moist cake and that unmistakable Mediterranean touch. Freshly squeezed orange juice and a hint of orange blossom water bring even more sunshine to every bite, while a dusting of sugar on top bakes into a delicate, crackly crust and pop of sweetness to contrast with the dollop of honey mascarpone cream. A sprinkle of salty pistachios and extra orange zest are the final touch for a dessert that tastes like a Mediterranean escape.

---

1. **MAKE THE ORANGE BLOSSOM OLIVE OIL CAKE:** Position a rack in the middle of the oven and preheat to 375°F. Lightly oil the bottom and sides of a 9-inch springform pan, and line the bottom with parchment paper.
2. In a medium bowl, whisk the flour, cornmeal, baking soda, baking powder, and salt.
3. In the bowl of a stand mixer fitted with the whisk attachment (or in a bowl using a handheld mixer), add the sugar and orange zest. Using your fingers, rub the zest into the sugar until pale orange and fragrant, about 1 minute.
4. Add the eggs and beat on medium speed until slightly thickened, 3 to 5 minutes. Add the orange juice and orange blossom water and beat on medium speed until just combined.
5. Reduce the speed to low and slowly stream in the remaining 1 cup of oil. Raise the speed to medium and beat until combined, using a silicone spatula to scrape down the sides as needed, about 1 minute.

(recipe continues)

PERFECT PAIRING

A sweet and perfectly acidic late harvest Sauvignon Blanc or Sauternes would balance this cake beautifully.

HOT TIP

Orange blossom water is a special ingredient to say the least! Also known as orange flower water, or neroli water, it lends an unmistakable floral note that elevates everything from desserts to cocktails. You can find it online. Store tightly sealed in a cool and dark place (no refrigeration required).

6. Add about half of the dry ingredients and beat on low speed until just combined. Add the remaining dry ingredients and beat on low speed until no dry streaks remain. Don't overmix!
7. Pour the batter into the prepared pan and place on a sheet tray. Sprinkle a few generous spoonfuls of sugar over the top.
8. Bake for 15 minutes, until the cake just begins to rise, then reduce the heat to 350°F and continue to bake for 22 to 25 minutes (37 to 40 minutes total), until the top is golden and a toothpick inserted in the center comes out clean. Transfer to a baking rack and allow to cool completely in the pan before releasing from the springform pan and frosting.
9. **MAKE THE HONEY MASCARPONE CREAM:** In the bowl of a stand mixer fitted with the whisk attachment (or in a bowl using a handheld mixer), add the mascarpone, cream, honey, and vanilla and beat on low speed until smooth. Raise to medium speed and continue to beat until soft peaks form, 5 to 6 minutes.
10. Run a butter knife around the edge of the cake and release it from the springform pan. Remove the parchment paper from the bottom of the cake and transfer to a large plate or cake stand. Using an offset spatula or butter knife, spread the frosting in generous swoops across the top. Top with the chopped pistachios, orange zest, and flaky salt. Slice and serve.

Skillet Berry Crumble

SERVES 10 • **TOTAL TIME** 1 HOUR 35 MINUTES

FOR THE CRUMBLE TOPPING

- 1½ sticks (12 tablespoons) unsalted butter, melted, plus more for the skillet
- 1 cup lightly packed light brown sugar
- 1 teaspoon grated lemon zest
- 1¼ cups all-purpose flour
- 1¼ cups rolled oats
- ½ teaspoon ground cinnamon
- ¾ teaspoon kosher salt

FOR THE FILLING

- 1 teaspoon grated orange zest
- 1 teaspoon grated lemon zest
- 2 tablespoons fresh orange juice
- 2 tablespoons fresh lemon juice (about 1 lemon)
- 2 tablespoons cornstarch
- 2 teaspoons pure vanilla bean paste or extract
- 2 pounds mixed berries of choice
- ½ cup lightly packed light brown sugar
- 1½ teaspoons ground cinnamon
- 1 teaspoon ground ginger
- ½ teaspoon ground nutmeg
- Vanilla bean ice cream, for serving

PERFECT PAIRING

A sweet wine, like a fortified Muscat or a Sauternes, works great.

A bubbling, warm fruit crumble, crowned with melting vanilla bean ice cream, is pure comfort in dessert form. Its appeal lies not just in its golden, crisp topping or jammy fruit filling, but in its effortless versatility. I love the deep sweetness of mixed berries, but this crumble easily shifts with the seasons—apples and pears in the fall, peaches and stone fruit in the heat of summer, or a glossy, ruby sweet and tart blend of strawberries and rhubarb come spring. Frozen fruit works just as well; simply add an additional ¼ cup of all-purpose flour or 2 tablespoons of cornstarch to help absorb extra juices. It's a fuss-free, no-fail combination that delivers big flavor with minimal effort—ideal for a low-maintenance dessert that feels special.

1. Place one oven rack in the top third of the oven and one in the middle and preheat the oven to 350°F. Butter a 12-inch cast-iron skillet or 9 x 13-inch baking dish. Line a sheet pan with parchment paper or aluminum foil.
2. **MAKE THE CRUMBLE TOPPING:** In a medium bowl, add the brown sugar and lemon zest. Using your fingers, rub the zest into the sugar until pale orange and fragrant, about 1 minute. Add the flour, oats, cinnamon, and salt and, using a wooden spoon or silicone spatula, mix well. Add the melted butter and mix until evenly combined and pea-sized crumbles form.
3. **MAKE THE FILLING:** In a large bowl, whisk the orange zest, lemon zest, orange juice, lemon juice, cornstarch, and vanilla until no clumps remain. Add the berries, brown sugar, cinnamon, ginger, and nutmeg and toss with a spoon until evenly coated.
4. Transfer the berry mixture and all the juices to the buttered skillet and place on top of the lined sheet pan. Sprinkle the crumble evenly on top.
5. Bake for 35 minutes. Raise the heat to 400°F, transfer to the top rack of the oven, and continue to bake for about 35 minutes more (70 minutes total), until the top is golden and crisp and the fruit is thick and bubbly. If you want the crumble extra toasty, turn the broiler on high for the last 2 to 3 minutes. Allow to cool for at least 5 minutes.
6. **TO SERVE:** Divide among serving bowls and top with a big scoop of vanilla bean ice cream.

Spiced Date Bread Pudding
with Salted Butterscotch Sauce

SERVES 8 TO 10 • **TOTAL TIME** 1 HOUR 30 MINUTES

FOR THE SPICED DATE BREAD PUDDING

1 stick (8 tablespoons) unsalted butter, plus more for the pan

8 Medjool dates, pitted and coarsely chopped

½ cup dark spiced rum

1 cup lightly packed light brown sugar

5 large eggs

2 cups heavy cream

1 cup half-and-half

1 tablespoon pure vanilla bean paste or extract

2 teaspoons pumpkin pie spice (see Hot Tips)

½ teaspoon kosher salt

1 loaf day-old stale brioche (about 1 pound), cut or torn into 1-inch pieces (see Hot Tips)

¾ cup chopped pecans

FOR THE SALTED BUTTERSCOTCH SAUCE

1 stick (8 tablespoons) unsalted butter

1 cup lightly packed light brown sugar

1 cup heavy cream

2 teaspoons kosher salt

2 teaspoons pure vanilla bean paste or extract

FOR SERVING

Vanilla bean ice cream

Flaky sea salt

This bread pudding is brimming with warm spices, nutty brown butter, toasty pecans, and rum-soaked dates adding an almost toffee-like sweetness. Drenched in salted butterscotch sauce and crowned with vanilla bean ice cream, it's both indulgent and comforting. Need I say more? Pillowy brioche (stale or oven-dried, see Hot Tips) soaks up a spiced custard creating layers of caramelized bits and golden crust. Even better, it improves overnight—just reheat in a 350°F oven or pop it in the microwave. One last tip: Seriously consider making a double batch of the sauce! I drizzle it on everything.

1. **MAKE THE SPICED DATE BREAD PUDDING:** Preheat the oven to 350°F. Butter a 9 x 13-inch baking dish.
2. In a small bowl, soak the dates and rum while you make the pudding.
3. In a small saucepan, melt the butter over medium heat, stirring constantly, until golden brown and the aroma is nutty, about 4 minutes. Immediately pour into a large heatproof bowl, including all the browned bits from the bottom.
4. Whisk in the brown sugar and eggs until combined. Add the cream, half-and-half, vanilla, pumpkin pie spice, and salt and whisk until smooth. Add the bread to the custard mixture and, using your hands or a large spoon, toss until coated.
5. Using a slotted spoon or small mesh strainer, strain the dates and transfer to the pudding mixture. Discard the rum (or save for a cocktail!). Add the pecans and mix until evenly distributed.
6. Transfer into the prepared baking dish and spread into an even layer. Bake for 60 to 70 minutes, until the liquid is absorbed and the custard is mostly set. Allow to cool for 10 minutes in the pan before serving.

(recipe continues)

PERFECT PAIRING

Madeira, a fortified wine from Portugal, with semisweet flavor and notes of cloves, caramel, and toasted nuts—or the Blackberry Bourbon Smash (page 292).

7. **MEANWHILE, MAKE THE SALTED BUTTERSCOTCH SAUCE:** In a medium pot, melt the butter over medium-low heat. Add the brown sugar, cream, and salt and bring to a boil over medium-high heat. Cook, stirring constantly, until light golden brown, the aroma is nutty, and it's thickened enough to coat the back of a spoon, about 5 minutes. Off heat, stir in the vanilla.
8. **TO SERVE:** Spoon warm bread pudding into shallow bowls and top with vanilla bean ice cream, butterscotch sauce, and a sprinkle of flaky salt.

HOT TIPS

Have a fresh loaf of brioche, but nothing stale? Bake the bread pieces on a sheet pan at 350°F until dried and slightly crisp, about 15 minutes. Using oven-dried bread may require less final bake time: Start checking the pudding for doneness at 50 minutes.

To make your own pumpkin pie spice, use ½ teaspoon ground cinnamon, ½ teaspoon ground ginger, ½ teaspoon ground nutmeg, ¼ teaspoon ground cloves, and ¼ teaspoon ground allspice.

If your pudding is set but not crisp, turn the broiler on high and cook until the top is golden brown and lightly crisp, 2 to 3 minutes. Cool for 10 minutes before serving.

Peaches & Sour Cream Upside Down Cake

SERVES 10 TO 12 • **TOTAL TIME** 1 HOUR

- 1 stick (8 tablespoons) unsalted butter, at room temperature, divided, plus more for greasing
- 2 medium yellow peaches, pitted and sliced ¼-inch thick
- ¼ cup lightly packed light brown sugar
- ¾ teaspoon kosher salt, divided
- 1½ cups all-purpose flour
- 1½ teaspoons baking powder
- ¾ cup granulated sugar
- 2 teaspoons grated lemon zest
- 2 large eggs, at room temperature
- 1 cup sour cream, at room temperature
- 1 teaspoon pure vanilla bean paste or extract
- Vanilla bean ice cream, for serving

PERFECT PAIRING

One of the world's best sweet wines, Sauternes, would be phenomenal; a white Zinfandel would be fun as well!

What to do with all those gorgeous fresh summer peaches? Bake a tender sour cream upside down cake. It's beautifully moist, with a bouncy, delicate crumb, and decadent caramelized fruit on top. Serve warm with a big scoop of vanilla bean ice cream, wake up to it for breakfast, or let it revive you as an afternoon snack with coffee. Bring this to a summer BBQ or potluck or to anyone in your life who needs a little more sweetness in their day. This recipe works well with plums, too.

1. Preheat the oven to 350°F. Butter a 9-inch round cake pan.
2. Arrange the sliced peaches in concentric circles in the bottom of the prepared pan, overlapping the slices as needed to fit the pan. Place the pan on a sheet pan.
3. In a small saucepan, combine 4 tablespoons of the butter, the brown sugar, and ¼ teaspoon of the salt over medium-low heat. Cook, stirring constantly, until the butter and brown sugar melt and turn golden brown and foamy, 3 to 4 minutes. Immediately, pour the mixture evenly over the peach slices in the pan.
4. In a large bowl, sift together the flour, baking powder, and the remaining ½ teaspoon of salt.
5. In the bowl of a stand mixer fitted with the paddle attachment (or in a bowl using a handheld mixer), add the remaining 4 tablespoons butter, sugar, and lemon zest and beat on medium-high speed until light and fluffy, about 3 minutes. Add the eggs one at a time on medium speed, fully incorporating one before adding the next. Add the sour cream and vanilla and beat on medium-low until incorporated, about 1 minute.
6. While beating on low speed, gradually add the dry ingredients, scraping down the sides of the bowl as needed, until no lumps remain. Don't overmix! Pour the cake batter over the peaches in the prepared cake pan. Evenly spread the batter to the sides.
7. Bake for about 40 minutes, until golden brown and a toothpick inserted in the center comes out clean. Transfer to a wire rack to cool for 15 minutes.
8. Run a knife around the edge of the cake to loosen it from the pan. Place a flat serving plate on top of the cake pan and carefully invert the cake, pouring the juices over the top. Let the cake cool completely, then slice and serve with vanilla bean ice cream.

POPPIN' BOTTLES

Cocktails are liquid confetti—the first pour sets the tone, the bubbles keep things lively, and every sip is an invitation to celebrate. This chapter is all about colorful, stylish, and effortlessly fun drinks that bring people together. Whether it's a fizzy spritz at golden hour, a citrusy margarita that tastes like vacation, a nostalgic icy martini, or a deep, spiced sangria perfect for slow sipping, these cocktails are here to elevate the moment.

I've gathered my favorite fruity, vibrant, and unfussy sips—some built for one, others for a crowd to enjoy with friends and family while cooking, over a meal, or at a party. Their bright flavors and fresh ingredients are conversation starters themselves. It's all about drinks that flow effortlessly with the dishes in this book, each one designed to complement the flavors and keep the good times going, including individual cocktails, larger servings, and batch recipes for easy entertaining.

All you need is a cocktail shaker, a muddler (or the end of a wooden spoon!), a strainer, a blender, and the right glass in hand. And because the best celebrations are inclusive, nearly every recipe here can be made into a nonalcoholic mocktail—because good vibes don't need booze, just great company and something delicious to sip.

These drinks are as much about flavor as they are about feeling: a Cucumber Basil Martini (page 288) cooling things down alongside Foolproof Date-Night Steak with Creamy Peppercorn Sauce (page 108), Summer Berry Sangria (page 287) swirling around while Spiced Chicken & Black Bean Taco Salad (page 75) comes together, or a Spicy Watermelon Pine-Aperol Margarita (page 284) kicking off the party with Mom's Secret Salsa (page 31) and a never-ending bowl of chips. And if a Limoncello Spritz (page 291) over a plate of Amalfi-Inspired Spaghetti al Limone (page 153) doesn't scream summer in Italy, I don't know what does. Cheers!

Spicy Watermelon Pine-Aperol Margarita

SERVES 2 • **TOTAL TIME** 5 MINUTES

Tajín, for the rim (see Hot Tip)

Lime wedges, for the rim

4 slices fresh jalapeño pepper, plus more for garnish

1 ounce agave nectar or honey

1 ounce fresh lime juice (about 1 lime)

Ice

6 ounces watermelon juice (store-bought or blended and strained from 1½ cups cubed watermelon)

4 ounces pineapple juice, fresh if possible

4 ounces blanco tequila (I love LALO)

2 ounces Aperol

¼ teaspoon kosher salt

Before this margarita came along, I was loyal to a cucumber jalapeño marg. But the moment I mixed up this spicy, sweet, and citrusy dream, it shot straight to the top of my Margarita Hall of Fame. The inspiration? Our wedding cocktails—Andrew's was a watermelon mint margarita (he not-so-secretly loves a fruity drink), while mine brought the heat with spicy pineapple mango. This version blends the best of both, with a surprise twist: Aperol. Its orange, rhubarb, and herbal notes add just the right depth, like the missing puzzle piece every margarita's been waiting for. Andrew's hot tip? Swap tequila for mezcal if you're feeling smoky.

---

1. On a small plate, sprinkle a few tablespoons of Tajín. Run a lime wedge around the rim of two rocks glasses. Dip the rim of each glass into the Tajín to coat.
2. In a large cocktail shaker, using a muddler or the end of a wooden spoon, muddle the jalapeño, agave, and lime juice until slightly broken down, about 45 seconds. Add a large handful of ice along with the watermelon juice, pineapple juice, tequila, Aperol, and salt. Seal the shaker and shake vigorously until the outside is frosty, about 30 seconds.
3. Fill the prepared glasses with ice and strain the margarita between the glasses. Garnish with the jalapeño rounds.

HOT TIP

No Tajín? Use a chile lime seasoning (with salt) or make your own using 1 tablespoon fine chile flakes, ¾ teaspoon kosher salt, and 1 teaspoon lime zest.

Summer Berry Sangria

SERVES 6 TO 8 • **TOTAL TIME** 5 MINUTES (PLUS CHILL TIME)

12 ounces blueberries

2 ounces simple syrup (recipe follows)

2 bottles dry red fruity wine (I use Rioja)

6 ounces raspberry liqueur (such as Chambord)

6 ounces raspberries

1 medium orange, sliced and quartered

3 ounces fresh orange juice (about 1 orange)

½ cup fresh mint

Ice

I fell in love with sangria's effortless charm of wine and fruit in Barcelona a decade ago, and I've been making seasonal versions ever since. It's the ultimate hosting hack—quick to batch, easy to mix, and only gets better as it sits. This summer take is loaded with juicy blueberries and raspberries, raspberry liqueur, fresh orange juice, and a hit of mint. Refreshing, vibrant, and dangerously smooth, it pairs beautifully with just about anything on the table. For the best flavor, let it meld for at least six hours; twenty-four is even better. Short on time? An extra splash of simple syrup mimics the jammy sweet depth of long-macerated fruit, no wait required.

1. In a large pitcher, add half of the blueberries and all the simple syrup. Using a muddler or the end of a wooden spoon, muddle until slightly broken down and the juices release, about 30 seconds.
2. Stir in the remaining blueberries, red wine, raspberry liqueur, raspberries, orange slices, orange juice, and mint until well combined.
3. Cover and refrigerate for at least 6 hours and ideally overnight, for up to 3 days. Serve in large ice-filled wine glasses.

Simple Syrup

MAKES 1½ CUPS • **TOTAL TIME** 10 MINUTES (PLUS CHILL TIME)

The base recipe used to smoothly sweeten many of your drinks. Experiment and simmer with cinnamon, citrus peel, herbs, ginger, and even peppercorns. Strain any flavorings before storing.

In a small pot set over medium-high heat, combine 1 cup granulated sugar and 1 cup water, stirring constantly until the sugar is completely dissolved. Let cool and refrigerate in an airtight bottle or container for up to 2 weeks.

Cucumber Basil Martini

SERVES 2 • **TOTAL TIME** 5 MINUTES

1 small Persian cucumber

1 cup basil, plus sprigs for garnish

1 ounce simple syrup (see page 287)

Ice

4 ounces gin (or vodka)

1 ounce elderflower liqueur (such as St. Germain)

1 ounce fresh lemon juice (about 1 lemon)

This is without question my favorite martini—the kind that has your friends and fam begging for the recipe after the first sip. It's loosely inspired by a basil smash Andrew and I had in Portofino, Italy, where basil (and focaccia!) reign. But here, I took that herbaceous vibe and gave it a fresh twist with crisp cucumber and a splash of elderflower for a subtle floral lift. The result? Smooth, fragrant, and refreshing, landing somewhere between a classic gin martini and a garden-fresh spritz. With its intense green hue and layered botanicals, this martini is stiff enough for martini purists, but easygoing enough for those who usually shy away from them. Whether you shake it up for an elegant cocktail or sip it at a breezy summer dinner outdoors, it just works. Pair it with a plate of Faux-caccia (page 36) for a faux seaside trip to the Ligurian peninsula—no passport required!

---

1. Chill 2 coupe or martini glasses.
2. Using a vegetable peeler, peel 2 thin strips of cucumber and ribbon each strip onto a cocktail pick, then set aside. Slice the cucumber into ¼-inch rounds.
3. In a large cocktail shaker, add 8 cucumber rounds (snack on any leftovers), the basil, and simple syrup. Using a muddler or the end of a wooden spoon, muddle the ingredients until broken down and well combined, about 45 seconds.
4. Add a large handful of ice to the shaker, along with the gin, elderflower liqueur, and lemon juice. Seal the shaker and shake vigorously until the outside is frosty, about 30 seconds.
5. Using a fine mesh strainer, strain the mixture into two chilled glasses. Garnish each with a cucumber-ribboned cocktail pick and a basil sprig.

Limoncello Spritz

SERVES 6 • **TOTAL TIME** 5 MINUTES

- Ice
- 1 bottle Prosecco, cold
- 12 ounces limoncello
- 6 ounces fresh lemon juice (about 6 lemons)
- 6 ounces sparkling water
- 3 ounces simple syrup (see page 287)
- Lemon slices, for garnish
- Fresh mint sprigs, for garnish

If you're true lemon lovers like us, this is the best way to spritz. I had my first limoncello spritz while visiting Amalfi, and it was love at first sip. Limoncello, a southern Italian liqueur made by steeping lemon peels in alcohol and sugar, is intensely aromatic and packed with citrus oils—sweet, slightly tangy, and just the right amount of punchy. Mixed with dry Prosecco and a splash of soda, it's crisp, effervescent, and effortlessly drinkable. One sip takes me straight back to Italy's southwestern coasts and islands, where lemon trees dot the hillsides and every café serves a chilled glass of something citrusy. Paired with Amalfi-Inspired Spaghetti al Limone (page 153)—as I first had it—and you've got the next best thing to dining seaside. I've included both individual spritzes as well as a party version that guarantees very happy guests.

1. Fill 6 wine glasses with ice and pour 4 ounces of Prosecco into each glass.
2. Add 2 ounces of limoncello, 1 ounce of lemon juice, 1 ounce of sparkling water, and ½ ounce of simple syrup to each glass.
3. Stir and garnish with a lemon slice and a sprig of fresh mint.

Blackberry Bourbon Smash

SERVES 2 • **TOTAL TIME** 5 MINUTES

- 1 lemon
- 6 ounces blackberries
- 20 fresh basil leaves, plus sprigs for garnish
- 1 ounce honey
- Ice
- 4 ounces bourbon
- 4 ounces ginger beer

Inspired by our community favorite Peach Bourbon Smash, we were craving a bourbon cocktail that offered a bit more complexity. Enter blackberry and basil. The berries bring natural sweetness with enough tang to cut through bourbon's rich oak, smoke, and vanilla, while the basil adds a fresh herbal and earthy contrast that keeps every sip interesting. Shake this cocktail at summer barbecues, picnics, and poolside hangs. If bourbon's not your jam, swap it for a dark rum or tequila—it plays just as well.

1. Using a vegetable peeler or paring knife, peel 2 thin strips of lemon rind. Spear 3 blackberries each onto 2 cocktail picks or toothpicks and set aside with the lemon rind for garnish.
2. Halve the lemon and squeeze into a large cocktail shaker; discard any seeds. Add the remaining blackberries, the basil, and honey. Using a muddler or the end of a wooden spoon, muddle the ingredients until broken down, about 45 seconds. Add a large handful of ice and the bourbon, seal the shaker, and shake vigorously until the outside is frosty, about 30 seconds.
3. Fill two rocks glasses with ice and strain the mixture into the glasses. Divide the ginger beer between the glasses. Twist the lemon strips directly over the glass, then drop the strips in, and garnish with a blackberry-skewered pick and a basil sprig.

Frozen Coconut Mojito

SERVES 2 • **TOTAL TIME** 5 MINUTES

- $^2/_3$ cup coconut gelato (such as Talenti)
- 3 ounces coconut rum (such as Malibu)
- 3 ounces light rum
- $^1/_3$ cup fresh mint, plus sprigs for garnish
- 1 ounce pineapple juice
- 1 ounce cream of coconut (such as Coco Reàl)
- $^1/_2$ ounce fresh lime juice (about $^1/_2$ lime)
- 2 cups of ice

This beachside-inspired cocktail is what happens when a piña colada and a mojito collide—in the best possible way. Creamy, citrusy, and impossibly smooth, it blends the richness of coconut with the freshness of mint and lime for a sip that's both indulgent and refreshing. My secret ingredient? Coconut gelato. It gives the drink a velvety texture and just the right amount of sweetness, balanced by cream of coconut, pineapple, lime juice, and mint, plus a mix of coconut and light rum. Blended to slushie perfection, it's the ultimate summer drink made for your next pool party, backyard barbecues, or any excuse to bring a little tropical energy to a dinner party.

---

1. In a blender, combine the coconut gelato, coconut rum, light rum, mint, pineapple juice, cream of coconut, lime juice, and ice and blend until smooth, 20 to 30 seconds.
2. Pour into 2 highball glasses and garnish with the mint sprigs.

Slice of Heaven Rossini

SERVES 4 • **TOTAL TIME** 5 TO 10 MINUTES

- 1 pound strawberries, hulled
- ¼ cup granulated sugar
- 1 ounce fresh lemon juice (about 1 lemon)
- ¼ teaspoon pure vanilla bean paste or extract
- 1 bottle Prosecco, chilled
- Edible flowers, for garnish (see Hot Tip)
- Fresh mint sprigs, for garnish

One sip will melt your cares away! The first time we visited Positano, what should have been a smooth journey turned into an eight-hour car trouble saga. By the time we arrived, carsick, exhausted, and bleary-eyed, one thing was clear—we had landed in heaven. Il San Pietro di Positano, with its gorgeous views, welcoming staff, and signature Rossini quickly made it our favorite place on earth. The Slice of Heaven Rossini is my take on the perfect drink—effervescent, lush, and tasting like the ripest, juiciest, most perfectly boozy strawberry. I've added a touch of vanilla bean, fresh lemon, and mint while keeping it so easy to make. Use fresh strawberries, pour generously, and sip slowly—you deserve your own slice of heaven.

1. In a blender, combine the strawberries, sugar, lemon juice, and vanilla and blend until smooth, about 30 seconds. You should have about 2 cups of puree.
2. Pour ½ cup of the strawberry puree into the base of 4 wine glasses. Top each glass with 6 ounces of Prosecco and gently stir to combine. Garnish with edible flowers and a mint sprig.

HOT TIP

Look for edible flowers packaged near the fresh herbs in your local grocery store or farmers' market.

MENUS:

FOR CELEBRATING, GATHERING & INSPIRING

These menus are here to spark ideas—whether you're hosting, unwinding, or just looking for something deliciously different. I've shared many dishes, so feel free to mix, match, or go wild and make them all. And, of course, add your own twist!

LA DOLCE VITA DINNER PARTY

Limoncello Spritz

Faux-caccia

My Big Fat Italian Chopped Salad

Spaghetti alla Nerano (Fried Zucchini Pasta)

Amalfi-Inspired Spaghetti al Limone

Tagliatelle Bolognese

Easy Burrata Lasagna

Magic Meatballs & Marinara

Famous Brown Butter Lemon Chicken

No-Churn Cannoli Ice Cream

Limoncello Tiramisu

TACOS AND TEQUILA

Spicy Watermelon Pine-Aperol Margarita

The Holy Trinity

Chile Mango Halibut Ceviche

Sweet & Spicy Mexican Fruit Salad with Tajín Vinaigrette

Camarones al Mojo de Ajo (Mexican Garlic Shrimp)

Spice-Rubbed Fish Tacos with Cilantro Cabbage Slaw

Mexican Rice

Brothy Frijoles de la Olla (Mexican Beans)

Mom's Cheesy Calabacitas (Mexican Squash)

No-Mayo Esquites (Mexican Street Corn Salad)

YOU FETA BELIEVE IT (TRIP TO THE MEDITERRANEAN)

Summer Berry Sangria

Green Goddess Hummus with Feta

Zesty Fattoush Salad with Lemony Feta Vinaigrette

One-Pan Sicilian Baked Cod with Roasted Tomatoes & Olives

Crispy Garlic Butter Smashed Potatoes with Feta

Burrata Broccolini with Calabrian Chili Romesco

Orange Blossom Olive Oil Cake with Honey Mascarpone Cream

BOOZY BRUNCH

Slice of Heaven Rossini

Sweet & Savory Balsamic Peach Bruschetta

Kitchen Sink Breakfast-for-Dinner Skillet

Mom's Classic Chilaquiles Verdes

Sweet & Spicy Mexican Fruit Salad with Tajín Vinaigrette

Peaches & Sour Cream Upside Down Cake

Sisterhood of the Traveling Zucchini Carrot Cake

HOLIDAY FAVES

Blackberry Bourbon Smash

Cheesy Baked White Bean & Artichoke Dip

Auntie Bug's Caramelized Almond & Orange Baked Brie

Easy Brussels Sprouts Salad with Honey Shallot Vinaigrette

The Only Roast Chicken You'll Need

Family Favorite Pot Roast

Honey & Chile Roasted Carrots with Labneh

Spiced Date Bread Pudding with Salted Butterscotch Sauce

STEAKHOUSE AT HOME

Cucumber Basil Martini

Little Gem Caesar Wedge with Lime-Zested Breadcrumbs

Seared Scallops with White Wine Butter Sauce & Crispy Pancetta

Foolproof Date-Night Steak with Creamy Peppercorn Sauce

Auntie Bug's Shortcut Asparagus Risotto

Perfect Green Bean Salad

Key Lime Pie with Pecan Graham Cracker Crust

SUMMER SOIRÉE

Frozen Coconut Mojito

Mini Pineapple Teriyaki Meatballs

Summer Stone Fruit Salad with Basil Mint Vinaigrette

Best Ever Pasta Salad

Italian Smash Burger

Jalapeño Cornbread with Maple Butter

Spicy Lemon Parm Cauliflower Bites

Skillet Berry Crumble

CRAVING COMFORT FOOD

Loaded Twice-Baked Broccoli Cheddar Potatoes

Roasted Carrot Tomato Soup with Garlicky Grilled Cheese

Mom's Modern Pozole Rojo (Mexican Pork & Hominy Soup)

Guinness Irish Beef & Veggie Stew

Green Mac & Cheese

Creamy Chicken Tortilla Soup

Yellow Chicken Curry & Coconut Rice

Red Wine–Braised Short Ribs

Easy Creamy Parm Polenta

Loaded Brown Butter Chocolate Chip Cookies

ACKNOWLEDGMENTS

To My Online Family: Never in my wildest dreams did I believe that this book could be a reality, and not a day goes by where I don't realize that it is all because of you. I hope you can feel the love that I poured into this cookbook, because every single page, every ingredient, every story is for you. Your endless support and encouragement inspired me to make this journey a reality. Thank you for making my recipes (even back in the day when I was still learning!), for sharing them with your loved ones, and for welcoming me into your homes and kitchens. And lastly, I'm sorry if I haven't DMed you back! I just about drove myself crazy writing and testing recipes to make this book the best it could possibly be for you. If you're reading this and I still owe you a message, slide into my DMs!

Nana: You are one of a kind. The strongest, most courageous, and most resilient woman I know. Thank you for inspiring me and for encouraging me to go after my dreams. You've overcome adversity while retaining the softest and kindest heart. Your sacrifice is the reason I am here. This book, and the life we've created, wouldn't be possible without all that you've done. I love you more than I can say, and hope that you know this book is—every word of it—dedicated to you (and Mom!).

Mom: You taught me how to cook, and more importantly, how to show love through food. You taught me that kindness and how you treat others is always the most important thing. You're my best friend, role model, and the most selfless, giving, caring, and thoughtful person I know. You've been there for me through it all, especially when I needed an infinite amount of support with creating and recipe testing this book. I love spending hours in the kitchen with you (glasses of wine, a bonus!), watching you work your magic and attempting to decode all of your and Nana's secret measurements. I would not be doing what I'm doing today without you, and your devotion makes it all possible.

Dad: Thank you for being you, for being my biggest motivator, and for nudging me to take the risks and be fearless in following my dreams. You taught me by example that it's all about enjoying the journey and focusing on the present, instead of worrying so much about the destination. You've touched so many lives through coaching and teaching, and inspired me to find true fulfillment in what I do for a living, always striving to do the same. You and Mom shaped me into the strong (and sassy) woman I am today, and I am so proud to be your daughter. Let's take another hike up to one of our favorite spots, Chantry Flats, sometime soon.

Andrew: I love you. This would simply never be possible without you. You learned to wear at least a dozen hats at once, working right beside me every single day (and too often long into the night). Thank you for being not just a 50/50 partner in marriage, business, and friendship but a true 100/100. Without hesitation and with never one complaint, you rolled up your sleeves and helped make this book a reality in any and every way possible—from helping with boatloads of dishes and ingredient measurements, to making sure this book would work for anyone even if their signature dish is boxed mac & cheese (and yes, yours is the best version I've had).

You've shown up for me in ways I never knew possible, and I can't begin to express how grateful I am for you. Thank you for making me a better person.

Auntie Bug: All I can say is that I am so blessed to have you as my aunt. Granted, not by blood, but by something that is often stronger, the family we are able to choose. I'm forever grateful that you and my mom became friends in grade school and cultivated the beautiful relationship you share today. Thank you for always encouraging me, supporting me, and for never failing to make me laugh my ass off. If the instructional recipe videos you would send me during the pandemic so that I could learn more and share more with my community isn't love, I don't know what is. I am so proud to be able to include some of your most coveted recipes in this book. Can't wait to cook from it together!

Gina, Armen & Levon Pilavjian: Thank you for being constant pillars of support for Andrew and me. You have been there for us through it all, and we could not be more thankful.

Alix Frank: Thank you for putting this book into motion and for being there for me every step of the way—for always taking my calls (even on NYE when this book manuscript was due in a few short hours) and for calming me down during the many moments of high stress. Thank you for believing in me and this project from the very beginning, for being the best advocate, and for always having my back as we work together to reach my pie-in-the-sky goals. I'm so grateful for you and our friendship.

Andrea Barzvi: Thank you for coming all the way from Long Island to NYC during rush hour traffic to meet me in Manhattan at the very beginning of this book journey. You understood who I was from day one. Thank you for always believing in me, supporting me, and championing this book as it came to life. Your guidance and advice in every step of the process put me at ease and made it all possible.

Lily Diamond: Where do I begin? Thank you for being such a wonderful teammate (and friend). I am so thankful to have had your guidance during the process of bringing this book to life. Thank you for pouring your heart, soul, and creativity into this book and for seeing my vision. Not to mention, lending your big sister advice along the way. I'm forever grateful.

Lauren Deen: How can I say thank you a million times over? Thank you for jumping in full speed ahead during the eleventh hour to help me make this book as amazing as it could possibly be. Somehow you knew my voice immediately, and more importantly, you saw the parts of me, my family, and my community that make this project unique. Thank you for bringing those nuances to the surface. You're a mastermind and I am beyond grateful to have had you on my team and in my corner.

Thea Baumann: Thank you for testing every single recipe in this book, providing the most insightful and specific feedback along the way, thinking of things from every angle, and for being so wonderful to work with. And to my entire recipe testing crew: **McKenzie Mitchell, Kelly Orr, Sophie Clark & Danielle Whichard**. Thank you for your ideas, your vision, and your taste buds, all of which helped shape this book.

Matt Armendariz & Adam Pearson: Thank you for bringing my vision to life and for making this book, and the recipes I hold closest to my heart, even more beautiful than I could have ever imagined. Your talent is unmatched, and I feel so lucky to have worked with you on this project. Thanks for making it so much fun. I wish we could relive our photoshoot—it was one of the most magical parts of this process. Love you guys. And to the best photo team, Wade, Sophie, Diana & Elle: You guys are INCREDIBLE. Thank you for making the process so efficient, effortless, and special for us.

Helen Johannesen: Working together on this project was a dream! Thank you for helping me demystify the complex world of wine, and most importantly, for making it so much fun. You are seriously the coolest, and I'm grateful for your kindness, expertise, and friendship more than I can express. You rock.

Matt Feil: Thank you for ALWAYS having my back and for providing such sound advice. I can't tell you how much I appreciate your friendship and guidance. You're the best.

Justin Schwartz: To my editor, Justin, thank you for believing in me and for allowing me the creative freedom to make this book exactly what I always dreamed it could be. Your passion for food and cookbooks is inspiring, and I'm grateful to have an editor who is so involved and cares so deeply. Thank you for your patience and guidance as I've navigated this (crazy!) process for the first time. And thank you for pushing me—I know it's because you believe in my vision and what we can accomplish together.

Simon Element Team: Thank you to the entire team at Simon Element, including Jen Wang, Gina Navaroli, and Farzana Razak for your vision, support, and genius. I'm so honored to have been able to collaborate with you, and I appreciate all your hard work in making this book so incredible.

Renée Schillaci & Kyle Grasso: Words can't fully capture our gratitude. Thank you for your generosity in opening your beautifully designed, one-of-a-kind home for the most special part of our cookbook photoshoot. It's a true testament to your impeccable taste and the vision behind your design and architecture firm, iElements in San Marino, California. Everyone couldn't stop raving about your warm, unique oasis (and how they never wanted to leave!). Beyond that, your kindness and support have meant the world to our entire family throughout the years. We love you guys.

To my friends (Jenna, Hope, Ali, Danielle, Xochi, Rachel, Christy, Jessica, Monica, Kelly, TJ, Pat, Mateen, David, Doug, Josh, Ryan, Ed & Mike): Thank you for being the best cheerleaders and support system, and for always understanding when I said no to plans and went days (ok . . . weeks), without texting back. True friends are rare and I'm so lucky we get to navigate life together.

Gaby Dalkin: Thank you for not only lending me your surrogate husbands, Matt and Adam, but for encouraging me and never hesitating to lend the best advice along the way. Having someone that I can fully trust and have looked up to long before I got into this crazy line of work (I'll never forget winning one of your giveaways as an early WGC fan!) has meant more to me than you know. Love you.

Armen Sarkissian & Hazel Perera: Thank you for teaching me to be assertive and disciplined while we worked together in real estate and beyond, and for cheering me on from the moment I told you all about the crazy dream I had to become a cookbook author one day. I know that we will always be in one another's lives and I'm forever grateful for that.

Ellie & Dani Bamford: If it weren't for your beautiful wedding in New York, I may have never tried the Lil' Frankie's Limone and taken the leap to step away from real estate. I'm forever grateful that tequila shots on the beach in Mexico brought us together, and value your friendship and advice beyond measure. Now, let's plan another trip!

Danny & Jen: Thank you for being the most wonderful neighbors and friends, and for lending us your taste buds at any and every time of day. Your (extremely) detailed feedback helped me perfect everything.

Ellen Bennett: You are a force. Thank you for welcoming me into your world with open arms, and for sharing so much warmth and inspiration. You are the true definition of wonder woman. I'm still not exactly sure how you do it all, but you make me believe it's possible to do the same. Thank you for reminding me to dream first and sort the details out later.

Jessica, Courtney, Alyssa, Rosie & Winnie: Thank you for your friendship, getting me camera ready, and for making me feel my best!

And finally, Izzy: To my favorite little sous chef (and good luck charm), who has been by my side since the very beginning. Your sassiness and spunk bring me so much joy, and we are so lucky to have you. Thanks for putting up with all the late-night recipe testing that took away from you being the center of attention (as usual).

INDEX

An Imprint of Simon & Schuster, LLC
1230 Avenue of the Americas
New York, NY 10020

Illustrations by Nari Creative
Food Stylist: Adam Pearson
Assistant Food Stylists: Sophie Clark, Diana Kim, and Elle DeBell
Photo Assistant: Wade Hammond

First Simon Element hardcover edition May 2026

Interior design by Farzana Razak

Manufactured in China

1 3 5 7 9 10 8 6 4 2

Library of Congress Control Number: 2025939103

ISBN 978-1-6680-7716-0
ISBN 978-1-6680-7717-7 (ebook)